An investigative reporter specializing in national security affairs, and formerly a senior editor at *U.S. News & World Report*, Steven Emerson is the author of *The American House of Saud* and *Secret Warriors*, winner of the Investigative Reporters and Editors Award for best book in 1988. He is also a former investigator for the Senate Foreign Relations Committee. Brian Duffy is assistant managing editor of *U.S. News & World Report*, in charge of its investigative reporters. He won many awards for his reportorial work with the *Miami Herald*. Both authors live in Washington, D.C.

STEVEN EMERSON AND BRIAN DUFFY

The Fall of Pan Am 103

Futura

A *Futura* Book

First published in the United States by G. P. Putnam's Sons
in 1990
This Futura edition published in 1990

Copyright © 1990 by Steven Emerson and Brian Duffy

ISBN 0 7088 8347 8

Typeset, printed and bound in Great Britain by
BPCC Hazell Books
Aylesbury, Bucks, England
Member of BPCC Ltd.

Futura Publications
A Division of
Macdonald & Co (Publishers) Ltd
Orbit House
1 New Fetter Lane
London EC4A 1AR
A member of Maxwell Macmillan Pergamon Publishing Corporation

CONTENTS

ACKNOWLEDGEMENTS

We are deeply grateful to the many people who gave unstintingly of their time and assistance, who endured our endless questions with grace and good humour, and who steered us away from more potentially embarrassing mistakes than we would happily admit. For necessary reasons many of those who assisted us and to whom we owe some of the biggest debts of gratitude must go unnamed. A detailed note on sources and methodology appears at the end of the book; we alone are responsible for the book's contents.

Here we would like to thank especially those who, while not sources, provided invaluable contributions to the book and without whose help it might well never have been completed. To Barry Rubin, Patrick Clawson, Daniel Pipes and Orli Low, who kindly agreed to read the manuscript and suggested changes. To John Walcott, whose encouragement, help and guidance throughout were prodigious. To Robin Knight and Richard Z. Chesnoff, whose assistance in and enthusiasm for the project were unfailing. To Brian Reid and David Beveridge of the Scottish Lord Advocate's staff, whose kind help in arranging interviews long-distance was more than generous. To David Ben-Aryeah, for help and guidance on several reporting tasks in Scotland. To Ola Liljedahl, Leif Brannstrom and David Bartals, whose assistance in reporting in Sweden was invaluable. To Gavin Hewitt, whose help throughout was extraordinarily kind. To Merrill McLoughlin, Michael Ruby and Roger Rosenblatt, without whose indulgence in so many absences from the office the book surely would not have been finished. To Robin Hoehn and Christina Staehle, whose translations of German and Swedish documents were timely and meticulous. To Susan Lavine, for organizational and research help. And to Gillian Sandford and Doug Pasternak, whose reporting and research assistance in so many areas were truly exceptional, and to whom we will be eternally grateful. To Anna Jardine, whose attentiveness during the copyediting of the manuscript is to be marvelled at. To Suzanne Herz of G. P. Putnam's Sons, whose encouragement and good humour were unfailing. To our agent, Esther Newberg, whose enthusiasm for the project kept us going throughout. And finally, to Neil Nyren, our editor at Putnam, whose wise counsel, kind words and unfailing optimism made the whole thing worthwhile.

February 1990

CHAPTER 1

A few hours earlier, the sun had dipped to 23 degrees, 27 minutes south latitude and, for what it was worth, winter had officially begun. According to the calendar, December 21 would be the shortest day of 1988, but one would hardly know it from the people of the village of Lockerbie. In late December, in the tumbled valleys of southern Scotland, the days all seemed short and the nights dark and endless. *Dreich* nights, the Scots called them, and the night of the twenty-first was a perfect specimen: wild and breezy, with a fine, misty drizzle that conferred a strange penumbra on the streetlamps and gave chill encouragement to the odd pedestrian to get indoors. The cold enveloped like a cloak, and this time of year all Scotland seemed to smell of wet wool.

Approaching 31,000 feet, a clean sheath of white metal kept the rain and the wind at bay. The odd lines of Boeing's 747 jumbo jet give even some veteran travellers pause. From the tip of the tail, the lines are clean, smooth, what one expects. From the wings forward, however, the metal swells, as if concealing some strange growth beneath the skin. It seems a bit perverse and ungainly. And yet as one of the big Boeings climbed to cruising altitude on this evening just south of Lockerbie, buffeted by winds of nearly 100 miles per hour, its passengers, on Pan Am Flight 103 to New York, never even noticed. The aircraft is a sure and steady performer.

At 6:00 P.M., its scheduled departure time, Flight 103, the clipper *Maid of the Seas*, had been pushed back from

Heathrow's newly remodelled Terminal 3. Under its own power, it had begun taxiing towards the airport's main east-west runways to await a takeoff slot from the air traffic controllers in the tower. Heathrow is typically a mess at this time of night, with too many planes coming and going. Many evenings, the 103 to New York is held up on the taxiway. It had happened again tonight, the result a twenty-five-minute delay. Finally, the runway clutter had been swept away. After another evening's brief fling with chaos, Heathrow had managed to sort itself out once again, and the *Maid of the Seas* had been cleared for takeoff.

On the darkened flight deck, Captain James McQuarrie had revved the four Pratt & Whitney turbofan engines to full power. Inside the cabin, thick insulation had cut the jet engines' scream to a dull whine. The flight attendants had issued the usual safety instructions, a few tardy passengers had snapped their seat belts shut, and seconds later, the 740,000-pound jet, with 259 people on board, had lumbered down runway 27L and lifted into the night, west into the slate-grey skies over Scotland.

Winter had held off longer than usual this year, and there had been an odd bright autumn, with days of high blue skies and precious little rain. Now, though, in the narrow lanes and bald hills around Lockerbie, there would be nothing but dank cold and *dreich* nights until spring came and the lambing began. In Lockerbie this night, only by the bright lights winking in holiday windows and the burble of voices issuing from pubs along the High Street was some of the winter gloom lifted.

In the council houses of Rosebank Crescent, just above Lockerbie's town hall, it was a bit easier to muster some holiday cheer. At 124 Rosebank, at Robin and Sally Devlin's home, gifts had been bought, and now supper dishes had been cleared. There was still holiday baking to be done, though, and Sally had gone next door to her mother's to borrow some butter. Another neighbour, just leaving, asked the time, but no one needed to consult a watch. From a television in the living room came the theme from *This Is Your Life*. It was going on seven. Butter in hand, Sally Devlin hurried back home.

A few doors away, at 71 Park Place, Ella Ramsden was feeling blue. Her Christmas had already come and gone. Ella's son, Jimmy, a Royal Air Force corporal stationed in West Germany, had left with his family at midday. He was due back at Gütersloh the next afternoon and had a full day of travel ahead. It had been a wonderful visit, the first time the whole family had been together in three and a half years. Ella Ramsden's husband had died eight years before, and all she had now was her three children, but it always seemed so hard to get everyone together. This time had been special. Kate had come from Aberdeen with a friend, Ian. Louise was always close by, just a few miles away in Dumfries. But Jimmy and his wife had made it all the way from Germany. And the boys too: Steven was just ten months old, and Ella had barely recognized James. He was big for a five-year-old. But now they were gone. For company, there was Cara, the Jack Russell terrier, Chirpy, the bird, and the three nameless goldfish in the tank. Somehow none of them could lift Ella's spirits. Little James had left his new teddy bear on the bed in the spare room, and Ella gave it a last look before heading downstairs to open Christmas cards and watch television. It seemed that nearly everyone in Rosebank Crescent was watching *This Is Your Life*. It was a silly show about ordinary people to whom nothing much ever happened.

People in Lockerbie loved it.

Three miles away, in the roomy old kitchen of Tundergarth Mains Farm, Jimmie Wilson sat drinking coffee with his wife, June, and one of their three daughters, Lesley, the twenty-three-year-old. A friend, Liz Young, had joined them for supper, and they had dined

13

well: lamb chops, roast potatoes, carrots and broccoli. In the kitchen of the handsome farmhouse, the lights shone against the varnished wood. The place had been built nearly 140 years before, of stones from the surrounding fields. Tonight the Christmas tree occupied the place of honour in front of the big window in the dining room, where it could be seen by passersby on the road outside. The lights glowed.

Aboard the *Maid of the Seas*, from the business travellers who had been gone just a few days to the college students returning after months away, the anticipation of home and holidays was evident. Gifts in gaudy packages jammed the overhead racks. Nearly everyone aboard Flight 103 was heading for some kind of reunion with friends and family, and that simple fact managed to obscure another: that the passengers, as is true on most commercial flights these days, were of vastly different backgrounds. Old and young. Well-to-do and working-class. But tonight, in the bright warmth of the plane, away from the cold and the rain, the differences didn't seem to matter. The destination for almost everyone, after all, was home.

In the front of the plane, in 10B, sat Joseph Miller, age fifty-three, a prominent American philanthropist and active supporter of American and Israeli causes. He was returning home to Woodmere, New York, to see his wife and four children after a hectic thirty-hour business trip to London.

James Fuller, fifty, was returning with a colleague from a meeting in West Germany. A vice-president of Volkswagen of America, Fuller was used to shuttling back and forth between his office in Troy, Michigan, and that of the parent company in Wolfsburg. He had taken Flight 103 before. It was simply a matter of convenience. After a first leg, Frankfurt to London, the 103 made a stop at Kennedy in New York, then continued on to Detroit, where his wife, Georgeanne, usually met

14

him. Tonight, Fuller was travelling first-class, sitting in 3H.

Behind him, in 4H, was Ingrid Smith. Pretty, with an elfin grin and lively blue eyes, Ingrid had been working as a chiropodist with the British Health Service when she met Bruce Smith, a veteran Pan Am pilot, while on vacation in Majorca five years before. One year later they'd been married. Instead of tending tired feet now, thanks to Bruce's generous Pan Am travel benefits, Ingrid flew. She had travelled in Europe, South America, the United States. Tonight she was flying to New York to meet Bruce, who was already there, waiting. They would spend the first part of the holidays in the States with his children from a previous marriage; then they would fly to Tel Aviv.

Across the aisle, also in first class, was Diane Maslowski. Just thirty years old, she had already achieved remarkable success. A broker for Drexel Burnham Lambert in London, Diane owned property in England and the United States. One of four children of a New Jersey clothing retailer, Diane, for all her wise investments and far-flung adventures, had never lost touch with her roots. Each year she returned to her parents' home for Christmas. It was a Polish tradition, her father reminded her. Diane didn't need the hint; she would not miss Christmas with her family for all the world.

Farther back, in seat 14J of the coach section, was Matthew Gannon. And in 15F, one row back on the other side of the aisle, was Charles McKee. Of all those on Flight 103, no one could have been more pleased about going home this night. With another passenger, Ronald LaRiviere, Gannon and McKee had left Beirut for Cyprus early in the morning. Another State Department employee, Daniel O'Connor, had also flown from Cyprus that day. At Heathrow, the four men had killed time making phone calls, buying gifts and generally just waiting to board. Two among the four were U.S. intelligence operatives, and in their chosen line of work,

15

there was no more difficult place to be than in the strife and confusion of Beirut. Having left it behind, however briefly, they were eager to be with their families again.

In row 23 was one of Flight 103's youngest passengers. Suruchi Rattan was all of three, and she was winding up her biggest adventure ever. With her parents, grandparents and her two-year-old brother, Anmol, Suruchi had attended an uncle's wedding in New Delhi. She had worn pretty clothes and eaten wonderful food. Like a tiny queen, she had behaved with studied grace in accepting the endless blandishments of her extended family, some of whom had seen her before this only in fuzzy snapshots from America. Suruchi's father had returned to the States a day earlier, and now she and the rest of her family were following. They had boarded the first leg of Flight 103 in Frankfurt, and Suruchi, in bright red tunic and pants, had spent most of the brief flight to Heathrow recounting to a man in the row behind her the details of the wedding and everything else she could remember from her long trip. At Heathrow, Suruchi had waved good-bye to her new friend. Now she and her family were airborne again.

Karen Hunt, in 31H, was one of thirty-eight Syracuse University students aboard Flight 103. An English major in her junior year, Karen had just completed four magical months in London. It had been only a semester, but in some ways it had seemed much longer. She had seen so much and done so much. She had had a wonderful time, but it had been enough. Her mother had come to visit, but Karen had missed her family and friends, and she was glad to be heading home tonight. Her bags were jammed with gifts, for her younger sister, Robyn, for her boyfriend, Mike, and especially for her parents.

Michael Bernstein, in seat 47D, seldom used the words to describe his profession, but he acknowledged the accuracy of the description: Nazi hunter. His official title was Assistant Deputy Director, in the Office of

16

Special Investigations, U.S. Department of Justice. The OSI's mission is to track down Nazi war criminals and see that they are prosecuted. In his three years in the department, Bernstein was the only lawyer to have extracted a confession from a former Nazi. He was good at his job, but now, most of all, he was tired. For the past three days he had been haggling with authorities in Vienna over the deportation of a former guard at Auschwitz. Earlier in the day, the Austrians had finally agreed to allow the man to be deported into their country. Unexpectedly, they had consented to consider still other cases. Bernstein was happy but exhausted. Having missed his scheduled flight from Vienna, he had jumped from one Pan Am connection to another and finally made it to London, barely in time to board the 103. With luck, he would be home by midnight. Joey, four, and Sarah, seven, would be sound asleep. He would wait until morning to see them.

In seat 53K was Khalid Jaafar. The handsome twenty-year-old had spent the past two months with friends near Frankfurt and visiting relatives in Lebanon, some of whom he had not seen in years. He'd spent time with his mother too. Divorced from his father, she still lived in Beirut, and Khalid had not seen her in a long while. It had been a good visit, but he had been thinking about home, about enrolling in an automotive trade school. Perhaps when he completed the course, he could go work for his father. Once a lawyer in Beirut, Nazir Jaafar had fled in 1974 and had since opened a truck stop near the Canadian border. Such things could happen in America, maybe even for Khalid. He had called his father the day before. He would be on Flight 103, and his father would meet him in Detroit.

Business people and college kids. Immigrants and government employees. It was, in a very real sense, a microcosm of America on Pan Am Flight 103.

Like so many of his passengers, Captain MacQuarrie, the skipper, was heading home. Westbound transatlantic flights are odd-numbered, eastbounds even-numbered. Although there were few better assignments than the nightly 103 to New York and its sister route, the 102 to London, it sometimes got tiring: the same hotels, the long time away from family. A devoted father of two, MacQuarrie, fifty-five, had become accustomed to the long absences from home. Besides the flying, mainly on routes to the Middle East and Europe, MacQuarrie had been active in the pilots' union, the Air Line Pilots Association. It was a lot of work, MacQuarrie often said, and he would be pleased to leave the *Maid of the Seas* in New York this time and stop moving around for a while.

But first there was the business of getting the 103 to New York.

'Good evening, Scottish.'

It was Captain MacQuarrie calling the Scottish Air Traffic Control Centre in Prestwick. 'Clipper One Zero Three. We are level at three one zero.' The 103, MacQuarrie was confirming, had levelled off at its cruising altitude of 31,000 feet.

'Good evening.'

It was Alan Topp in Prestwick. 'Squark, zero three five seven, ident please.' Topp was checking the identification code that MacQuarrie's crew had punched into the jet's transponder before leaving Heathrow.

Alan Topp was a master of the machines that keep so many different-size aircraft aloft and out of each other's way. For eight years he had been a radio operator abroad more different Royal Air Force planes than he could remember. Then he had decided to take a look at the flying business from the other side. By the night of December 21, when he picked up Flight 103 on his flickering radar screen at Prestwick, Topp had been an air traffic controller for twenty-three years. He was fifty-three years old, his wife had left him recently, and except for Ted, his small border collie, all he had to worry about was his job. He took it with the utmost seriousness.

Perhaps that was why, although he was assigned to work the high-level traffic that night, above 25,000 feet, Topp had already been tracking the Pan Am jumbo jet for several minutes before it entered his air space at 6:45 P.M.

The 103 had just come off a standard routing from Margo – this was the code name for its first reporting point on its route across the Atlantic. Margo is just north of the town of Penrith, in the hills of Cumbria. Having passed it, MacQuarrie and his crew were heading north towards Glasgow. On Topp's dark-green radar screen, the 103 appeared as a small bright-green cross inside a square box about two millimetres across. Topp continued to track the 103, but it was still London's responsibility. At 6:56 P.M., the London controller, at Polehill Sector in West Drayton, spoke with the 103 a final time.

The 103 was Topp's business now.

After MacQuarrie confirmed the 103's code to Topp, it was automatically reconfirmed by Scottish radar at Prestwick. As if by magic, the signal 'PAA 103' blossomed in bright green letters on Topp's screen. Beside the image of the green cross in the tiny box, Topp's screen now showed the flight number, 103; the plane's altitude of 31,000 feet, abbreviated as 310; and its destination code, 59, for New York's Kennedy Airport.

Topp confirmed all this information to MacQuarrie: 'One Zero Three, you are identified, and after Margo, route direct five nine north, one zero west.' This routing would take the 103 directly over Lockerbie.

Topp turned to other things, but only for a moment. The pilot of a London shuttle requested permission to descend towards Glasgow. Topp approved but cautioned that the 103 was at 31,000 feet. 'Okay,' he radioed the shuttle, 'but the clipper's the traffic.' He turned back to his screen.

19

'I had the two aircraft, both well set, both going direct,' Topp recalled. 'There wasn't much to do. I just sort of gently watched them. Despite that, I was watching the clipper quite closely.'

Suddenly, on Topp's screen, the green cross in the tiny box vanished.

Then, in its place, there were 'four or five' bright blips. 'It struck me immediately that they looked like Christmas tree lights because they were winking,' Topp remembered later. 'In a sense, they were twinkling.'

'Clipper One Zero Three, Scottish,' Topp called. Perhaps it was a trick of the radar, he thought. A blind spot of some sort. Such things happened but not, God knew, very often. Alan Topp tried again.

Nothing.

'Clipper *One* Zero Three, Scottish!' Topp appealed.

Silence. It seemed endless. But just a couple of minutes had elapsed since the lights had begun twinkling on Alan Topp's radar screen.

He called across the room to his watch manager, Adrian Ford. Ford waved him away. He was on the radio with the London–Glasgow shuttle. Descending to 24,000 feet, the pilot had spotted an enormous fire.

'I've got a report of an explosion on the ground,' Ford called to Topp.

'You're kidding,' Topp said. His stomach began churning. 'I've lost the clipper, One Zero Three. That must be him.'

Bodies had begun to rain on the roofs of the people of Lockerbie.

It is a small place, tucked into the narrow valley of the Annan River. The village of Lockerbie boasts of ancient churchyards, handsome sandstone homes and some of the best lambing fields in Great Britain. Some 3,000 people live in Lockerbie, and virtually everyone knows everyone else and, usually, a good deal more about their business. There had been big doings in

Lockerbie's past, but that was a long time ago. Ancient history. In the later Border Wars with England, which had ended with the Union of the Crowns in 1603, Lockerbie had seen some of the bloodiest fighting. Thousands had died. A century earlier, clan wars had claimed hundreds of lives. The Maxwells had held the lower end of the Annandale and the Johnstones the middle. Stabbings and burnings were the principal means of dialogue. In one fight, a Johnstone lady, pretending to surrender to a Maxwell lord, withdrew an iron castle key from the folds of her garment and smashed him in the head. It is reported that the lord died of his wounds. Still further back, the Romans had come through the Dale of Annan, leaving a slender road along the river, two forts and a camp in which to practise laying siege to forts and castles.

The forts, the road and the scenes of the worst of the clan and border fighting may all still be viewed, but the great attraction for the few visitors who found their way to Lockerbie before December 21, 1988, was more ancient still. In a quarry that supplies much of the town's construction materials, fossil hunters have had much success excavating footprints of dinosaurs. Each new find was an event.

That was pretty much the most exciting thing that had ever happened in Lockerbie. Many of the people of the village tended to look on the events of the world with a mixture of wry amusement and sad incomprehension. Mrs. Thatcher, the troubles in Belfast, America's carny politics: all were matters of great interest and little consequence. Lockerbie, like most small towns, was happily self-contained. But if there is merit in eliminating squalor, living at peace with one's neighbours and seeing to the needs of one's family, Lockerbie was a far better place than most. Life was simple, and it moved at a comfortable pace. It ambled, and to many of the good people who call Lockerbie home, that seemed just about right.

Until the night of December 21.

Ella Ramsden's dog growled. Then people began to hear the noise. To Sally Devlin, at first it sounded like one of the great big trucks that sometimes rumbled down the hill to the village from the A74, the four-lane highway that skirts Lockerbie as it wends its way north to Glasgow. The noise grew louder. 'It was like the lorry was going to hit the house,' Sally Devlin said. 'Then it was just outside the window. Then it was as if the roof was coming off.'

Ella Ramsden's dog, Cara, jumped into her lap just as the explosion hit. 'I saw all this orange,' Ella said.

A garden shed crashed through a bedroom window at the Devlins'.

Ella Ramsden's house began to fall. 'There was this terrible swell of wind, which brought up the dust, whooshing, whooshing. Then I looked up and I could see the stars.'

At Jimmie Wilson's farm, the lights went out. Then, as he clutched his teacup, the cockpit of the *Maid of the Seas* fell in his field.

On the other side of Lockerbie, a Pratt & Whitney engine came to earth. It had just cleared the A74 and landed in the cul-de-sac of Sherwood Crescent, on Maurice and Dora Henry's house. The Henrys were getting on in years, but they kept a pin-neat home with a nice garden bordered by heavy blue paving stones. Maurice Henry had ordered them specially.

At the tiny police station three blocks away, one of the paving stones came through the roof. Some cars were aflame on the A74.

It was just after 7:00 P.M., and the village of Lockerbie was burning.

But there was not much anyone could do about it. Alan Riddet, an assistant fire officer, raced to Sherwood Crescent from his parents' home on the other side of the village. He had been mending a balky radiator when the roar of noise engulfed the village. What had been the Henrys' home was now a vast crater. A gas main had ruptured, aviation fuel was burning in trees and on roofs. Even the ground was ablaze. 'Number of casualties unknown in Lockerbie,' Riddet called in on his portable radio. 'Make pumps ten.'

In issuing this command, Riddet was activating the Major Disaster Plan for the Dumfries and Galloway region, which provided Lockerbie with fire and police protection. In calling for pumps 10, Riddet was summoning every piece of fire and police equipment in the district and alerting all hospitals in the area to be prepared to treat survivors from the crash.

There would be none, though.

The bodies of Joseph Miller, James Fuller, Ingrid Smith, Diane Maslowski, Matthew Gannon, Suruchi Rattan, Karen Hunt, Michael Bernstein and Khalid Jaafar lay scattered across an ancient Scottish town that probably none of them had even heard of. There were bodies everywhere in Lockerbie.

Robin Devlin found a handsome young man in his yard. He had tight blond curls. A signet ring shone on a finger. 'There was barely a mark on him,' Robin recalled. 'But from the way he was lying, like a rag doll, you knew all his limbs were broken.' He checked the young man's pulse, but there was nothing.

Neighbours led Ella Ramsden from her shattered house. They had heard her shouts, she recalled later in wonder: 'Will someone come get my wee dog?' A young man had pushed a sagging wall aside. 'She's fucking alive, lads,' Ella Ramsden said the young man had yelled. 'Let's get her out!'

In the road was another body. 'Who is it?' Ella asked. No one knew. They had never seen the pretty young woman before. On Ella's roof was another young woman, partially clothed and still strapped in her airplane seat. In a tree across the road was still another. All dead.

Jimmie Wilson and his family had donned Wellingtons and clambered into their sturdy Austin to see what strange hell had descended on them. Far across the field, they could make out the shape of something beyond imagining. Like the head of a great bird fatally stricken in flight, the broken cockpit of the *Maid of the Seas* lay on its side in the grass. Lights burned inside. Maybe, miraculously, someone was still alive, the Wilsons thought. But there was no sound. The cattle, terrified, had fled to a far hill; the lambs were still farther afield. In the wreckage were three bodies. Captain MacQuarrie's body had been ejected from the cockpit and lay a short distance away. Clearly, the two members of his crew still inside the cockpit were dead. But June Wilson saw the stewardess move. Desperately, she searched for a pulse. There was nothing. What she had seen was a last twitch, a spasm of the nerves.

Eerily, the lights continued to glow in the cockpit, powered by an emergency backup system. Across the field were scattered thousands and thousands of pieces of debris: luggage and airplane parts, and steel rivets by the hundred, which had popped like corn from the aircraft's skin. There were more bodies too. Some, as June Wilson remembered, were 'like waxen dolls', still and pallid. There was a baby, naked. And a pretty girl in a pink sweater.

Other bodies were wretchedly dismembered. Feet were missing from some. Others had been horribly compressed by the impact of the fall from 31,000 feet.

June Wilson went back to the house to phone Dr. Hill. He lived close by, and if there were some who had survived, he could probably help them. Jim Hill made it to the Wilsons' in eight minutes, but no one could find anything for him to do. They went back to the cockpit for a last look.

As June Wilson pointed a bright flashlight, Dr. Hill crawled inside for a look. June kept warning him to mind the jagged metal all around. The doctor finally crawled back out with a briefcase. It bore a crisp blue-and-white label:

PA 103

CHAPTER 2

To anyone who knew him, it would come as no surprise that Oliver 'Buck' Revell would be among the first
at FBI headquarters to learn of the crash of Flight 103.
A native of Muskogee, Oklahoma, who had left to join
the Marines, Revell had spent nearly a quarter-century
in the Bureau, climbing the ranks under J. Edgar
Hoover, directing the Bureau's efforts against organized crime, government corruption and white-collar
criminals. He had run numerous undercover operations, and in June 1980, he had been promoted to
executive assistant director of the FBI. Revell oversaw
not just the Bureau's criminal investigations but also its
investigations into terrorism against U.S. citizens and
property, and relations with Interpol, the international
police agency. A rumpled and sometimes irascible task-
master, Buck Revell had acquired a reputation in his
years with the Bureau as something of a bulldog and a
rule-bender, but those who know him well say he is
scrupulously fair and intolerant of corner-cutting by his
agents. Over the years, the 'tough guy' label had
proved its value: among many in the law enforcement
and intelligence communities, he was alternately feared
and respected, and as a practical matter, that made it
easier for him to do his job.

The phone call to the FBI's spectacularly ugly headquarters on Pennsylvania Avenue had come in at
3:47 P.M. Washington time, alerting officials to the
crash of a Pan Am 747 bound for New York. Revell had
already made three phone calls by then. He had let

the FBI director, William Sessions, know. Then he had alerted the Bureau's criminal investigation and intelligence divisions. It was no secret how Revell had learned of the crash. Oliver North, another can-do type who many would say helped tarnish Revell's reputation during the Iran-contra affair, often chuckled that he got word of trouble around the globe not from spy satellites or secret agents but from CNN. 'CNN,' North liked to say, 'was faster than NSA,' the National Security Agency, which eavesdrops on electronic communications around the globe. Like North, Revell was an inveterate watcher of the twenty-four-hour Cable News Network. On the afternoon of December 21, as he was working in his office on the fifth floor of headquarters, cleaning up some paperwork before a brief Christmas vacation, Revell had the television set against the wall tuned to CNN with the volume turned down. Every once in a while he glanced absently at the screen, but there was not much to interest him. There was talk of snow, and winter storms bloomed like strange flowers on the TV weather map.

Revell wasn't interested in the weather, however. His son, an Army combat engineer in West Germany, had been scheduled to fly home that day with his wife. Chris Revell was being stationed stateside, and his wife would be joining the Bureau. By a stroke of luck, the couple had been able to leave Germany a few days earlier than expected. They had been scheduled to take Pan Am Flight 103 from Frankfurt on December 21, but they had managed to change their tickets several days before. Revell remembered the flight number. And when it came across on CNN, with word that the aircraft had crashed in Scotland, he knew it was bad.

'It was a 747,' Revell remembered telling Sessions. 'And usually, this time of year, they're all full.'

A few minutes later, Bill Chorniak, a supervisory special agent, telephoned across the street to the Justice Department. Bill Braun, a lawyer who worked terrorism cases in the department's General Litigation Division, took the call. Chorniak told Braun that a Pam Am jet had gone down in Scotland. We don't know anything yet, Chorniak said. Stand by.

In London, Darrell Mills had just left the U.S. embassy on Grosvenor Square to meet his son. Mills, an FBI veteran like Revell, was the Bureau's legal attaché in London, and like Revell, he had acquired something of a reputation over the years. Except that where Revell was regarded as a hardcharger with barely disguised disdain for the bureaucracy, Mills was known as a charmer and a bit of an operator. 'A character' was the nearly universal description of Mills around the Bureau. He had been a terrific street agent, working organized-crime and bank-robbery cases, and his many successes had won him one of the most coveted and prestigious jobs in the FBI. By any measure, the LegAtt's job in London was a plum. For all that, however, for all the high-flying social life of the embassy and the top-drawer diplomatic contacts, Darrell Mills still talked fondly of his days on the street. It was no act. He genuinely missed the tumult and the action of a field agent. But he also moved easily in all kinds of society. He had friends among congressmen as well as beat cops, not to mention a rare gift of blarney, which he was ever putting to good use on the Bureau's behalf. As the LegAtt in London, Mills was supposed to work closely with Scotland Yard and with local police officials throughout Great Britain. His turf extended as far as Scandinavia, and it was the rare chief of police there or in the United Kingdom who had not shared a pint with Mills at one time or another to talk about police business.

The LegAtt programme was something new for the FBI, one more indication that the old bureaucracy created by Hoover was changing to meet the newer, more complex demands of fighting crime in the late twentieth

28

century. By 1988, it was not just the Ten Most Wanted list and kidnappers that concerned the Bureau, but insider trading on the financial markets, terrorism in the skies and on the seas, and illegal transfers of high-tech equipment to the Soviet Union. FBI agents still went after bank robbers, of course, and there was no police agency better at solving kidnappings. But there were new challenges. More and more crime within the United States had international dimensions – from narcotics and gun smuggling to white-collar financial crimes. The Bureau found itself having to deal more and more with law enforcement agencies overseas, and the LegAtts were intended to facilitate that process. And to those most familiar with the Bureau, none was better at it than Darrell Mills.

Before grabbing a taxi from the embassy, Mills had left word where he could be reached. It was standard procedure, and with a skeletal staff and so many on holiday leave, it was important to know where everyone could be reached. Mills's son had just graduated from college in the States, and he had flown over earlier in the day to join his parents for Christmas. They were going for dinner that night at a place in South Kensington.

Before they even had had a chance to order, however, Mills was summoned from the table. Something about a plane crash, he explained, before dashing out of the restaurant. A quick taxi ride back to Grosvenor Square, and Mills was back at work in his third-floor office. He would not leave for days.

Special Agent Tim Dorch was leaving almost immediately. Mills had called him at home and told him to get to the embassy as quickly as possible. By the time Dorch arrived, a U.S. Air Force jet had already been fuelled and was waiting for ambassador Charles Price II and a group of U.S. embassy security and consular officials. There would be no time to pack. Within hours of the crash of Pan Am 103, Tim Dorch would be on the ground in Lockerbie, the first FBI representative on the scene. He had no earthly idea what he was going to do there.

Dorch was younger than Mills and Revell. Slender and easygoing, with a ready smile, he was the father of two teenage boys. He and his wife had loved their time in London. The boys were pretty much split on the matter, but the whole family agreed that the chance to live abroad, especially in a place like London, was something to be cherished. In another year Dorch's tenure as an assistant LegAtt would be up, and it would be time to return to the States. Before this overseas stint, Tim Dorch had made a name for himself in the FBI's New York office, a sprawling place on the upper floors of the Jacob Javits Building at 26 Federal Plaza in lower Manhattan, where hundreds of agents worked in cramped cubicles and the few lucky ones got a small office. New York was the largest of the FBI's fifty-nine field offices, and in the 1980s it was busier than it had ever been. The New York field office was, and is, unlike any other in the FBI system. The others were run by special agents in charge, or SACs; the New York office by an assistant director, James Fox. Under Fox, the New York field office had led the way into wider investigations of foreign counterintelligence operations; organized-crime busts of unprecedented scope; and groundbreaking inquiries into fraud in the financial markets of Wall Street, which was several blocks downtown from the Javits Building, and corruption in City Hall, which was even closer.

The latter was Tim Dorch's specialty. The government-corruption cases in which U.S. Attorney Rudolph Giuliani had taken so much pride, and on which he would build his unsuccessful campaign to become mayor of New York, had been the product of the investigative work of Tim Dorch and his colleagues. As impressive as that work was, however, it was no preparation for dealing with the horror of a jumbo jet-liner crashing to earth in an ancient Scottish village.

In Lockerbie, Dorch just did what he could.

Back in Washington, alarms were going off. They always do when a plane goes down, but even with the very first sketchy reports, this seemed an especially awful tragedy. Within minutes of Buck Revell's phone calls, Larry York, the FBI's assistant director for identi-fication, had put his disaster team on alert. These are forensic specialists, the experts assigned the grisly busi-ness of identifying bodies from air disasters and other tragedies. Within hours, they would be airborne across the Atlantic.

It was too soon to tell, but everyone was puzzled by the sudden disappearance of the 747. The big Boeing was one of the safest jets in the skies. But there had been no communication from the flight deck before it had vanished. Just silence. In the first hour in Washing-ton, FBI officials attempted to confirm a report that there had been a midair collision with another aircraft. Flight 103 was at 31,000 feet, however, and a collision at that altitude seemed highly improbable. That left a catastrophic mechanical failure of some kind.

Or a bomb.

To cover the latter possibility, Special Agent James T. Thurman, one of the Bureau's best explosives tech-nicians, was ordered to leave for Scotland immediately. Across town at the Federal Aviation Administration, senior executives were having similar thoughts. Walter Korsgaard, a retired Army lieutenant colonel, was a special agent with the FAA and one of the most experi-enced authorities in the world on aircraft explosions. He was already packing a bag. A tall, rangy man, hard of hearing, Korsgaard was the FAA's senior explosives expert. In his trademark long-billed cap with the FAA insignia on the front and his special agent's badge pinned to the beak, Korsgaard had poked through the

31

dismal wreckage of virtually every suspicious air crash of the past decade. If there was evidence of a bomb, the FAA executives knew, Walter Korsgaard would probably find it.

Like Korsgaard, Tom Thurman was regarded by his colleagues as a pro. Described by friends and coworkers as serious-minded and intense, Thurman had acquired a master's degree in forensic science from George Washington University and was a graduate of the United States Naval Explosive Ordnance Disposal School. Even after all his highly specialized training, the FBI still did not consider Thurman quite ready to work in its Washington crime laboratory, one of the most advanced forensic labs in the world. At the Bureau's request, Thurman undertook more than a year of intense lab study on explosives and explosive devices. That was in 1977. Thurman had been a special agent with the Bureau ever since, and according to those knowledgeable about the dangerous arcana of explosives, he was among the very best investigators in the field.

As Korsgaard and Thurman prepared to leave for Scotland, they ran over the few facts they knew about the crash of the 103. A plane exploding at altitude. Chance for survivors? Virtually nil. Chance of finding what caused it? Somewhat better. The jet had come down over land. There would be debris, and in the debris, no doubt, clues. The only trick would be finding them. What else? The plane had vanished without a sound. No Mayday distress call. No final communication from the flight deck. It smelled bad.

At National Airport, on the other side of the Potomac, an FAA pilot had already rolled out the agency's ageing Gulfstream 3 from its special hangar at Butler Aviation and begun running the usual preflight checks. Within ninety minutes, the jet would ferry Thurman, Korsgaard and more than a dozen other officials from the alphabet-soup agencies usually summoned after an air disaster. Besides the representatives of the FAA and the FBI, the NTSB, the National Transportation Safety Board, was obliged to send investigators. There were also people from Boeing and Pratt & Whitney on the Gulfstream as it beat through the night towards Lockerbie. They could help immensely in the search for clues. Among the professionals on board, as they tried to grab a few hours of fitful sleep, all thoughts of a happy holiday had already been scrapped.

All across Washington, the same thing was happening. On the seventh floor of the State Department is an operations centre for managing foreign emergencies and, when that isn't possible, simply keeping track of them. With its secure telephone and cable facilities, the operations centre had been used to monitor emergencies from revolutions in Latin America to government crackdowns in Beijing. On the afternoon of December 21, a group of officials under the lead of the State Department's European bureau convened in task-force rooms 2 and 3. In TF2, officials were assigned to coordinate with officials in Lockerbie and handle inquiries from relatives of those who had been on the aircraft. The people in TF3 were assigned to start looking for the causes of the crash. The secure phones linked them to the FAA, CIA and FBI. But the best information source, however, was still CNN. None of the government agencies knew very much at all.

In London and Lockerbie, officials were similarly in the dark. Cabinet ministers in Whitehall made no move to convene a session of COBRA, the government's crisis committee, which took its name from the cabinet briefing room. A highly secret gathering of senior officials from intelligence branches, the Foreign Office, the Home Office and various cabinet ministries, COBRA is convened in times of national emergency. It most closely resembles an emergency session of the National Security Council and its senior staff. In recent years, COBRA has been convened most often to handle

33

terrorist threats such as the seige of the Iranian embassy in London. This time, it was decided, there was no need for COBRA. A plane had crashed, people had died, the appropriate emergency services were being provided. End of story.

Even in the first minutes and hours, however, as the shattered Pan Am clipper and its passengers and crew were hurtling to earth, there were strange inklings that this was not the end of a very brief and tragic tale, but the beginning of a much longer and more terrible story.

John Boyd had never investigated an air disaster. He rarely even flew, but he felt it: Something was horribly wrong.

Boyd is a slight man with an unfashionable crew cut and a perpetually quizzical look. His entire professional life, twenty-six years, had been spent as a police officer in Scotland, and in spite of his quiet way and abhorrence of public speaking and just about any kind of publicity, he had done quite well for himself indeed. For the past three years, he had been the chief constable in the Dumfries and Galloway district, in which Lockerbie was located. Just weeks before, he had been named Her Majesty's Inspector of all Scottish police. It was among the most prestigious police positions in Great Britain.

The promotion would not take place for several months, but it would mean that Boyd and his wife would have to sell their comfortable home in the village of Dumfries and get something smaller, and certainly more expensive, in Edinburgh, ninety minutes' drive away. On the night of December 21, in expectation of the move, Boyd was standing somewhat precariously on a counter in his kitchen, attempting to hang wallpaper. He was not having much luck. His wife was out, visiting her mother in a nearby rest home, and Boyd had the volume of the TV in another room turned up. There was some kind of documentary on, but it was interrupted suddenly by a news announcer. Hurriedly, the man read a brief statement that a Boeing jumbo jet had landed on Lockerbie. Boyd recalled thinking, 'My God, that's wrong, there's something wrong there.'

A minute later the phone rang. Headquarters confirmed the crash.

Boyd sped from Dumfries to Lockerbie. It was just fourteen miles, and in the few minutes in the car, John Boyd realized he would need help, and plenty of it. Lockerbie had a police force of only twenty-two officers, plus a traffic bureau. But the Dumfries and Galloway Constabulary couldn't handle the emergency either. It was the smallest police force in all the United Kingdom. From headquarters in Dumfries, Boyd had already summoned help from two neighbouring police districts, Lothian and Borders, and Strathclyde. After London's Metropolitan Police district, Strathclyde, in Glasgow, was the largest force in Britain, with some 7,000 officers. Until his promotion to the top job in Dumfries, Boyd had been in charge of the criminal investigative division in Strathclyde. He had many friends there, and now he wasted no time in calling them for help.

Once he reached Lockerbie, however, Boyd realized he would need much more help than any police force could provide. The destruction was beyond belief.

Under a circular issued by Her Majesty's Government, 'Military Aid to Civilian Powers,' local authorities in Great Britain may summon military assistance in times of emergency. In Lockerbie, John Boyd did just that. It is a strange thing, a local police chief mobilizing the vast resources of an army and air force, but that is precisely what happened. By 8:00 P.M. in Lockerbie, less than an hour after the *Maid of the Seas* had shattered in the sky, soldiers were boarding buses and troop carriers at several bases in England and Scotland. Royal Air Force helicopters were already en route from Prestwick, Pitreavic and Bulmar, in the north of England.

In the dark of December 21, in the rain and the mist, Boyd had a sickening feeling that none of the emergency help would matter. There were bodies everywhere, he remembered, but no survivors.

And the debris, scattered so far and wide. The devastation, so total.

'We knew in our hearts,' Boyd recalled, 'that it was not a natural thing that caused the aircraft to break up like that.'

CHAPTER 3

A smoky dawn greeted Lockerbie on the twenty-second of December.

Through the night, nearly 500 police officers and soldiers had poured into the village to help in the search for survivors. Now, with small fires still burning in parts of Lockerbie and the smell of aviation fuel heavy in the air, they awakened to a mild grey day. Many of the soldiers had slept in fields around the village, huddling under ponchos. This far from Lockerbie, with mist still thick on the hills in the first dim light, it was almost possible to forget the surreal scenes of the night before. But it took just a few minutes before they came flooding back.

In Sherwood Crescent, where Maurice and Dora Henry's house had been, firemen had had no water to fight the flames that leapt like demons from one house to the next. One of the Pratt & Whitney engines had landed on a water main at Neatherpeace Farm and crushed it like a sipping straw. Said Lockerbie police inspector George Stubbs, 'I'll never forget it. There were these firemen standing there with hoses and no water coming out.'

Someone had had the presence of mind to dash out to Express Dairies, just outside Lockerbie, and soon milk tankers filled with water from a main on the other side of the village were descending on Sherwood Crescent. It was hours before the fires there were brought under control. But then the hard work was just beginning.

One of the first things John Boyd did on arriving in

Lockerbie was to appropriate an enormous map of the village and surrounding areas. If there were survivors, he knew, they would have to be found fast. In this weather, they would die quickly of exposure. Boyd marked off six search areas, and police and soldiers were assigned to each. Volunteers had also begun arriving by the score. Ham radio operators. Men and women from a Scottish organization that trained dogs in mountain rescue work. Townspeople who showed up with pots of tea and coffee for the emergency crews.

Because the police and soldiers couldn't communicate over their different radios, the ham operators had proven invaluable. Each had been assigned to a search-and-rescue team, and they communicated with each other through the night as they made their way across the pitch-dark fields. Their job was to make sure the search teams wasted no time going over the same areas twice. By maintaining a steady dialogue and consulting their maps constantly, they had kept the search teams from stumbling into each other in the dark. Still, all they could do was flag bodies. It seemed so hopeless.

In Rosebank Crescent, outside Ella Ramsden's ruined house, men with rescue dogs had spent hours clawing their way through piles of debris, searching vainly for some sign of life. The dead had been marked with strips of white paper or bunting. Through the night, they had fluttered like frail ghosts, as the dogs padded back and forth poking their noses into hedgerows and under drifts of aircraft debris and broken-down houses. Flight 103 had been carrying a consignment of sewing needles, of all things, and many of the search dogs in Rosebank Crescent had gotten needles stuck in their paws. A veterinarian who lived nearby had set up an impromptu clinic, extracting the needles with tweezers and putting ointment on the dogs' paws. Whining and tugging at their leashes, the dogs had been sent back into the gardens of Rosebank Crescent that had, just weeks before, been home to the last fading flowers of autumn.

At Sherwood Crescent, the fires extinguished, the crater that had replaced the Henry's house was awash in aviation fuel. Houses and bodies had evidently been vapourized; things and people had simply vanished. Soldiers, police and firefighters had combed the charred and sagging houses around the crater for some evidence of life. At No. 15, the Somervilles', everyone had died: John, Rosaleen and the children, Paul, thirteen, and Lindsey, ten. At No. 16, across the street, Tom and Kate Flannigan had evidently perished, and so had little Joanne. The bodies had simply disappeared in the fireball of gasoline and flaming metal. But where was Steven? The youngster had nipped around the corner to a neighbour's to repair a bicycle. When Sherwood Crescent exploded in flames, he had been a half-block away.

He was the only one of his family to survive. The rescue dogs found no other signs of life.

By midnight, John Boyd had finally moved the teams of police, security men and accident investigators into Lockerbie Academy. Tim Dorch had established an FBI beachhead in the chemistry lab. Other U.S. embassy personnel had been assigned some kind of science classroom; mice and chipmunks clattered away in cages. Pan Am people had been given a classroom directly below the FBI. There were no phones yet, but Dorch had begun making lists of things they would need. For Dorch, a secure communications link with Darrell Mills in London and FBI headquarters in Washington. For Pan Am personnel, a clearing-house operation, so relatives could check with police and the airline in New York, London and Frankfurt on names of passengers on Flight 103. Boyd had already issued orders for telephones to be installed in the next few hours. Scottish police had a computerized phone bank, the Crisis Casualty Bureau System, for just such an emergency. Boyd had asked his old police friends in Glasgow to establish the phone bank, so that Alan James Berwick, manager of security for Pan Am, and fellow employees could begin fielding relatives' calls as quickly as possible.

Through the night, fourteen RAF helicopters had scissored the sky around Lockerbie, scattering livestock as they shuttled police and soldiers to outlying portions of the search areas established by Boyd. In the first hour, he had realized they would have to search fields as far as fifteen miles east of Lockerbie. He needed men with lights and radios out there right away. Not long afterward, Boyd recalculated, the search area would have to be extended, perhaps by as much as 100 miles. Bodies and debris were scattered across the valley of the Annan River. One man had phoned the town hall to report a woman in a plane seat in his yard. He lived more than ten miles from Lockerbie.

By 1:00 A.M., with search teams in each of the six areas, soldiers and police were still pouring into Lockerbie. In the confusion, they had been directed first to the town hall, an old primary school gymnasium that had been remodelled years before into a graceful high-ceilinged room with white crown mouldings and elegant mullioned four-foot windows. The town hall had been used most recently for a dance. Now farmers and searchers carried in the first of the bodies, and it was transformed into a mortuary.

At 2:00 A.M., Boyd had convened the first meeting of the investigators. There were over 200 bodies and tons of general cargo out there, he had told them. He had stressed the need first to locate any survivors. With so many people searching already, however, it was important that the hunt be conducted carefully so that no bit or scrap of debris was unaccounted for. In his usual manner, Boyd had taken time to introduce the representatives from the various agencies and the military services and thank them for their prompt response to his calls for help. The soldiers, the RAF chopper jockeys, the police officers from outlying districts: Boyd had forgotten no one. Then he had introduced Tim Dorch.

'The FBI is here,' Boyd had said, 'and they are fully operational.' It was a simple statement, a gesture of courtesy. But for the FBI it was an important moment. For the past five years, the Bureau had had the statutory authority to go after criminals who targeted Americans or American property overseas. Yet it had been blocked nearly every time it attempted to exercise that authority. In August 1988, a Pakistani military jet with President Mohammed Zia ul-Haq on board had crashed shortly after takeoff; Zia, U.S. ambassador Arnold Raphel and several senior Pakistani military officers on the C-130 Hercules had all perished. Pakistani authorities had immediately suggested sabotage, but at the last minute the Bureau had been expressly prohibited from sending its counterterrorism team to investigate. With its expertise in forensic and criminal investigative work, the Bureau had been the U.S. agency most qualified to examine the cause of the crash. State Department and Pentagon officials had persuaded the White House that an investigation by the FBI would not, in the words of Robert Oakley, Raphel's successor in Islamabad, 'add any expertise to the team [already investigating the crash] and that it might create complications.' Only later, during congressional hearings, would the State Department concede publicly that it had erred in prohibiting the FBI from assisting the Pakistanis with the investigation. Typical of Foggy Bottom, the officials referred to the whole episode as a 'misunderstanding.'

In the event, the investigation resembled an old Mack Sennett comedy. More than 1,000 people had been rounded up and questioned, and at least ninety placed under arrest. Finally a report had been completed. Despite the fact that Arnold Raphel had died in the crash, U.S. officials say they never received the full text of the 350-page report; instead, they got a flimsy summary of the findings. And what had the investigators concluded was the cause of the crash? Despite evidence of mechanical problems in the hydraulic elevator-control system of the C-130, they determined that sabotage was probably responsible. A sophisticated device had released a colourless, odourless gas into the cockpit, and this had led to the 'insidious incapacitation of the flight-deck crew,' the summary said. It was not a bomb that had done it, and not, in a part of the world where shoulder-fired surface-to-air missiles are about as hard to come by as woven rugs, a missile. It was a mysterious gas. And the evidence for that? Nothing, No autopsies had been performed on the crew members who had been so insidiously incapacitated. No trace of a chemical agent was ever found. And if someone had managed to incapacitate the plane in an attempt to kill Zia? Thanks to the botched investigation, that would never be known. It was, by any measure, a complete disaster.

It stuck in the minds of many in Washington, who pledged that such an inquiry would never be repeated. Within the upper reaches of the FBI, there was not just anger but acute frustration over the Zia investigation. With news of the crash of Pan Am 103 in Lockerbie, even at this very preliminary phase, the anger and frustration came flooding back. It was impossible to tell so soon what had caused the jet to crash, but this time, Oliver Revell vowed, there would not be 'another Zia.' If he and other senior FBI officials had their way, they would not be shut out of another terrorism investigation overseas. An important corner had been turned.

Before John Boyd had adjourned the meeting in Lockerbie Academy, just before three on the morning of December 22, he stressed again the importance of an exhaustive search. There was no chance anyone had survived the crash of Flight 103, he had concluded privately. But if they were careful, some good might yet come of a tragedy as awful as this. Since he had arrived in Lockerbie seven hours before, Boyd had been given more information about the Pan Am flight. He had learned of the twenty-five-minute delay at Heathrow. A student of police work, Boyd had recalled the downing of an Air-India jet some years earlier. Sikh terrorists had placed the bomb on board in Vancouver, but it had not detonated until it was over water. No one was ever prosecuted.

'If Flight 103 had left Heathrow on time,' Boyd said later, 'it would have blown up in the sky over the Atlantic, and there would have been no evidence. Here, we had a chance to get evidence, and it was important to gather as much as we could. We had a chance, and an obligation, to make those people responsible for this tragedy pay for it.'

In nearly three years in London, Darrell Mills had made innumerable friends. At Scotland Yard, in the Home Office and in the down-at-the-heels government offices of Whitehall, he had people who knew and liked him and who knew they could rely on him if and when the need arose. In Ireland, Scotland and Scandinavia, this was also the case. On his frequent trips, playing his horrid brand of golf or sharing the odd pint, Mills was a hard man not to like.

On the night of the twenty-first, in his comfortable office on Grosvenor Square, he soon had a pretty good fix on where the Pan Am jet had gone down. Strathclyde police had to be handling it, Mills figured. He was wrong, but not by much. Lockerbie was not far from the Strathclyde district, but Lockerbie and its outlying areas were in the jurisdiction of Dumfries and Galloway. As Mills checked his private phone directory, he was astounded. He knew every chief constable in England and Scotland, but not John Boyd. He had dined with most of the others, and he knew their children's names. But somehow he had never managed to meet Boyd. It was just one of those things.

This was a hell of a time to be making introductions, Mills thought, but he phoned Boyd immediately. The call went to Dumfries, then Lockerbie. Somehow, in the confusion, a police officer had located Boyd, disentangled him from yet another impromptu meeting and brought him to the phone. 'Whatever you need,' Mills said, 'however we can be helpful, just let us know.'

Already, Boyd knew he would need plenty of help from the Bureau. Flight 103 had been full of Americans, and if any one agency could help him with identification of the passengers, it would be the FBI. In the United States, the Bureau keeps millions of fingerprints in a computerized filing system. On countless occasions the computer had come up with a critical piece of information in investigations of kidnappings, murders and even domestic disputes. Boyd needed that kind of help on Lockerbie, and he needed it quickly.

Mills gave his word, got off the phone with Boyd and called Buck Revell in Washington. The FBI's Ident team was already moving. The assistant director, Larry York, and his boss, Bill Garvie, had sent agents home to pack bags. They were to be back at headquarters in a few hours, and a plane was being readied to fly them to Scotland. Garvie and York had an ace up their sleeve, and neither Revell nor Mills knew anything about it. The Ident Division had been experimenting with an expensive new piece of equipment that could transmit and receive razor-sharp images of fingerprints and other identifying body marks over commercial phone lines. It was called a phototelesis machine, and it worked on the same principle as the ubiquitous fax, but its resolution was so fine, and its cost so great, that it had not even been put into production yet. The Bureau had a prototype that could send and transmit colour images. Garvie and York ordered it readied for shipment to Lockerbie immediately. Another, a black-and-white machine, would be set up in Mills's office in London. This would later become the source of several

44

jokes and much muttering. The LegAtt's office in the embassy was so badly wired that every time Mills or someone else turned on the shredder to destroy sensitive documents, the other office equipment – computers, clocks, Dictaphones – would all cut out and then come back on, machines beeping and blinking cacophonously. The new phototelesis machine would only add to the chaos.

Like Oliver Revell and the others who would be charged with investigating the crash of Pan Am 103, relatives of the passengers, most of them, heard the grim news on television.

At home in Bethesda, Maryland, a prosperous suburb of Washington, D.C., Stephanie Bernstein was riding her exercise bicycle in the family room and wondering whether to go out to the airport to pick up Michael. It was just about 10:00 P.M., and a news bulletin had come across the screen. A Pan Am jet from London had crashed somewhere in Scotland, the announcer said; there was no word yet about survivors. Sarah, seven, and Joey, four, were asleep upstairs. Determined to remain calm, Stephanie Bernstein tried to recall the details of Michael's flight home. A co-worker had phoned to say Michael would be arriving after midnight, but he didn't know the flight number. At eleven, Stephanie phoned Pan Am. They could not confirm the passenger list yet, a woman said. Two hours later, they called back. Michael Bernstein had been on Flight 103. In the flood of emotion, Stephanie Bernstein wondered briefly whether she should go to Scotland. But who would watch Sarah and Joey?

His twenty-one-year-old son telephoned Bruce Smith in New York City with the news. He had just seen a news bulletin. Bruce went out and hailed a cab – he was going to Scotland. When he arrived at Pan Am's operations centre at Kennedy Airport, Smith found out that his wife, Ingrid, was on the plane. He demanded

45

a seat on the next flight to London. He was determined to see what had happened to the plane carrying his wife. Jets just don't fall out of the sky.

Shachi Rattan, Suruchi's father, at first was unsure what to do. His family was not supposed to have been on Flight 103, after all. After a day of waiting, he decided to go to Lockerbie with his brother-in-law Sudhakar. Pan Am staff tried to dissuade the two, but they wanted to go, if only to help identify the bodies. 'We told them, "We are both physicians and, hopefully, we will be able to cope with the situation."'

Diane Maslowski's grandmother was the first to hear the news on TV. The family frantically began checking Diane's travel plans. A local travel agent confirmed that Diane had been on board, but perhaps she had missed the flight; Diane was so busy, she was often running late. A phone message on Suzi Maslowski's answering machine crushed what small hope the family had left. Evidently, Diane had left her younger sister's number with Pan Am as her contact number in New York. When Suzi Maslowski checked her machine later in the day, a pleasant voice, that of a Pan Am employee, said: 'This is to inform you that Diane Maslowski was on Pan Am Flight 103 and that it has crashed.' It would be another two weeks before the Maslowskis could bring themselves to get on a plane and go to London to begin collecting Diane's effects.

At the State Department, the Pentagon, the Central Intelligence Agency and the Justice Department, bureaucrats staffing the operations centres knew what they had to do. They assumed, correctly, that the families of Matt Gannon, Chuck McKee, Dan O'Connor and Ron LaRiviere had already heard the news of the air crash. But the men were government employees, and they had served their country at considerable hazard to themselves. It was only proper that the families should be notified, officially, in person. It was also imperative to get an intelligence officer to the crash scene as soon as possible. The four agents on Flight 103 had been carrying sensitive documents in their carry-on bags, and they would have to be retrieved as quickly and quietly as possible. In the embassy in London, Darrell Mills was alerted to the problem. Through its own separate communications link, CIA headquarters in Langley, Virginia, communicated an urgent request to the London station chief. Within an hour of the crash, U.S. officials say, at least two CIA officers were en route to Lockerbie.

John Boyd awoke thinking of helicopters and HOLMES. He had gone to bed just two hours before, and now at 6:00 A.M., on the twenty-second, he was racing back to Lockerbie from Dumfries through the lifting mist with a thousand things on his mind.

First were the choppers. Boyd knew next to nothing about helicopters, but he did know that the big RAF birds were not right for the job he had to do. They were too big, too noisy and too hard to manoeuvre. At Lockerbie Academy, one of his first calls was to the Glasgow airport. It was a strange request, but Boyd informed the man at the other end of the line that he would have to requisition the privately owned helicopters there. All of them. Boyd wasn't sure how long he would need them. The airport official assured him it didn't matter. He promised Boyd the helicopters would be available immediately. He would start calling around, he said, to line up pilots.

HOLMES was another matter. Boyd had thought of it almost as soon as he had learned of the crash the night before, but it had been too late, and the need for haste too great, to do anything about it. HOLMES was named after the great detective; the name was an acronym for 'Home Office Large Major Enquiry System.' A sophisticated computer software package designed especially for British police, HOLMES had a capacious and well-ordered memory for classifying virtually every bit of

47

information from a large disaster. Data on location of a body, type and nature of injury, clothing colour and style: all would be logged and sorted. For the accident investigators, those responsible for finding the cause of the crash, HOLMES would prove especially valuable. The only way to determine precisely what had happened to the big Boeing jet was to rebuild it, part by part.

On their way into Lockerbie the morning of December 22, Tom Thurman and Walter Korsgaard already knew there would be thousands and thousands of parts. Thank God for computers.

The FAA's Gulfstream 3 had landed at Newcastle just a few hours earlier. While Thurman and Korsgaard dozed, knowing it might well be the last sleep they would get for the next few days, the Gulfstream had transited the Atlantic on a beeline course from Washington to Scotland. By 5:30 A.M., with Boyd fielding calls and issuing orders almost nonstop, Thurman and Korsgaard were getting themselves organized in Lockerbie Academy before they took to the fields in search of whatever it was they would find. Evidence, they hoped. But the wreckage was spread so far and wide. Korsgaard scrunched his battered FAA cap hard down over his eyes. It would not be easy.

The rest of Lockerbie was in chaos. For the first time in its history, the ancient village was experiencing gridlock. Emergency vehicles, police vans and army trucks jammed the narrow roads and spilled off into fields and onto sidewalks. More than 1,100 police officers and 600 military personnel had descended on Lockerbie by this morning. The FBI's Ident team had already arrived from Washington. With Tim Dorch's help, they had begun setting up shop and unpacking the new phototelesis machine. The RAF had dispatched a team of morticians. Twenty-one months earlier, an overloaded British ferry had capsized in the Belgian port of Zeebrugge. Captain Tony Balfour of the RAF and his wing commander, Ian Hill, had directed the scores of autopsies. There were none better in handling the grim business of disaster. Now Balfour and Hill and their team of medical technicians had arrived in Lockerbie. Late the night before, Scotland Yard, assuming it would handle the investigation, had also ordered a team of agents from SO 13, the elite anti-terror squad, to Lockerbie. They too were converging on the town this morning, along with a team of deputy constables from London's Metropolitan Police. The DCs would help with security. John Boyd would need every one of them.

A brief tour by chopper had convinced him, his senior investigating officer, John Orr, and Superintendent Stuart Henderson, one of the most important members of the investigative team, that the search area would have to be expanded immediately; there was wreckage scattered as far as the eye could see. The six search sectors would have to be expanded. Ultimately, teams would be assigned to eleven sectors covering 845 square miles. There was no rhyme or reason to the way debris had scattered. Maurice and Dora Henry's home had vanished in the fireball of Sherwood Crescent, for instance, but searchers would find household papers in a field sixteen miles away.

In the basement of the town hall, Balfour and Hill had begun setting up the mortuary. Some bodies had been brought in overnight. There was a small girl, in red tunic and pants. A farmer, tears coursing down his cheeks, had brought Suruchi Rattan's body into the makeshift morgue the night before. He had held her ever so gently until a police officer had helped him set the body on the floor. Earlier, a social worker had obtained wide spools of plain brown paper from a merchant's shop. The police officer had cut a sheet from the spool. Carefully, he had drawn it over the small girl in the bright red outfit. Still sobbing, the farmer had gone back into the night, to help look for more bodies.

49

Before the search teams had been sent out, at 8:00 A.M., Boyd had passed the word. He wanted all bodies recovered by the evening of December 24. The terrain was rough, and there was plenty of it, he knew. But for the sake of the families, they must try to find and identify every body before Christmas Day.

Even before the new recruits were sent into the fields, the people of Lockerbie had begun bringing bodies and bits of wreckage in.

Foster Dodd farmed 105 acres up on Banks Hill in Tundergarth, near where the cockpit of the *Maid of the Seas* had come to rest. He had tried to search his fields the night before, but in the pitch dark he had found only debris. Early on December 22, one of Boyd's men called to ask if he would help in the search. He said he would, and summoned his three children. Dodd took Laura, nine, in one tractor. Stuart, fourteen, drove the other with Robbie, who was a year younger, and a friend. There were shards of metal everywhere but, strangely, no bodies. They had found a door of the plane, unbroken, on the ground. A bit further on was a huge piece of the fuselage, maybe eight by twenty feet. The cabin windows shone dully against the grass. Still further on, through a strip of woods, and a field of rushes, a bright silver sheath had caught their eye. It was actually a piece of metal, two feet wide by about four and a half feet long. It was attached to a box with a metal carrying handle. The box measured two feet by six inches, and on its side was printed: 'DATA REPRO-DUCER 1972.' The Dodd boys had recovered Pan Am 103's black box.

Since they had actually found it on their neighbour's land, they brought it to his house. Chris Graham called the police. The boys went back out to see what else they could find. A few hours later, they returned with money. Or at least that's what they thought it was. What they had actually recovered, from a buff-coloured airmail envelope that had burst on impact with the ground, were cancelled cheques, hundreds of them. There was one for $200,000 and another for $547,000. Later they would learn from the police that these were cheques from one bank to another for credit-card accounts. At the time the boys were dumbfounded by the amounts. But as they pored over the cheques, something even stranger happened. Below them, in a field a half-mile away, a helicopter landed and a man jumped out. Quickly he grabbed a bright orange mail bag that had been lying on the ground. Then he threw it in the chopper and flew away.

I wonder what that's all about, Stuart said to Robbie.

In Lockerbie proper, while soldiers searched the close-in fields, residents awoke to scenes of horror. A few bodies had already been pulled out of trees and off roof-tops, but many others remained. A fire truck with a man on an extended ladder drove up and down the High Street, to Sherwood Crescent and up to Rosebank. He was looking for bodies on roofs, and he found quite a few. In Rosebank Crescent, near Ella Ramsden's house, there were bodies all over the place. Most looked like young people, from what Ella could see. Sally Devlin was sure about the young man in her yard. He could have been one of hers, a handsome blond lad. For some reason his body lay there for days. Sally called him 'our boy.' She pleaded with her husband. 'I kept on saying, "Maybe he's just unconscious, is there nothing we can do?"'

On Alexandra Drive, a few minutes north of the High Street and the town hall, Police Superintendent Douglas Roxburgh, one of John Boyd's key deputies, was unlocking the big double doors of an empty plant that belonged to Dexstar Chemicals Ltd. On Boyd's orders, Roxburgh had assembled a team of forty police officers who would receive, check, sift and tag the debris that residents such as Foster Dodd and his sons were turning over to police. On the morning of the twenty-second, police officers had begun distributing clear plastic bags for people to put debris in, but it would be days before it was all picked up, and weeks before Roxburgh and his men could make sense of it all. After sweeping the plant clean, Roxburgh's officers had divided the plant into six sections, one to correspond to each of the search areas. On one wall of the plant, between the small offices to the side of the warehouse area, officers hung a five-by-three-foot map of Lockerbie and the surrounding area. The search areas were marked on the map, and when Boyd extended them to a total of eleven sectors, the officers relined the floor of the Dexstar plant accordingly. As they came trickling in through the double doors, the socks, battered suitcases, Bibles and crushed Christmas gifts would begin to fill up the cavernous old warehouse on Alexandra Drive.

That first day, however, Boyd and Roxburgh agreed that aircraft debris should be kept separate from personal effects of passengers. RAF specialists were due to arrive that morning from London, as were investigators from the Air Accident Investigations Board. The AAIB is the British equivalent of the FAA, and its technicians are among the best in the world at sorting through aircraft disasters and determining their cause. With Korsgaard and Thurman, they would want to examine every last piece of the Boeing jet, as would the technical experts from Boeing and Pratt & Whitney. Often their expertise was critical in helping government investigators learn what had caused an engine to fail or a plane to fall from the sky.

Roxburgh had sent another police team to the garages of Blue Band Motors, on Bridge Street. These men would take charge of the aircraft wreckage recovered from Lockerbie, but today they had little to do. The black box had already been spirited off to London for analysis. And the searchers were still looking for survivors and retrieving bodies.

Besides, Margaret Thatcher was due any moment. When she had learned the extent of the disaster late on the evening of December 21, the British prime minister had decided to go to Lockerbie to express her condolences and offer whatever she could by way of moral support. In addition to everything else he had to do on December 22, John Boyd had to make time for the PM and be sure she had adequate security when she spoke to the press. More than a hundred journalists from radio, television and print media had descended on Lockerbie during the night, and more were flooding into the village each hour. Boyd chose the community centre as the best place for Mrs. Thatcher to address them. In fact, it was the only place. Every other building of size in Lockerbie was filling up with dead bodies and aircraft debris.

The community centre was also a busy place. Mike Combe, a social worker in Lockerbie, had unlocked the front door the night before, and it had been filling up ever since. Residents in shock, searchers in need of warm food and drink, and police officers exhausted from carrying bodies in from shattered homes and distant fields: all had come in for a bit of sustenance during the night and the early-morning hours. Now, with many of the searchers back at work by late morning, the crowd of policemen and accident investigators had thinned out considerably. There would be enough space to accommodate Mrs. Thatcher and the press corps. It would have to do.

Earlier, the prime minister had been given a helicopter tour of the village and the surrounding hills. She had been visibly moved by the sight of so many bodies in the fields, and especially on seeing the cockpit of the *Maid of the Seas*, crumpled on the wet earth of Tundergarth. Afterwards, as she entered the community centre with Combe and Boyd, she noticed a sign that read: 'Quiet, Please. Examinations in Progress.'

'Surely not,' Thatcher whispered to Combe.

'No,' Combe replied. 'The police are in there.'

Not long after Mrs. Thatcher departed, shortly after noon, the HOLMES technicians arrived from London, and FBI specialists began working on a secure communications link between Lockerbie and Washington. British Telecom, the butt of so many jokes because of its alleged sluggishness, had already begun installing phones in Lockerbie Academy; more helicopters had begun arriving from Glasgow; and the families and friends of those who had boarded Pan Am Flight 103 at Heathrow only eighteen hours before were finally coming to accept the awful truth.

For the Fullers, the Smiths, the Maslowskis, the Gannons, the McKees, the Hunts, the Bernsteins and the Jaafars, for all those who had loved ones on Pan Am 103, there would be no holiday, no joyous reunions, just a terrible sense of emptiness and loss. How to articulate such things? The man on the flight from Frankfurt to London who had listened so kindly to Suruchi Rattan's account of her great adventures at her uncle's wedding in India sent flowers to Lockerbie. He didn't know Suruchi's name, so he asked that the bouquet be delivered to the town hall, with a brief note:

> To the little girl in the red dress,
> who made my flight from Frankfurt so much fun:
> You didn't deserve this.

CHAPTER 4

It is a strange and unsatisfying business, the sorting of half-clues, the parsing of whispered hints and the grasping after odd bits of hard information – the rare fact that one knows absolutely to be true and yet, in and of itself, tells almost nothing. Such is the work of cops and spies.

In the first few hours after the Boeing 747 disintegrated over Lockerbie, virtually no one, either police investigators or intelligence officers, believed it was an accident. Before he left FBI headquarters on the evening of December 21, Buck Revell had spoken with John Boyd in Scotland. The conversation had been hurried but friendly, Revell solicitous of the Scottish policeman's needs, Boyd grateful for the offer of assistance from the world's most distinguished investigative agency. Besides explosives expert Tom Thurman and the Ident team, agents from the FBI's Criminal Investigative Division were already en route to Lockerbie, Revell had told Boyd. They would be there to help process evidence, provide expertise, whatever Boyd needed. Boyd said they would be most welcome.

At home, the television still tuned to CNN, Revell continued to monitor the news from Lockerbie. Bureau technicians swept his office at home regularly for bugs. The phones, fax and computer all had dedicated, secure lines that linked Revell directly with headquarters. He would be using them constantly over the next few days. Christmas would have to be sandwiched in somewhere.

The very first news reports had almost no useful information. Reporters, unable to reach harried police officers and accident investigators, stuck closely to the one piece of information on which they knew they could rely: A Pan Am jet had crashed in Scotland with a lot of people on board. For a long time that's pretty much all anyone outside Lockerbie knew for sure. Three hours after the crash, the Associated Press was moving its eleventh version of the story:

BC-BRITAIN – CRASH: 11th LD –

WRITETHRU

URGENT

Pan Am Jumbo Jet Crashes With 258 Aboard

Eds: New thruout with more from eyewitnesses. No pickup. Adds byline.

BY EDITH M. LEDERER
Associated Press Writer

LONDON (AP) – A New York-bound jumbo jet carrying 258 Christmas travellers crashed in a Scottish village Wednesday night, sending up a towering ball of flame raining burning debris on houses and cars.

The Department of Transport said it had no immediate information on casualties or survivors from the crash of the Pan Am Boeing 747. One witness said the plane may have been on fire before it crashed.

Subsequent versions would place the number of passengers, correctly, at 259. In the first few hours, no one had any idea that eleven more people – among them, the Henrys, the Somervilles and the Flannigans – had died in Lockerbie, bringing the number of casualties to 270.

As is the case with virtually every aircraft disaster, some of the very first news stories would focus on the age and condition of the doomed plane. Typically, CNN was among the first to disclose that, of a total 710, the *Maid of the Seas* had been the fifteenth oldest 747 delivered by Boeing to U.S. and overseas carriers.

Federal records showed that the jet had had a history of trouble: cracks and corrosion in the fuselage, an onboard fire, smoke in the cabin. A year earlier, the plane had undergone an extensive overhaul. From April to September, it had been retired to a Boeing repair hangar in Wichita, Kansas, for extensive work on the engines, fuselage, landing gear and structural support system. It was possible that some of the problems cited in the FAA records, especially the cracks and corrosion in the fuselage, had been discovered during that time. In any event, an overhaul that thorough made one thing quite obvious. Whatever structural or mechanical problems the *Maid of the Seas* had had before 1987, they were 'invalidated', in the words of one aircraft maintenance specialist, by the repairs and modifications made in Wichita. Still, the early news reports focused on the plane's earlier problems; it was one of the few reliable bits of information reporters could lay their hands on.

Buck Revell knew a red herring when he saw one. A former pilot, he now flew more than 100,000 miles a year on commercial jets in the course of Bureau business. He had flown on plenty of 747s, and he knew the reputation of the aircraft as one of the safest in the sky. One that had been reoutfitted so recently would be especially reliable, Revell knew. There had been one occasion, years before, in which a faulty bulkhead repair had led to a 747 crash in Japan. But as a matter of course, the big Boeings simply did not fly into pieces like that.

Unless someone put a bomb on board and blew it up.

At the CIA, intelligence officers assigned to the counterterrorism centre were already scanning their computers for clues. The U.S. intelligence community has a specially designated computer system for terrorism investigations. Known as DESIST, it contains what is believed to be the world's most comprehensive database on terrorists and terrorism. Analysts and investigators using the system at the CIA, FBI, Pentagon and State Department can communicate with each other on another system, known as FLASHBOARD. There are three FLASHBOARD terminals at the CIA, two at the National Security Agency in Fort Meade, Maryland, one at the FBI and several more at the various intelligence agencies housed within the Pentagon. The system is manned twenty-four hours a day. The busiest cog in the FLASHBOARD network is the CIA. In late 1985, President Reagan had signed an intelligence directive, known as a finding, authorizing the Agency to hunt down and kidnap terrorists. To do so, Agency officials created the counterterrorism centre, or CTC. Many senior administration officials, including several at the CIA, had questioned the wisdom, and the legality, of 'snatch and grab' operations conducted overseas. Revell himself had been a dissenter. But despite complaints from other intelligence agencies that the CTC was too insular, it served as a valuable clearinghouse on terrorist groups from Belfast to Beirut. All of that information found its way into the DESIST system, and within an hour of the crash of Pan Am 103, CIA computer operators were scrolling through reams of data on bombs, bomb- makers and bomb threats against American air carriers. Sadly, there was plenty to look at.

Secure phones linked the CTC with the operations centre on the fifth floor of FBI headquarters and the seventh floor of the State Department. At the Bureau, the ops-centre team had been drawn from the violent-crimes and the counterterrorism sections. Robin Montgomery, who headed the violent-crimes section, had been in that job only two weeks. Neil Gallagher, in charge of the counterterrorism section, had been there a bit longer, but with just three weeks on the job, he could hardly be called a veteran in the arcane business of counterterrorism. Montgomery and Gallagher were joined in the ops centre by Dick Marquise, who headed the Bureau's Terrorism Research Analytical Center, and Bill Chorniak, one of Marquise's deputies. Like the specialists in counterterrorism at Langley, Marquise kept track of all sorts of hints, rumours and information about terrorists and terrorist organizations inside and outside the United States. Montgomery and Gallagher would stay with Marquise through the night and do whatever needed to be done. If there was no substitute for on-the-job training, Montgomery and Gallagher would learn their new jobs well. They would certainly learn fast.

At the State Department, officials from the Office for Combatting Terrorism and the Division of Intelligence and Research had voluminous files on terrorists and terrorist threats. They too would be working through the night. Frank Moss, who had been with the State for fourteen years, had served as a refugee coordinator in the Sudan before coming to the Office for Combatting Terrorism two years earlier. After he had learned of the crash of the 103, Moss dashed home for a shower and a change of clothes. Like Revell across town and John Boyd in Lockerbie, Moss had no evidence that a bomb had blown up the Pan Am jet. As far as he knew, no one had even suggested as much out loud. It was just that the way the jet had simply vanished and then scattered its remains across the Scottish countryside led to no more plausible explanation. Moss and his colleagues in the SCT, as the Office for Combatting Terrorism is known, had voluminous files on terrorist groups that had the wherewithal to plant a bomb on board a plane. They would spend the night reading over the data and conferring by FLASHBOARD with their counterparts in the CTC on the other side of the Potomac.

The last link in the communications net established on the night of December 21 was the Federal Aviation Administration. Technically, the FAA still had the lead role in determining what had happened to Flight 103. Officially, it was just another air crash, albeit an

59

unusually terrible one, if one considered the number of casualties and the time of year. But like nearly everyone else involved in the investigation, even at this early stage, FAA experts didn't doubt for a minute what had caused the 747 to crash and burn. Late that night, their investigators already airborne toward Scotland, they pulled their own files on bombs and bomb threats and began going through them for clues.

It took almost no time to come up with the first one.

Just over two weeks before, at 11:45 A.M. local time on December 5, a man with a deep, indistinct voice who'd spoken with a thick Arab accent had placed a call to the main switchboard behind the Marine guard-post in the U.S. embassy building near the Helsinki waterfront. The man had said something about a bomb and a Pan Am jet in Frankfurt. The operator could barely understand the man, but she had been trained well, and she knew exactly what to do. She'd routed the call to the embassy's Regional Security Office. A State Department employee named Kenneth Luzzi was filling in for the regular embassy security officer, and he'd taken the call, but for some reason he neglected to tape it.

Start over again, from the beginning, Luzzi told the man on the phone. Several times Luzzi asked the man's name. His voice sounded odd, and he would not give his name. His message, he told Luzzi, was simple. Sometime before the end of the year, operatives of the Abu Nidal terrorist organization would smuggle a bomb on board a Pan Am flight from Frankfurt to the United States. He mentioned a Mr. Soloranta in particular. 'Mr. Soloranta' was actually Samir Kadar, a master bomber from the Abu Nidal organization. Many police and intelligence officials believed he had died in an explosion in Athens in July 1988. But no one could prove it. If Kadar were involved, this would be a threat to take seriously. But the caller gave no why or where-fore, no dates. Luzzi tried to press him; the man hung up. Luzzi quickly alerted embassy security officials. A CIA officer in the embassy was told of the threat. So were Finnish intelligence officials.

They said it was a false alarm. The man with the Arab accent was Samra Mahayoun, they said, an unfortunate creature. Finnish security officers told U.S. officials and representatives from Pan Am that they had been watching Mahayoun for weeks. They had tapped his phone, and they had listened as he had made other bomb threats. He had called the Israeli embassy in Helsinki several times. The man was a Palestinian, believed to be in his late twenties, and he said the bombing was to be carried out by another man, Yassen Gharadot. Samra Mahayoun had come to Helsinki to attend the university, and he was living there on a student visa. He was a little old for a student, and his studies had gotten sidetracked when he had fallen in love. Unfortunately for Mahayoun, the object of his affections had recently dumped him for someone else. That someone else, Finnish police say, was Yassen Gharadot. It was believed Samra Mahayoun wanted revenge.

He went about it in a strange way, though. According to intelligence officials familiar with his activities, Mahayoun figured that by threatening to blow up planes he would cast suspicion on his old lover's new friend. Finnish security officials couldn't believe the young man was quite this dumb, so they kept following him around and listening in on his phone calls. The police said they had picked up some references to the drug business. But it was clear that Mahayoun knew nothing of airplane bombings. He would be hard-pressed, one policeman joked, to change a flat tyre on his car. No mad bomber he. At least that's what they thought at the time.

At the CTC in Langley and the ops centres at State, the FBI and the FAA, Mahayoun's story was well known, but it would have to be looked into again. And even if it was bogus, as the investigators believed, that

61

did not mean it was not a problem. Although Mahayoun's story had been discounted by everyone who had reviewed it, the FAA had issued a bulletin on December 7 to air carriers and airports throughout Europe advising them to step up security measures. Pan Am security officers had been alerted to the phone call on December 5, and they had concurred with the judgement of the intelligence officials: It was meaningless, pure nonsense. There had been universal agreement on that point, but the State Department had forwarded the FAA bulletin to its embassies and consular offices throughout Europe. On December 13, in Moscow, in the cramped and drafty pile of cut stone that served as the American embassy, William Kelly, the embassy's administrative counsellor, had ordered that the notice be posted.

TO: All Embassy Personnel
SUBJECT: Threat to Civil Aviation

Post has been notified by the Federal Aviation Administration that on December 5, 1988, an unidentified individual telephoned a U.S. diplomatic facility in Europe and stated that sometime within the next two weeks there would be a bombing attempt against a Pan American aircraft flying from Frankfurt to the United States.

The FAA reports that the reliability of the information cannot be assessed at this point, but the appropriate police authorities have been notified and are pursuing the matter.

In view of the lack of confirmation of this information, post leaves to the discretion of individual travellers any decisions on altering personal travel plans or changing to another American carrier. This does not absolve the traveller from flying an American carrier.

Moscow was the only embassy that had posted the FAA warning, but it didn't really matter. Too many people had seen it, or knew of its existence. It was only a matter of time before it leaked.

At the State Department and the FAA, this meant trouble. On the night of the twenty-first and in the early morning hours of the next day, when officials could have spent more time looking for leads to real terrorists, many were planning damage control for a terrorist threat that never was, preparing for nasty questions about a supposed screwball bomber who, if the truth were really known, probably couldn't change a tyre on his car. A waste of time. But it was true: The questions would come, and the heat would be intense.

As they were anticipating this unhappy prospect, Moss and his colleagues at State got the first whiff of what looked like a real clue. It came across sometime around 5:00 A.M., and the all-night crews at the FBI, CIA and FAA all heard it within minutes of each other. In London a man had placed two quick calls, to the offices of Associated Press and United Press International. He wanted to read a statement, he said, about the crash of the Pan Am airplane: 'We, the Guardians of the Islamic Revolution, are undertaking this heroic execution in revenge of blowing the Iran Air plane by America a few months ago and keeping the Shah's family in America.'

If syntax counted for anything, there was probably something to the claim; for some reason Iranian terrorists always seemed to have such a hard time with English. The content was also interesting. The business about the Shah's family could pretty much be discounted right away. All sorts of people had reason to hate the late and unlamented inhabitant of the Peacock Throne; his family was no bargain either. But in the reference to the Iran Air jetliner that had been shot down in the Persian Gulf a few months before, there was the genuine seed of a clue.

63

The incident involving the Iranian aircraft is one of the most unfortunate and bewildering in the history of the U.S. Navy. On July 3, 1988, at 10:54 A.M. local time, the USS *Vincennes* had loosed two surface-to-air missiles while on patrol off Iran in the Persian Gulf. The missiles had exploded directly beneath an Iranian commercial airliner, blowing off one wing and the tail and sending 227 adults and 63 children cartwheeling to their deaths in the warm waters of the gulf. All, by any definition, had been noncombatants.

The *Vincennes* is one of the Navy's most advanced warships. It had been dispatched to the Persian Gulf earlier in the year as part of a U.S. mission to protect reflagged Kuwaiti oil tankers from attack by Iran as they transitted the Strait of Hormuz. The *Vincennes* is equipped with the Aegis computerized combat-control system, regarded by naval experts as the most advanced in the world. On the morning of July 3, all seventeen computer consoles in the *Vincennes*'s CIC, or command information centre, were manned. It was still early, but it had been a busy morning already. Iran had somehow acquired a small but deadly fleet of Swedish-made Boghammer speedboats, and outfitted them with missiles and machine guns. For months they had been playing havoc with shipping in the Persian Gulf.

On this particular morning, they were playing havoc with the *Vincennes*, but staying just out of range of her antiship guns. Captain Will C. Rogers III, the commander of the *Vincennes*, had been in the CIC most of the morning. Sometime after 10:30, an ensign manning one of the seventeen digital-display consoles reported an unidentified aircraft descending toward the *Vincennes* in an 'attack mode'.

Rogers could not assume the aircraft was hostile, but everything about it – its course, angle of descent and point of origin, from somewhere inside Iran – made him edgy. And there were still the Boghammers out there to be dealt with. Rogers ordered *Vincennes* radio operators to contact the mystery aircraft. Normally, in combat situations, this is done with a simple, universally acknowledged electronic signal, IFF: Identify, friend or foe. Over the next five minutes, the *Vincennes* sent out ten messages. But the anonymous jet, now believed by the computer operators in the CIC to be a hostile F-14, failed to respond. And it kept on coming. Later the Navy would say that the jet was 'squawking' on the Aegis's Mode II system, which is used only by military aircraft, and that it was emitting a code that had been used previously by an Iranian F-14 fighter jet. In fact, a review of the Aegis computers would show the jet was squawking on Mode III, the proper channel for civilian aviators.

What Captain Rogers's CIC technicians had in their sights was Iran Air Flight 655. It was a regularly scheduled flight, from Bandar Abbas to Dubai, and usually it was filled with Iranian shoppers off to spend wads of hoarded money on fancy electronics in Dubai's well-stocked department stores. On July 3, Iran Air was using an Airbus 300, a handsome and highly efficient French-made plane, to ferry the passengers to Dubai. Only later would it become clear that on the morning of July 3, Flight 655 was in the proper civilian air corridor, identified as Track Number 4131, or TN 4131. It would also become clear afterward, mainly from another ship, the USS *Sides*, which was less than twenty miles from the *Vincennes* when the Iranian aircraft was shot down, that the plane was not descending but ascending. The only known anomaly, as far as investigators could determine after the tragedy, was the timing of Flight 655. The plane had left Bandar Abbas about twenty minutes behind schedule. Evidently a passenger's problems with immigration authorities had delayed the flight.

But there was no gainsaying the real danger the *Vincennes* was in. Intelligence officials, through the Navy command, had issued an alert to the gulf fleet to be prepared for some kind of attack during the July 4 weekend. This was not unusual. According to one Navy official, such alerts were issued 'nearly every other day' in the Persian Gulf. Things seemed to be getting more tense by the day. On April 14, the USS *Samuel B. Roberts* had struck a mine planted by an Iranian navy vessel, and the U.S. Navy had struck back four days later, destroying two Iranian oil platforms, the Sassan and the Sirri-D, both of which were believed to have been used for Iranian military surveillance and communications operations. Within hours after Sassan and Sirri-D erupted in flames, the U.S. Navy had sunk or damaged six Iranian vessels, and things had not let up much since then. On the weekend of July 4, however, no one seemed to know what kind of attack to prepare for. There were the Boghammers to be mindful of – they were not there for sport. But there were any number of ways Iran might attack.

For all the dangers facing U.S. forces in the Persian Gulf, it is impossible to understand precisely what happened between the *Vincennes* and the Iranian airbus on the morning of July 3. Because Captain Rogers was clearly in combat conditions, he needed no permission before he fired on hostile aircraft, either on the sea or in the air. Inaction had led to heavy damage and loss of life on the USS *Stark* more than a year before. The *Stark* had waited before responding to a hostile attack from Iraqi warplanes and missiles, and suffered grievously for it. Nevertheless, on July 3, Rogers waited a bit longer before taking action against the still unidentified plane. Despite that, some would say later that the *Vincennes* had been irresponsible and incautious. David Carlson, the Navy commander in charge of the USS *Sides*, said afterward that the *Vincennes* had been consistently overaggressive during its gulf mission. In the wardrooms of the gulf fleet, the *Vincennes* had acquired an unflattering nickname, 'RoboCruiser'.

At twenty miles out, however, the aircraft was within

missile range of the *Vincennes*. Captain Rogers announced his intention to take it out. The *Vincennes*'s fire-control radar had been illuminated several minutes earlier. Now the two surface-to-air missiles were launched. On the Aegis monitors in the CIC, the computers recorded a direct hit. The airbus and its passengers spilled into the gulf moments later.

Why did the Iranian plane never respond to the *Vincennes*'s warnings? Much later it would be discovered that seven of the ten messages from the *Vincennes* had been transmitted on a frequency no civilian airliner would pick up. The remaining three had been sent out on a frequency the U.S. government had instructed civilian airliners operating in the Persian Gulf to monitor, but it was unlikely many flight crews would readily be able to identify their aircraft relative to the position of a U.S. warship steaming around the gulf. Flight 655 may have never known that any of the *Vincennes*'s messages were intended for it. Only one message, sent by the *Sides*, probably got through. The radio operator on the *Sides* had sent a message using the same code being transmitted by the Iranian plane, and was fairly certain that it had reached its destination. But that message was sent only thirty-nine seconds before the *Vincennes* launched its missiles. A final, tragic irony is that even if the Iranian aircraft had been a hostile F-14, it could not have done much damage to the *Vincennes* or its heavy armour; the F-14 is just not much of a threat to ships. In Pentagon parlance, it has no significant anti-surface warfare capability.

Within an hour or two of the crash of the airbus into the gulf, Iranian navy helicopters were flying over the wreckage, training long-lens videocameras on the bodies bobbing in the waves. Captain Rogers issued a statement later, expressing his grief and that of his crew and taking personal responsibility for the tragedy. A thoroughly honourable man, according to those who know him, he had been suddenly caught up in a horrible nightmare. The death of those innocent people, he said, was something he would live with for the rest of his life. That night in Teheran, however, no one was interested in the captain's expressions of apology. From the Iranian videocams, the grisly images of bloated bodies were broadcast around the world. And across Iran once again, nearly a decade after inflamed mullahs ransacked the U.S. embassy and snatched 240 American hostages, impassioned shrieks against the 'Great Satan' split the night. The Iranian plane had been shot down for the Fourth of July holiday, the mullahs believed, to celebrate America's independence.

The caller to AP and UPI had struck a chord with his reference to the ill-fated Iran Air flight. He had also wasted little time. He had called just before 10:00 A.M. London time, fifteen hours after Pan Am Flight 103 had fallen on Lockerbie. Some two hours before John Boyd had sent the newest search teams into the most distant fields around the village. Now, in his chaotic office in the Lockerbie Academy, he got word of the two phone calls. Boyd remembered the shooting down of the Iranian jet. This confirmed his gut reaction of the night before. But who in the name of God were the Guardians of the Islamic Revolution?

In Washington, it would be at least another two hours until sunrise. An unhappy time, indeed, to be contemplating the identities of terrorist bombers. To the all-nighters, in their operations centres in different corners of the city, the link to Iran Air Flight 655 made a lot of sense. But the Guardians of the Islamic Revolution were another story. Pushing aside crushed coffee cups and ashtrays full of crumpled cigarettes, intelligence officers at the CTC in Langley, up on the seventh floor of the State Department and at FBI headquarters, began to pull together what they knew.

It wasn't much.

CHAPTER 5

The thing about terrorism, besides the fact that it is a crime of cowards against defenceless people like Suruchi Rattan, James Fuller and the others on Pan Am Flight 103, is that it is maddeningly hard to counter. Ordinary police work is difficult enough, an unhappy business of chasing leads that go nowhere and relying on informants who are themselves criminals and so by definition unreliable. Police work as it involves terrorism is infinitely more complicated. It tends to blur the lines of responsibility between the intelligence officer, who gathers and analyses information to make sense of the world, and the criminal investigator, who must use whatever information he can find to apprehend a suspect and make a case against him in a courtroom. It can lead to hellishly messy investigations.

Nowhere are the difficulties greater for the forces arrayed against terrorism than in the Middle East and, especially, Iran. For the Ayatollah Khomeini, and now for his successors in Teheran, terrorism is a tool of government. If war is diplomacy by other means, as Clausewitz said, then terrorism is just another means of waging war. Hostage-taking, aircraft bombings – all could and should be used against the West, the Imam Khomeini instructed his followers: it is the only way a small and impoverished nation could hope to bend the United States and its allies to its will, and so spread the great Islamic revolution throughout the world. Khomeini, as it turned out, had it just about right.

Three days before Christmas, and a man phones a

news office to say that 'guardians' of Khomeini's revolution had blown up an American jet, killing hundreds of innocent people in response to a tragic mistake in which hundreds of innocent Iranians had died months before. The 'guardians' had shown, in the most graphic way possible, that they would watch over the Ayatollah's followers and avenge any wrongs done to them. Iranians die in the Persian Gulf? Now Americans die in Lockerbie. Tit for tat. It was that simple.

But who were these 'guardians'?

In Iran, as in so much of the Middle East, nothing is ever quite as it seems. Names of individuals overlap with names of ancestral villages, which are commingled with the terrorists' noms de guerre, which in turn are mixed up with plain old aliases.

In no place are the terrorists' name games played with more maddening guile than Lebanon. For the international community, one consequence of permitting the existence of a land in which virtually no law applies is that the land becomes a convenient refuge for the lawless. Witness the events of the past decade in the wastes of Lebanon's Bekaa Valley. Near Baalbek, an ancient crossroads village, the world's biggest terrorist training camp is doing a terrific business. There is instruction in bomb-making, in hand-to-hand combat and in small-weapons fire. Call it a finishing school for the foot soldiers of Khomeini's Islamic revolution.

The camp's history is not complicated. Within months after his victory over the 'Great Satan' in 1979, Khomeini had dreamed of coming to the aid of his downtrodden Shiite brethren across the Middle East. Until Israel invaded Lebanon in the spring of 1982, however, Khomeini had been forced to restrain himself. Syria controlled the overland routes in the Bekaa, and President Hafez-al-Assad would have no truck with a revolution of Islamic fundamentalist crazies in his backyard. The Israeli invasion changed that. The Israelis had promised not to attack Syrian troops, and now they had done just that. If the Iranians wanted in, Assad concluded, so be it: it would make for more firepower against the Jews.

In the summer of 1982, along a rutted mountain road from the Syrian border, a contingent of fighters from the Iranian Revolutionary Guards made their way slowly to Baalbek. There they set up camp in an old Lebanese army post, which they renamed the Sheikh Abdullah Barracks. In downtown Baalbek, a command post was established for the Revolutionary Guards at an old traveller's inn known as the Hotel al-Khayyam.

Thus were the first seeds planted of the movement the West would come to know by so many different names. Its founders called it Hezbollah. In English this means 'Party of God'. But the fighters of Hezbollah use other names: Islamic Jihad, or Holy War; the Revolutionary Justice Organization; the Organization of the Oppressed on Earth. These were just a few. Under the umbrella of Hezbollah, and at the direction of Iran's ambassador to Syria, a fanatic named Mohammed Mohtashemi who had lost several fingers in a letter-bomb attack in Syria, the movement would grow rapidly. Western intelligence officials believe Khomeini poured as much as $100 million into Hezbollah over the next few years, and Mohtashemi was not shy about spreading it around. Through a senior official at Iran's Foreign Ministry, Hosein Sheikholislam, Mohtashemi began an intense recruiting drive among the disaffected young Shiites of Lebanon's slums. Sheikholislam was a good proselytizer. A former Berkeley student, he had led the siege of the U.S. embassy in 1979. This message was simple. With the Imam's inspiration, he had made a revolution happen and changed the course of history; in Lebanon, it could happen again.

But first, all Western influence must be expunged. The United States, in particular, would have to be driven out, Mohtashemi and Sheikholislam preached. It was not long before money and messianic zeal began

71

to achieve results. Hezbollah membership climbed to 3,000; the Revolutionary Guards contingent in Baalbek continued to grow. Then embassies in Beirut began to blow up, 241 U.S. Marines were murdered by a suicide truck-bomber, and hostage-taking in Lebanon began.

Surely the Ayatollah must have been pleased. The revolution was spreading.

But would Khomeini have ordered the destruction of the Pan Am jet so many years later? Or was this some free-lance 'guardian' worried that with Khomeini in failing health and after eight murderous years of war with Iraq, the revolution was finally running out of gas?

In the predawn hours of December 22 in Washington, the questions went around and around, and there were simply no answers. At the State Department and the CIA, the terrorism experts expected nothing less. They had been this route before, looking for clues to terrorist acts in which Iran was believed to have played a part. Confusion was inevitable.

The Iranian government, through a spokesman in Teheran, quickly denied that it had had anything to do with the crash of Flight 103. That meant very little, however; relations between Khomeini and Hezbollah had frayed somewhat since the glory days of the mid-1980s, but even with static on the line between Baalbek and Teheran, the connection was still fairly strong. Hezbollah terrorists could have carried out the bombing, and Iran still could have denied it. Other terrorists, working at Teheran's behest, also could have been responsible. Either scenario would give Iran 'plausible deniability', a phrase made famous, oddly enough, in some of the darkest days of the Reagan administration, when the president and his senior aides claimed they knew nothing of the rogue Iran-contra operation being run from Oliver North's cluttered office next door to the White House. If someone had blown up Pan Am 103 at the instance of Teheran, the odds were mighty long against anyone being able to prove it.

For the experts in Washington, what was fairly certain on the morning after the crash was that there was no separate and discrete organization known as the Guardians of the Islamic Revolution. The name had been used a few times before, but there was almost no reliable information about it in the DESIST computers. The name was just that, an inconsequent label in an exasperating shell game. The frustrating thing, for the all-night crews in Washington, as a pale sun began to glint off the newly painted Capitol dome, was that the shell game worked. There was no hard information about any group of 'guardians'. For all the investigators in Washington knew, the Guardians of the Islamic Revolution could have been a rock band in the lounge of the old Teheran Hilton.

What the investigators needed was evidence. And so far they had none.

That's why the investigators in Lockerbie were so important.

And this is what John Boyd and Stuart Henderson had tried to emphasize when they sent the search teams back into the fields earlier that morning. Now, at noon in Lockerbie, as his colleagues in Washington were completing the first of many sleepless nights to come, Boyd was not so sure that the cause of the crash could be determined. If it really was a terrorist bombing, as the caller to AP and UPI had claimed, could they really hope to recover the evidence to prove it? The volunteer radio operators, hams from a group called Raynet, were better organized this morning than the night before. An operator accompanied each of the search teams, while still others were scouring the countryside alone, on foot and in four-wheel-drive vehicles. As each new Raynet report landed on his desk in Lockerbie Academy, Boyd realized just what he was up against. Young striplings from the Royal Highland Fusiliers had arrived by bus from Edinburgh at first light that morning, and Boyd had sent them farthest afield. They were in splendid physical condition and could cover more of the rough terrain than out-of-shape beat cops and tank soldiers. From the Fusiliers, through the Raynet hams, came word that debris from the 103 was scattered through the thick woods of the Kielder Forest. This is the largest forest in Great Britain, and in places it is virtually impenetrable, with dense stands of elm and oak rising alongside of each other like a great beard on the craggy land. How to search such a place?

And the distance over which the debris had scattered! Lockerbie is in the southwest corner of Scotland, yet on the morning of the twenty-second, word had already come to Lockerbie Academy of plane debris and clothing that had been found in villages at the edge of the North Sea. A watch from a body that had fallen in the fields of Tundergarth would later be recovered way up in Northumbria, over eighty miles away. Perhaps, Boyd wondered to himself, the search for evidence would prove impossible after all.

Still, they would have to try.

Normally, the noon briefing for reporters at the State Department is a semicivilized affair. The Department spokesperson strolls to the lectern, reads whatever prepared statements he or she has been given for the day, then fields questions on a range of subjects that may or may not have anything to do with the statements just read. To an outsider it at first seems a strange colloquy. A reporter interested in the Department's position on Bulgarian refugees spilling into Turkey, for instance, might ask: 'Anything on Bulgaria?' The spokesperson, unprepared for the question, would reply: 'No, we have nothing on Bulgaria.' And so it would go for some thirty minutes.

On December 22, the briefing room was jammed. Word of the Helsinki threat had already leaked, and the wire services had been moving speculative stories on the Guardians of the Islamic Revolution claim all morning. Already, families of those on board Pan Am 103 had been contacted by news reporters asking for their reaction to the earlier terrorist threat: Did they feel they were entitled to know of such threats? That was a typical question asked of the victims' families. Another was: Do you believe your husband/wife/son/daughter would be alive now if the terrorist warning had been made public? From the depths of their grief, many families responded with extreme bitterness. In the operations centre in Foggy Bottom, hundreds of phone calls from angry relatives had deluged the switchboard. The situation was made all the more impossible because the people fielding the calls still had very little information to go on. Late the night before, Pan Am's London office had faxed the passenger manifest for Flight 103. But the copy had been very poor in quality, and most of the passengers had been listed by last name only, with either a first initial or no initial at all. Besides, there was still no way to assess the accuracy of the manifest.

The families were furious. And the reporters, apprised of that fury, waited in the crowded briefing room armed with prickly questions. Spokesman Phyllis Crockett was no match for them. The nature of her job was such that she could say only what had been authorized beforehand. The State Department was looking into the Helsinki threat, she said. True. There was no way of corroborating the telephone claim by the Guardians of the Islamic Revolution. Also true. Very little was known with any degree of certainty about an organization of that name. Ditto. Crockett told the reporters that U.S. investigators were working closely with the Scots and that the investigation was continuing.

That was all.

At the State Department, the FBI and the CIA, the investigation *was* continuing, but it was, of necessity, something of a scattershot affair. Since the crash of

Flight 103, all sorts of people had called claiming they had put a bomb on board, or that they knew someone who had. Sociopaths, bored teenagers, extremist loonies: there had been strange calls throughout the night and all that morning. Several psychics had called with tips. Inmates had called from prison pay phones. Someone claiming to be from the Irish Republican Army had called. And the FBI's New York office had taken several calls, one from a man who said the jet had been bombed by a Puerto Rican separatist orgnaization; the caller could provide no details, however. In Miami, the FBI got a call from the brother of a convicted cocaine dealer. He would tell the Bureau who'd blown up the Pan Am plane, he said, if they would let his brother out of jail. The man would tell all, however, only after his brother was out of the slammer; otherwise, no deal. At a U.S. embassy in Europe, a businessman with impeccable credentials came in to offer information on the bombing. He seemed to know a great deal about Palestinian terrorists operating in Europe, and he was ushered in immediately to speak with the FBI's legal attaché and a regional security officer. During the course of a lengthy conversation, the man stopped and told his interviewers that he was receiving signals from outer space. He simply had to go, he said.

Another story came from a Long Island businessman, U.S. officials say. In March 1987, the man told investigators, he had been awarded a contract to supply U.S. ships in the Persian Gulf with fresh fruit and vegetables, and he had entered into the venture with an Iranian businessman in Dubai. In July, the man said, he had been approached by the CIA, who'd requested that he put an agency representative in touch with his Iranian partner. The Iranian man was evidently quite successful. He had an established trading company in Dubai and a membership in the Dubai Hilton Beach Club.

According to the Long Island businessman, his partner had met with a CIA officer in New York in March or April 1988 when, the businessman said, 'they struck up some deal involving U.S. citizenship' in exchange for the Iranian's assistance with some other, unspecified work.

On a business trip to Dubai between November 6 and December 12, the Long Islander said, he had been at the Hotel Intercontinental with his partner and a third man, an Iranian named Zadeh. The discussion had turned to relations between Washington and Teheran and, inevitably, to the shooting down of the Iranian airbus by the *Vincennes* in July. Zadeh, according to the man from Long Island, had said it would be avenged. 'Pan Am,' he had said. 'Boom. Before Christmas.'

Then Zadeh had gone on to say that the bombers would be paid nearly $700,000 from a Swiss bank account controlled by the brother-in-law of a high Iranian official. The bomb would be fed onto the plane at Frankfurt, Zadeh said, according to the man from Long Island; the courier would get off in London, before the explosion occurred somewhere over the Atlantic.

The businessman says he never did anything with the information, that he assumed his partner would pass it on to the CIA. After the crash, he called the FBI, detectives in Lockerbie, even *The Washington Post*.

Although elements of the businessman's story seemed plausible, he offered no evidence to support it, and his Iranian partner from Dubai disputed significant parts of it. Evidently, investigators didn't take any of it seriously.

'All these things,' said the State Department's Frank Moss, summing up the views of other intelligence officials, 'appeared to be junk.' But that didn't mean they could be dismissed. Each one would have to be checked out.

At FBI headquarters, the dimensions of the task were just becoming clear. But which things should be checked first? The Looney Tune leads would have to be investigated, to be sure, but there were other things to look at first. For one thing, there had been nineteen no-shows on Flight 103, only one of whom actually checked in, but then missed the flight. That passenger immediately became a suspect. Then there were the passengers who had boarded the doomed aircraft. Every one had to be considered a potential target. Possible motives ranged from a lover's revenge to an insurance scam. It was also possible that someone among the passengers or crew had brought a bomb on board unwittingly. Someone else could have given one of them a package, perhaps a holiday present, to carry to the States. If it wasnt actually ticking, no one would ever have known there was a bomb inside. All that would have to be checked too.

Two hundred and seventy people had died in the crash of Flight 103, and the only ones who could be immediately discounted as suspects were the eleven Lockerbie residents killed on the ground. There were also airport personnel who had access to the plane. According to Bob Ricks, the FBI's deputy assistant director of counterterrorism who coordinated the U.S. end of the Lockerbie investigation with the CIA, the FAA and other agencies, the universe of potential suspects extended to well over a thousand people. In the twenty-four hours before it arrived in London to carry the second leg of Flight 103 to New York, the *Maid of the Seas* had made stops in Los Angeles and San Francisco. It was possible that a maintenance worker or baggage handler had slipped a bomb on board there. The flight crews from Los Angeles were dismissed almost immediately from the list of suspects, but there had been as many as a dozen professional couriers on the flight from Los Angeles to London, and they were a great source of suspicion. Couriers are usually free-lance messengers who will carry a package, or even a letter, to a destination in exchange for free or discounted travel. Every one would have to be checked.

Then there were the airport personnel at Heathrow.

Pan Am shared Terminal 3 with four other carriers: MAS, the Malaysian government-owned carrier; Qantas, from Australia; Zambia Airways; and Iran Air. Twice a week, a London-to-Teheran flight left Heathrow, and Iran Air often used unoccupied Pan Am ticket counters to handle the crush of passengers. Not a hundred feet from the Pan Am security checkpoint in Terminal 3, an oversize photograph of the Ayatollah Khomeini glowered from the offices of Iran Air. Was there some way an Iran Air employee had hefted a bag with a bomb in it onto a conveyor belt or into an empty baggage hold? That would have to be checked.

Finally, there was Frankfurt. The first leg of Flight 103 had begun with a small Boeing 727 at the West German airport, where the possibilities for committing mayhem were even greater. Frankfurt Main is the busiest airport in Europe, and the investigators would have to examine scores of connecting flights. Of special interest, for obvious reasons, were Iran Air Flights from Teheran, Middle East Airlines flights from Beirut, and flights of Pakistan International Airlines, Syrian Arab Airlines, Royal Jordanian Airlines and Libyan Arab Airways. Passengers on Flight 103 who were continuing on from London to New York and Detroit would, theoretically, have had their bags checked again at Heathrow. Something else for the investigators to look at. If the checks had been incomplete, a bomb from Frankfurt could have made its way into the hold of the *Maid of the Seas*.

All told, the way Buck Revell figured it on the morning of December 22, the FBI was looking at a universe of maybe 1,200 suspects. Anyone who could have had contact with the *Maid of the Seas* in the previous seventy-two hours would have to be interviewed – from the flight crew to the baggage handlers to the people who cleaned the aircraft. This would mean bringing agents from every one of the Bureau's fifty-nine U.S. field offices into the case. It was a massive undertaking, but for the FBI it was important that the right tone be set from the outset. Because the Pan Am jet had crashed in Great Britain, America's closest ally, there would be no problem for the Bureau operating there. In introducing Tim Dorch to the other investigators in Lockerbie the night before, John Boyd had demonstrated that. The botched inquiry into the aircraft bombing that had killed Pakistan's President Zia and U.S. ambassador Raphel had left a sour smell in much of official Washington.

If the Bureau acted quickly now and simply assumed it would handle the investigation into the crash of Flight 103, perhaps no one would try to stop it. 'I was determined,' Revell said much later, 'that we were not going to face another Zia.' Coordination with John Boyd and the Scots could be worked out as they went along.

In Lockerbie late in the day on December 22, despite the State Department's breezy assurance to reports that 'the investigation is continuing', Boyd was unsure just how it would continue. Aircraft wreckage had been found at the edge of several far-flung lochs. The freezing waters would have to be searched by divers. Boyd would have to see to that tomorrow.

CHAPTER 6

Newspapers and food wrappers, the detritus of tired travellers, littered the empty terminal, awaiting the brooms of the night crews who moved like slumberous ghosts through the airport, shining and wiping, making ready for the next day's crush of tired fliers and waiting families. For hours a single bag had sat in the area reserved for unclaimed luggage, having been forwarded from London more than twelve hours before. It was late, and bags from the last arriving European flight finally had been claimed. Customs officers assigned to the Pan Am terminal at Kennedy Airport in New York were preparing to quit for the evening. The next day would be another long one, the airport regulars knew: the day before Christmas Eve, and Kennedy would be chock-a-block with holiday travellers. Unclaimed baggage would just have to wait.

For some reason, though, the solitary piece of luggage had caught one Pan Am employee's attention. Airport tags hung like tinsel from the handle of the apparently well-travelled bag. The newest ones were 'LHR', for London's Heathrow Airport, and 'JFK', for Kennedy. A check showed the bag belonged to a Daniel E. O'Connor. The alert Pan Am employee checked the manifest for the Pan Am flight that had crashed more than thirty hours before. Passenger 167 was an O'Connor, first initial D. Dan O'Connor had made the flight; his bag had not.

How come?

Even if O'Connor had been an ordinary passenger,

81

his bag's appearance would have raised red flags. Had someone swapped it with another, perhaps one with a bomb in it? Another piece of luggage, belonging to passenger Peter Raymond Peirce of Perrysville, Ohio, had turned up in London after the crash of Flight 103. But because O'Connor was no ordinary passenger, the question about his luggage carried a special urgency. A bright and ambitious young man, a native of Dorchester and resident of Boston, Dan O'Connor was an accomplished engineer who had worked for the State Department's Bureau of Diplomatic Security. In April 1988, he had been assigned to the U.S. embassy in Nicosia, Cyprus, as the State Department's regional security officer for the Middle East. In his nine months on the job in Cyprus, the new RSO had been a busy man, overseeing security planning for new U.S. diplomatic compounds in North Yemen and Lahore, Pakistan. In both places, the security risks were pretty much the same: terrorists. Had one gotten wind of O'Connor's travel plans?

And what of the other 'unusual' passengers on Flight 103?

In 1976, when George Bush moved into the big corner office at CIA headquarters in Langley, with its state-of-the-art phones and calming views of the Virginia woods, it had been like old-home week. Bush had never worked for the Agency before, but he had a lot of friends there. And he came from the right background: Yale, Skull and Bones, old New England money. From its origins in 'Wild Bill' Donovan's Office of Strategic Services, the 'oh so social' OSS, American intelligence had been the more or less exclusive province of the Eastern Establishment, of gentlemen.

That had been the case for the past thirty-five years, and it would not change during Bush's one year at the CIA, the most insular of the nation's intelligence services. In other parts of the intelligence community, vast changes had been under way for years. At State and the Pentagon – in the Defense Intelligence Agency and in the intelligence offices of the four services – analysts and officers were chosen more on the basis of brainpower than pedigree. On the technical side, among the cryptographers at the National Security Agency and the satellite specialists at the National Reconnaissance Office, this was especially true. With the exception of the CIA, every agency in the U.S. intelligence community had moved beyond the upper crust of the Ivy League to look for the nation's best minds wherever they might be found. In the mid-1970s, and more rapidly in the early 1980s, under Ronald Reagan's first director of Central Intelligence, William Casey, the CIA had begun to follow that route. In 1973, the Agency's analysts had badly misread the intentions of surprise attack by Egypt and Syria on Israel and the ensuing OPEC-driven oil crisis. Six years later, they had failed totally to anticipate the collapse of the Shah and the spread of Islamic fundamentalism, one of the defining forces of the next decade. These intelligence failures, among others, had led to a widely held view in and out of government that the CIA was an ossified bureaucracy in sore need of new blood. At the urging of Admiral Bobby Ray Inman, Casey's first deputy director of the CIA, and later, of Robert Gates, a successor, the Agency had intensified its recruiting efforts outside the Ivy League, focusing for the first time on state universities and even on technical schools. To its great surprise, the Agency had come up with some of its most able new recruits in little backwater colleges and in the big state schools of the West and Midwest.

It was largely for this reason that Matthew Gannon had found himself on board Pan Am Flight 103 on December 21. Of course it didn't hurt that Gannon had married the daughter of a senior Agency official, Thomas Twetten. A twenty-five-year veteran of the Agency, Twetten was the Near East division chief.

Gannon had been born in 1954 in Orange County,

California. He had been brought up in San Juan Capi-strano, where he'd attended Mission School. And after graduation from St. Michael's Prep in 1972, he'd matriculated at the University of Southern California. An exceptional student, Gannon had acquired degrees in international relations and Arabic. For a CIA recruiter, those were attractive credentials indeed. At age twenty-three, Matthew Gannon had become an officer of the Central Intelligence Agency. For the next eleven years, in postings in North Yemen, Jordan and Syria, Gannon would be listed among the embassy staffs as a 'political officer' of the State Department. To those he worked with, it was no secret who his real employer was, but the fiction was maintained for secur-ity reasons. In the chaos of Beirut, any cover, no matter how flimsy, was welcome. It could be the difference between life and death.

Gannon was in Beirut on temporary assignment. For obvious reasons of safety, his wife, Susan, had stayed home in Maryland with their two small children. There was never any question that they would do otherwise. It was simply too dangerous. The Gannon family knew the risks of Beirut for a CIA officer. On April 18, 1983, a delivery van had pulled under the front portico of the U.S. embassy and exploded in a fireball that collapsed the centre section of the unlovely eight-storey building. On the second floor of the embassy, almost directly above the portico, Robert Ames, the Agency's most respected Middle East analyst, had just convened a meeting of the CIA station officers when the bomb exploded. Everyone in the meeting had been killed. Eleven months later, William Buckley, the CIA's new Beirut station chief, was shoved into the trunk of a beat-up Renault as he walked to work. He died more than a year later, still the captive of his Shiite abductors.

No, Beirut was no place for the family of a CIA officer.

Charles McKee, another of Flight 103's more 'unus-ual' passengers, didn't have those kinds of worries.

McKee had entered the Army as a private eighteen years before. He had been married for a while, but now, approaching forty and the end of his Army career, he was still resolutely unattached. His family, perhaps for that very reason, worried about him. His mother and sister back home in Pennsylvania never quite knew where he was or what he did. And McKee never told them. He had come home for Thanksgiving. Then, on December 20, having purchased the tickets that would take him from Beirut to London and on to New York, McKee had called his mother.

'Is that you?' Beulah McKee had asked. The connection was bell-clear.

'Yes, it's me,' McKee had answered. 'I'm coming home for Christmas.'

'Well, where are you?'

Chuck McKee had laughed. 'I'm still here.'

Beulah McKee had no earthly idea where 'here' was. But she had been glad her son was coming home for the holidays just the same.

McKee was employed by an organization that did not exist, at least on paper. He was a spy. At six-foot-five and 270 pounds, however, McKee had certainly not been built for undercover work. His friends at the U.S. Army's Intelligence Support Activity, ISA, where McKee worked, called him 'Tiny'. McKee hadn't minded the nickname; he was one of the ISA's best agents.

The ISA had been created secretly within the Pentagon after the failure of the Iran rescue mission in 1980. The ISA would do for the military what the CIA either could not or would not do: gather information, so that if and when the Pentagon was authorized to conduct a similar operation anytime in the future, it would have intelligence on which it knew it could rely. For the intelligence community during the Reagan years, Beirut was at the top of its list of priorities. The president was deeply moved by the plight of the American hostages in Lebanon and viscerally angered by terrorism. Sooner or later, McKee and his buddies at the ISA had figured, their bosses at the Pentagon, aware of the president's concern, would want something done about it. As it turned out, they were right.

Despite his embarrassment over the shenanigans of Ollie North and the other Iran-contra schemers, Ronald Reagan was unwilling and emotionally unprepared to give up on the hostasges. If there was a way to get them out, he told his senior advisers, he wanted to try it. The only problem was that since the abduction of William Buckley, the U.S. had virtually no reliable intelligence on what was happening to the hostages. From time to time, word reached U.S. intelligence officers that some hostages were being held at a specific location. At one point, CIA technicians even worked up a $30,000 scale model of a house in which some hostages were believed to be held, so that they could begin planning a raid. The model was even replicated at Fort Bragg, North Carolina, where the Delta Force used it to practice a rescue mission. The only problem was that no hostages were ever held in that particular house. The hostages were moved by their captors so often and most of the information on their whereabouts was of such dubious value that a rescue operation was never attempted. They had to do better, Reagan insisted.

The secret warriors in the Pentagon certainly tried.

Sometime in 1986, the Defense Intelligence Agency had asked the ISA to supply an agent for an intelligence-gathering operation in Beirut. Chuck McKee had volunteered. He had been a near-perfect candidate. He spoke fluent Arabic, having learned it at the Defense Department's advanced language school in Monterey, California. McKee had spent four years as an officer of a classified program providing counterterrorism training to the security staff of the royal family of Saudi Arabia, where he had had a chance to improve his language skills. Since then, he had been posted for another four years in West Germany before being sent back to the Pentagon. McKee had quickly become frustrated with life in Washington and told a few friends at the ISA that he wanted to try something new. Beirut seemed like just the ticket. Enthusiastically, McKee had sold his car and given up his small apartment in suburban Virginia.

Before he left, he had told a few friends: 'I'm looking forward to my next opportunity to get my hands dirty.'

McKee had arrived in Beirut in January 1987. Just over a year later, on February 17, 1988, men with automatic weapons shoved Marine Lieutenant Colonel William Richard Higgins into a waiting car and drove off. Higgins wasn't even a combatant; he was unarmed, a member of a United Nations peacekeeping mission.

If Reagan was concerned about all the American hostages in Lebanon, many of the miltary men at the Pentagon were less so. The civilians who had stayed behind in Beirut had been warned by Washington to leave: their safety could not be guaranteed. They had stayed on, almost all for noble reasons, it is true. But the U.S. could not skew its policy for a few people who had defied the official warnings, much less the warnings of common sense. If there was a consensus within the Pentagon regarding the hostages, this was it.

It did not apply to Rich Higgins, however. Even in the chaos of Lebanon, all parties recognized his role as a peacekeeper. To find Higgins, the Pentagon would leave no stone unturned. Perhaps, with luck, they could rescue some of the other hostages as well. The abduction of Higgins placed enormous pressure on McKee, Gannon and the handful of other intelligence officers in Beirut. But try as they did, they had had no success.

Coming home on December 21, travelling with Gannon, Chuck McKee had plenty to think about. Over the past few months, the two had learned much about the people of Lebanon, and about the factionalism that stabbed like a wedge into the heart of the country that had once, not long ago, been rather beautiful and serene. For all the risks they took, and all they had learned, McKee and Gannon had not helped find a single hostage, however. A few weeks home with their families might help them forget the frustration.

Gannon had left Beirut by helicopter on the morning of the twenty-first with the U.S. ambassador to Lebanon, John McCarthy, and another American. Ronald LaRiviere was a year younger than Gannon. Like O'Connor, LaRiviere had been an officer with the State Department's Bureau of Diplomatic Security. LaRiviere had been no engineer, though. He was a decorated soldier, and his job in Beirut had been to protect McCarthy and the deputy chief of mission from the bizarre range of threats that existed only in Lebanon. Like Gannon and McKee, LaRiviere and O'Connor had volunteered for the dangerous Beirut posting. For the terrorists around them in the shattered Lebanese capital, any one of the four would have made an attractive target.

In Washington, intelligence officers at the State Department and the CIA, and investigators at the FBI had already begun speculating about that possibility. When O'Connor's suitcase, tag number CY188021, finally turned up in New York late in the day on the twenty-second, they began doing much more. But it seemed implausible. If someone had wanted to kill them, why not in Beirut? It would have been easier there. And the chance of retribution was virtually nil.

'That's what we all thought,' said one investigator. 'But still, if you think the 103 is a terrorist bombing, you've got to look at the spooksmen.'

An FBI agent was dispatched from the New York field office in downtown Manhattan to collect O'Connor's bag at Kennedy. Then a team of investigators from the FBI, CIA, FAA and State Department began trying to reconstruct the travel plans of the four men. If someone had wanted to kill them, they had gone to a hell of a lot of trouble in blowing up a jumbo jet over Scotland.

Thanks to the kindness of friends in the British embassy in Beirut, Gannon and LaRiviere had gotten the chopper ride out of the city just after first light on December 21. After landing at Akrotiri, site of an RAF base on Cyprus, the two men had been taken by car to the international airport at Larnaca. McKee had come out of Lebanon quietly and alone, on a ferry from the Christian port of Juniyah to Larnaca. It was risky, but McKee had made the trip before. He liked the ride.

From a company called Travel Masters, in Nicosia, the three men had booked tickets on Cyprus Airways Flight 504 to London. When they had checked in that morning they managed to get seats close to each other, McKee in 2D, Gannon in 2E and LaRiviere in 2G. The 9.30 departure would put them in London at 1:30 P.M. local time. They would have about four hours to kill before the Pan Am clipper was scheduled to board for the trip to New York.

So many people were trying to get away that Cyprus Airways had had to lay on another London flight that morning. For months, as the merciless shelling had continued in Beirut and basic necessities such as electricity and running water had become more and more unreliable, Cyprus had been filling up with refugees. Some were content to stay on the island, but many more wanted to move on. Estimates placed the number of Lebanese who had fled their country at more than a million, and most of them had passed through Cyprus. The managers at Cyprus Airways were used to it, and on the morning of the twenty-first they arranged for an unscheduled flight, 1364, to Heathrow.

Daniel O'Connor had a two-year-old daughter, Jessica, he was anxious to see. But there had also been a death in the family, and he was returning home sooner than he expected. With some luck, he had gotten a ticket on Flight 1364, with a connection to New York on Pan Am 103.

In Washington, investigators quickly confirmed that O'Connor had had only the one bag. McKee had had two, Gannon one and LaRiviere none. Security at the Larnaca airport was fairly thorough, but it was possible someone there could have exchanged bags with one of the four men. In London, the bags would have been offloaded from the Cyprus Airways flights at Heathrow's Terminal 2, sorted and transferred on the airfield side and then ferried over to the back of Terminal 3. Theoretically, the bags would have been X-rayed once again before they were loaded into the baggage hold of the *Maid of the Seas*. A Pan Am-owned company, Alert Management Systems, Inc., provided security for the airline's facilities around the world. Alert personnel should have examined all luggage in London, even if they were so-called interline bags from connecting flights and presumedly had been examined by the initial carrier.

Something else to check.

The request was passed on from Washington, but by the morning of December 23, investigators in London had already begun interviewing Pan Am and its Alert employees. At FBI headquarters, Buck Revell ordered that FBI agents assist with the interviews in London and Frankfurt. In London, Darrell Mills had already offered the Bureau's services. Mills's conterpart at the Bonn embassy, Dave Barham, did likewise. For now at least, that was about all that could be done from the Washington end. The real work was still in Lockerbie.

John Boyd was not at all sure he would be able to hold up his end of the bargain. At 5:00 P.M. on December 23, he had convened the evening meeting of the investigators in the big upper room of Lockerbie Academy. Windows ran down the left side of the room, but no light came through; it was already pitch-dark out. In two days the investigators had fallen into a routine. They were in the fields at the first faint glimmerings of dawn, just a bit after eight. And they worked until about four in the afternoon, until the light gave out. By five, most had recovered somewhat, with coffee or hot soup. Then Boyd reviewed the day's progress. On this evening the news was grim.

As the police and morticians slumped in their seats, looking ridiculous in their white and yellow paper coveralls smeared with Vicks VapoRub to combat the smell of formaldehyde, Boyd told them the obvious: Many bodies had been recovered, but many more remained to be found, and the identification process was going very slowly. Tony Balfour, the RAF pathologist, had set up a mortuary in the basement of the town hall. His men had not had a chance yet even to look at many of the bodies. The village ice-skating rink, just around the corner from Lockerbie Academy, had been opened up to store the bodies. As Balfour's mortuary teams were ready for them, the corpses were brought over one by one. The autopsy process was lengthy.

Boyd saw no way for all the bodies to be recovered and identified by Christmas Eve, as he had promised. And the families who had come to Lockerbie to identify their loved ones and claim their remains could not understand the delay. Their complaints dug at Boyd, and he felt helpless.

'It was Christmastime,' he said later, 'and I didn't want any of the relatives, in the U.S. or elsewhere, thinking we hadn't pulled out all the stops.' But there was only so much that could be done.

After the investigators went back to their hotels, Boyd sat in his office. He had not told them the worst of the news, and he scarcely knew how to deal with it himself. The BBC was reporting that the weather was closing in; snow was likely tomorrow. Worse, the army and air force troops who had been searching the fields around

Lockerbie were scheduled to go on holiday leave on the afternoon of the twenty-fourth.

'What the hell am I going to do?' Boyd recalled thinking that night.

Before he left his office to head home, he placed a call to an old police friend up north. The chief constable in Grampian was the only one he knew in all Scotland who had access to a snowmobile. If it was going to snow tomorrow, Boyd thought, he wanted the machine, for whatever good it might do. Over the telephone line from the north, the Grampian chief constable told Boyd that he could count on the snowmobile. 'I'll have it down for you tomorrow.'

Boyd, it turned out, need not have worried. December 24 dawned bright and clear. And from Whitehall came more encouraging news: The soldiers would continue searching as long as there were bodies still unrecovered. 'You'll have full coverage,' an army officer told Boyd, 'as long as you need it.'

In Lockerbie, the news was of little solace to the families of the victims. Bruce Smith had flown all day on December 22 and then driven to his home south of London to get Ingrid's dental records, and now he was at home with his three children in Bray, west of London, apoplectic at Boyd and his mule-headed investigators. Not only did he have the dental records, but he had something that could have been used to identify Ingrid immediately. Ingrid wore one half of a broken medallion on a chain around her neck, Bruce wore the other: it was not complicated. Besides, Ingrid had been sitting in 4H, in first class, right below the co-pilot's seat on the flight deck of the *Maid of the Seas*. Smith had driven up to his wife's parents' to bring them back to Bray. He knew his wife's body had been recovered, and yet the investigators would not identify her or even release any of her personal effects. Bastards, Smith thought, how can they hurt us so?

Most of the other families who had come to Lockerbie were not so forceful. Unlike Smith, they knew little about airplanes, and less about police work. FBI agent Tim Dorch spent an evening with Bert Ammerman, whose brother, Thomas, had died in the crash. Ammerman had flown from New Jersey, and he would later become an outspoken leader of the families of victims of Flight 103 and one of the most vocal critics of Pan Am and U.S. policy regarding aircraft security. In Lockerbie, however, Ammerman was mute with grief.

On Christmas Eve day, on the High Street outside the town hall, the victims' families passed each other numbly without greeting. The sun shone, church bells pealed, and to those who had lost loved ones in the crash, the whole of Christmas Eve seemed an exquisitely horrible form of torture.

To comfort the families of the victims, and to make sure they received information as soon as it became available, Boyd had asked another old police friend to come to Lockerbie. He also needed someone to handle the press, whose numbers had been increasing every day. Angus Kennedy, superintendent of police in Strathclyde, was more than equal to both tasks. A great friendly bear of a man, Kennedy had begun his police career over twenty years before in Glasgow, a brawling, hard-scrape city on the river Clyde where too many Saturday-night pub disputes ended in a clash of fists or knives. Since police officers were unarmed in Scotland, often the only way to make an arrest was by punching a troublemaker's lights out and hauling him bodily down to police headquarters. Kennedy still had the scars of those old wars, but somehow he had never lost his easy way with people, especially with children. A small girl whose father died on Flight 103 had come to Lockerbie with her family a day or two after the crash. Kennedy had accompanied the family up to Tundergarth to see the cockpit lying in the grass. It was the least gruesome of sights, and perhaps it would help explain it all somehow.

A reporter watching through binoculars described the scene afterwards: They looked at the cockpit for a long time, the police officer and the girl. When they finally turned away, her small hand in his big, calloused one, there were tears streaming down Angus Kennedy's face.

Kennedy, who would lose his own wife, Katie, to cancer in the coming year, could do little to ease the families' pain those first few days in Lockerbie. No one could, really.

On Christmas Day, at Lockerbie's Holy Trinity Church, the Reverend Patrick Keegans appeared on the altar to say Mass. The Flannigans and Somervilles had lived on Sherwood Crescent a few doors down from Father Keegans's house. They had been not just neighbours but friends as well. They had attended his church each week and listened carefully to his sermons. On the night of December 21, while the Somervilles and Flannigans had vanished in the fireball, Father Keegans's house had remained standing, slightly charred, at the edge of the crater. Father Keegans himself had not been injured, except in some strange, indefinable way that had left him hollow-eyed and ashen-faced this Christmas morning. He tried to continue with the mass, but he could not.

The text of his undelivered sermon said this, in part: 'As Christ did on the cross, we, too, scream at the Father: "My God, my God, why have you abandoned me?" He does not seem to answer. There is only silence.'

Nowhere in the sermon text did Father Keegans make any mention of Christmas.

CHAPTER 7

For the investigators in Lockerbie, Christmas Day brought a risk of bombs, rumours of AIDS, strange talk of spies and what looked very much like a large amount of drugs in a suitcase. Happy holidays.

At the Dexstar Chemicals warehouse, Superintendent Douglas Roxburgh watched glumly as his officers logged in the newest Yuletide findings: a crushed guitar, a sopping teddy bear, a stewardess's scarf and a surprising number of Bibles. Someone brought in James MacQuarrie's captain's hat. There was crumpled luggage that reeked of aviation fuel. And clothing caked with blood and mud.

The stuff was delivered by truck and by helicopter, and by village residents on their way into town for church services. In rubber gloves, surgeon's masks and their disposable plastic and paper jumpsuits, forty to fifty officers worked through the holiday. Each new find was run slowly through an X-ray machine when it first arrived at the Dexstar plant. John Boyd and his chief investigator, John Orr, had ordered every piece of debris and luggage checked for explosives or explosives residue. If there had been one bomb aboard the *Maid of the Seas*, there could easily have been several more.

After it was X-rayed, each item of luggage and clothing was passed over to the forensic specialists and explosives experts, Tom Thurman, Walter Korsgaard and their counterparts from the British Air Accident Investigation Board. Korsgaard and Thurman split their time looking through property and aircraft debris and treading across the sodden fields with the men handling the teams of bomb-sniffing dogs. Korsgaard had participated in more air-disaster investigations than probably any other American official, and whenever a bomb was the suspected cause, he did the same thing. In his travel bag were pictures and slides from previous aircraft bombings. If a bomb has been placed near the skin of the aircraft, the metal will become superheated as it blows outward. An explosion at an altitude of 30,000 feet or more, where temperatures are well below freezing, will cause the metal to remain in that position. There is no more clear and convincing evidence of an aircraft bombing than certain pieces of metal. Korsgaard's slides and photos showed untrained searchers exactly what to look for. Anyone, Korsgaard says, can be trained quickly to look for clues. Thurman, in his own patient way, said little and went about his business. Although the Scots warmed to Korsgaard first, they came to rely more and more heavily on the measured analysis of Thurman.

For both men, looking through clothing and broken luggage was another thing. It was an unhappy business, but it had to be done. Bomb residue could be found almost anywhere. Examination of the aircraft parts piling up in the garages of Blue Band Motors on Bridge Street was similarly important. An explosion with enough force to cripple a Boeing 747 would have left plenty of evidence. When a bomb explodes, it sends tiny fragments of itself and anything in its way hurtling at speeds of thousands of feet per second. Even the tiniest fragments could leave a trace in the side of a luggage bin or the hide of a jet. The fragments, Korsgaard said, 'will stick to their depth', in whatever they hit. So a tiny bit of metal or suitcase could become embedded in part of the plane, or perhaps in another piece of relatively undamaged luggage. Some specialists refer to this as 'high-speed particle penetration'. Thurman thought of it simply as evidence. Residue or soot recovered from a piece of luggage or part of the plane can usually be identified, even in the smallest quantities, by exacting laboratory analysis. 'If we get really lucky,' Korsgaard said, the lab boys could tell 'precisely what kind of explosive' was used. A *really* good investigator could pick out craters left in the metal by hot gases given off in the explosion. 'These are unique,' said Korsgaard. 'You don't find them in any other kind of impact.'

If Korsgaard, Thurman and the others could find such indications in Lockerbie, it would tell them about where the bomb had been on the 747 and, perhaps, how it had gotten on board. That was the necessary first step; without it, no matter what else they had, there would be no way to carry the investigation forward.

Finding the kind of evidence they needed, however, would mean sifting through mounds and mounds of scuffed and dirtied belongings, many of them contaminated with blood and other body fluids. The night before, on Christmas Eve, soldiers and police officers had been issued plastic gloves and plastic bags. Earlier that day, from an officer or medical examiner stationed at the temporary morgue in the ice-skating rink had come chilling news: One of the bodies recovered from the 103 was infected with the AIDS virus.

What else could go wrong?

Since the crash of the jumbo jet, up at his farm in Tundergarth, Jimmie Wilson had been trying to collect his lambs from faraway fields and get them calmed down. Since the night of the crash, the RAF's enormous Chinook helicopters had been crisscrossing the ancient hills around Lockerbie, swinging heavy searchlights to and fro from their undercarriages and driving the lambs to madness. Besides the one ewe that had been killed when it was hit by a body falling from the plane, twenty others had been crushed in wild stampedes as they raced frantically toward the darkness, trying to escape the searchlights that played crazily across his fields each night. On the morning of the twenty-fourth, Wilson had gone out to inspect the flocks to see what new damage had been done during the night. In a close-in field, he found a clot of sheep nosing cautiously around a burst leather valise. The bag had a red-and-white ribbon on it, indicating a searcher had already found it and marked it for pickup. But no one had come to collect it.

Wilson knew there were police at the end of the road that morning. There were police and news reporters everywhere around his farm, it seemed. The reporters were terrible, bothering his family at all hours of the day and night for comments or some new scrap of information. The police officers did their best to keep the news people in line, but they were badly outnumbered, and they had other things to worry about besides protecting local people's privacy. Besides, the locals were doing pretty well for themselves. The night before, in Lockerbie, a British television reporter, pretending to be a relative of someone killed on Flight 103, had edged his way into a private part of the town hall reserved for the victims' families. A Lockerbie man had spotted the reporter's tiny microphone, and he and several neighbours had ushered the man quietly outside, where they had administered a hearty pounding. Two people who witnessed the incident said a police officer and rescue worker had stood nearby but made no effort to interfere. The reporter, bruised and very dishevelled, found himself back out on the High Street later that evening with a broken microphone and no story. There was more than one way to keep unruly outsiders in line.

Jimmie and June Wilson wanted no part of any conflict with anyone. As much as they were annoyed by the harassment from the news reporters and worried over the disturbance to their animals, they grieved for those who had died in their fields. They had extinguished the lights on their Christmas tree the night the

98

jet crashed, and they were in no mood to celebrate. Like so many of their neighbours, the Wilsons wanted to do whatever they could to help make sure the bodies were recovered promptly and the belongings returned to the families of the deceased. It was the very least they could do, they figured.

Jimmie Wilson told a deputy chief about the unclaimed leather valise not long after he found it, and a short while later a junior officer was dispatched to collect the bag and its contents. Wilson said later that he did not know the officer or get his name. He recalled that the man gave him a plastic bag and asked him to hold it open while he shovelled the contents of the valise into it. Wilson was struck mainly by all the brightly coloured clothes in the bag. 'Every colour you can think of. Even coloured underpants.' Who would wear such things?

A label on the suitcase read 'Robbi', but a check showed that the name did not match, in whole or in part, with any of those on the passenger list for Flight 103. Anyway, the most interesting thing in it, Wilson said, was buried deep among the clothes. It was a khaki-coloured webbing belt, about nine inches wide.

'Uh oh,' Wilson remembered the officer saying. 'I know what we got here.'

'What have we got here?' Wilson asked.

Wilson never got a good look at what was in the belt, but he did catch a glimpse of what looked like white powder in plastic bags peeping out of its top pockets. He remembered that there was also a shorthand notebook in the bag, its pages smudged by rainwater. The officer never used the word 'drugs' but said only that the stuff in the belt, whatever it was, was 'of substantial value'. Wilson tried to press for information, but the police officer refused to have it drawn out.

'We know about this one,' Wilson recalled him saying. But the policeman would say no more.

What else could it be but drugs? Wilson wondered.

That was just one of several strange things going on as Christmas Day approached. Scottish and U.S. authorities would say afterwards that no drugs were found in the wreckage of Flight 103. As was not the case with the rumours about large sums of cash, which stemmed from the Dodd boys' retrieval of the stacks of cancelled cheques in Tundergarth, they had no explanations for the story about drugs.

And they were having nothing to do with any talk of spies.

By Friday, December 23, there were search teams at work in eleven sectors, A through K, with A at the crater on Sherwood Crescent and K extending all the way up to the Kielder Forest in Northumberland. John Boyd had designated the area around the Tundergarth as Search Sector D. It would turn out to be the most interesting of the areas by a long shot.

According to one official, on Friday, two days after the crash, senior police officers in Lockerbie were told that a CIA identification badge had been found by a searcher in Tundergarth. It seemed implausible that Matthew Gannon or any CIA personnel in such a sensitive posting as his would travel with CIA credentials, but the official insisted that at least one such item was found. A badge credential could have been used by Gannon to prevent a customs inspector from examining a packet of documents, for instance. In any event, searchers were given instructions to look for either badges or documents.

Since the crash of Flight 103, there have been various accounts of the recovery of CIA documents and materials, and no easy way to reconcile them. Two persons involved in the search of Sector D in the days just before and after Christmas, however, insist that a badge was recovered and, later, some documents that appeared to have something to do with negotiations concerning the American hostages in Beirut.

Lockerbie and Lebanon? It seemed preposterous.

Yet many details of the two individuals' account have been verified, and they have no apparent reasons for fabricating an outlandish tale of spy games in the Scottish hills. This is the story the two individuals tell: On December 23, there were roughly forty volunteer hill searchers and dog handlers walking the fields of Sector D alongside some sixty soldiers and 120 uniformed police officers. The Raynet men accompanied individual search teams, and a fleet of army and private helicopters flew back and forth overhead, helping direct them to still unrecovered bodies and debris. Bodies were still the priority. Suddenly, that changed.

That same day, after word had reached Lockerbie Academy that a CIA identification badge or seal had been found, John Boyd and his senior investigators were told that important papers were still missing. The papers were contained in a clear plastic bag with a red emblem on the outside. Evidently, only a very few people were told that the papers belonged to a CIA official who had been on the plane, but virtually all the searchers heard some variation of the rumour having to do with spies and hostages. In any event, searchers in Sector D were urged to look especially hard for the papers in the plastic bag with the red emblem. For some reason, officials were convinced the papers could be found in Tundergarth near where the cockpit had gone down.

Coincidentally, also on the same day, one piece of Charles McKee's luggage turned up. A Tundergarth farmer, Chris Graham, had found McKee's battered brown valise, split and with the handle broken, lying in his fields. He had stacked it with nineteen others he had recovered and phoned the switchboard at Lockerbie Academy to let the people know he had a bunch of bags for them to come and fetch. Later that day, a police officer and an RAF corporal in a Land-Rover drove out to Graham's farm and retrieved the bags. McKee's, with

101

all the others, was turned over to Superintendent Roxburgh's team of officers at the Dexstar warehouse. After it was X-rayed, examined and tagged, it was placed carefully into a cardboard box labelled 'Charles McKee'. And that is precisely where it sat until the early hours of Christmas morning.

The holiday had not affected the rhythm of the search one bit. 'It was,' John Boyd said afterwards, 'like Christmas never happened.'

On Christmas morning, police officers and soldiers were out in the fields just before eight. At ten, according to one of the two individuals who related this account of the CIA documents, a Raynet man summoned three or four police officials to Lockerbie Academy. There, after nearly an hour's delay, they were introduced to a man identified as a senior investigator for the British Air Accident Investigations Board and another man, identified only as 'Arnie', who was described as a Pan Am engineer. Arnie was wearing civilian clothes and a Pan Am ID badge. He said he was from New York.

With an explosives expert from the Home Office, a police photographer from Strathclyde and a Raynet wireless operator, the party went back up to Tundergarth. The two individuals who related the story of the CIA documents said they were told that McKee's bag had been found to have explosives residue on it, and it was away being tested; it was important, however, to determine exactly where the bag had been retrieved. That story was manifestly untrue. There was no evidence of explosives on or around McKee's luggage. Nevertheless, Arnie and his British sidekick were keen to know where it had been found, the two individuals who participated in the search said.

Arnie questioned the RAF corporal who had gotten the bag from farmer Graham. The RAF man said he didn't know where the bag had been found.

When Arnie asked farmer Graham, he couldn't

remember either. He had collected twenty bags, after all, and they all looked pretty much alike.

With few clues, the men began walking across the fields. They were told that they were looking for evidence of explosives, torn metal, charred clothing, those sort of things. They were also told to keep an eye out for any papers in a plastic bag with a red emblem on it. If they found such a thing, they should turn it over to Arnie immediately.

One of the two individuals said he saw Arnie pick up what looked like a piece of a baggage container and put it in his pocket. Otherwise, the searchers found nothing unusual. After several hours, they went back to Lockerbie Academy. They said they were told to keep quiet about the search and the questions that had been asked up in Tundergarth.

'Don't ask questions,' one of the two men was told. 'Just get on with your job.' The man remembered that Arnie had already disappeared by that time. He also recalled that Arnie did a pretty good job of interrogation. For an engineer, anyway.

John Boyd had other things besides drugs and spies on his mind. He had failed in his goal to recover all the bodies from the crash of the *Maid of the Seas* by Christmas Eve. At nightfall on the twenty-fourth, the four-man teams – each comprised of two police officers and two soldiers – were still bringing in bodies. They had been instructed to use plastic gloves to lift each corpse into a plastic bag, then to drop the gloves inside before they sealed the bag. In their exhaustion, many of the men had forgotten, and plastic gloves littered fields around Lockerbie like bunting after a fair.

The bodies went into black plastic bags. Everything else, aircraft debris and personal belongings, went into transparent ones. Everyone knew the difference. On his way to Christmas Eve services, Lockerbie police inspector George Stubbs overheard a conversation between a young mother and her three-year-old son. The child pointed to black bags in a nearby field, Stubbs recalled.

Dead people, the lad told his mother.

She told him, no, that was only rubbish from the plane.

'No, mum,' replied the youngster. 'Black bags is bodies. Clear bags is wreckage.'

After the transparent bags were X-rayed and emptied and their contents examined by the forensic specialists, they were passed on to other officers who tagged each item and entered it into the HOLMES computer. Police photographers then shot each item. The photographs would create a permanent record of the debris, but it was also a thoughtful gesture. For the families who would have to identify clothing and luggage, it would be less traumatic to examine a photographic image than the torn and battered objects that said so much more than words could about the violent explosion and the terrible crash to earth.

After being photographed, each item was sorted according to owner. Across the floor of the Dexstar warehouse, police officers had distributed 259 card-board boxes, each about the size of a large egg-packing crate. As an article of clothing or luggage was linked positively to a passenger, it was placed in the box with his or her name on it. It all seemed so simple, finding and cataloguing debris and examining it for clues. But there was no reason to expect Lockerbie, or any small community, really, to be able to respond as quickly and efficiently as it had after the crash of Pan Am 103.

As the smallest police force in Great Britain, the Dum-fries and Galloway Constabulary had had few encoun-ters with crime of any kind. Its report for 1987, for instance, noted that Dumfries and Galloway officers had captured a lot of stray dogs, 626 to be precise. And they had investigated 456 cases of suspected sheep anthrax; none was confirmed. There was the odd stolen car to be recovered and the rare spot of unpleasantness in one of the fine pubs along the High Street, but otherwise, very little violent crime of any kind. And yet the police force had responded swiftly to the crash of a jumbo jet in a small village and within hours begun the business of identifying the victims and investigating the cause.

'Had this happened in a small town in Oklahoma or in Texas,' said the FBI's Darrell Mills, 'I don't think we could reasonably expect a better job than they did in Lockerbie, and chances are we would not have done it as well.'

By Christmas Day, Mills had exchanged sleeping on his office floor in the embassy in London for a narrow bed in a chilly hotel room in Lockerbie. Unfortunately, hot showers were not among the amenities accorded paying guests. FBI agent Tim Dorch, who had been in Lockerbie since the night of the crash, had left London on the spur of the moment, without even a change of clothes. On the twenty-second, he had purchased a shirt, the very last one in a clothing store on the High Street. Since then, he had worked nearly around the clock, catnapping in a tiny hotel room, when it wasn't being used by the embassy consular officials with whom he had to share it. Several days before the crash of the 103, Dorch's parents had flown from the States to celebrate Christmas in London with Tim, his wife and their two sons. Mills, who knew this, ordered Dorch back to London by Christmas Day. He would go up to Lockerbie to take his place. It was bad enough that Mills would not be with his own family for the holiday, but that was the way he operated. If anyone had to be inconvenienced, Mills figured, it might as well be he. He sure wished someone would have told him about the shower situation, however.

In Lockerbie Academy, the FBI's Ident team had already set up the phototelesis machine, and it was working like a charm. Thanks largely to its ninety-

105

second turnaround on fingerprints, photographs of personal jewellery and the like, the first bodies from the crash of the 103 would be going back to the States the next day. It was small consolation to the majority of the families, who would have to wait days for the bodies of their loved ones to be positively identified and released, but at least it was a start.

As they filtered back into Lockerbie Academy at dusk on the twenty-fifth, Mills, Thurman and the investigators had little to lift their spirits but the prospect of a quick meal and bed. It had been another chilly, miserable day, made worse by each new retrieval of a dismembered limb and the thick stench of formaldehyde. On Christmas night, though, there was another smell in Lockerbie Academy. Members of the Women's Rural Voluntary Service had spent the day in the academy kitchen cooking. And when the soldiers and police officers filed in for John Boyd's evening briefing, they were greeted by the strange but welcome aroma of roast turkey and Christmas pudding. In their damp clothes, the men devoured the meal hungrily.

The intelligence analysts at the CIA's counterterrorism centre in Langley had spent the days since the crash assembling every bit of information they had on individuals and organizations with the capability of getting a bomb on board a plane and somehow triggering it after the plane was in the air. Their findings were anything but reassuring. In 1987 alone, the CTC analysts found, international terrorists had carried out 832 operations, attacking citizens and property of 84 nations, murdering more than 600 people and wounding at least 2,000. The toll was greater than in any year since the U.S. government had begun keeping records on terrorist activity, twenty years before.

In the autumn of 1988, just weeks before his election as president, George Bush had addressed an open letter on the subject of terrorism that had served as an introduction to the Defense Department's latest study of terrorist organizations. 'The difference between terrorists and freedom fighters is sometimes clouded,' Bush wrote. 'Some would say one man's freedom fighter is another man's terrorist. I reject that notion. The philosophical differences are stark and fundamental. . . . In seeking to destroy freedom and democracy, terrorists deliberately target noncombatants for their own cynical purposes. They kill and maim defenceless women and children. . . . The difference between the terrorist and the freedom fighter is as profound as it is obvious. To permit this distinction to become blurred is to play into the terrorists' hands.'

Hard words with which to disagree. But what did they mean, really?

No right-thinking person could doubt that killing innocent people was a heinous act, and that people who blew up planes were murderers plain and simple; airplane bombings had nothing to do with freedom fighting. For too long, however, American policy toward terrorists of all kinds had been more words than action. 'Let terrorists beware that when rules of international behaviour are violated, our policy will be one of swift and effective retribution.' Ronald Reagan had said those words on January 27, 1981, welcoming home the Americans who had been held hostage in Teheran for an agonizing 444 days. But 'swift and effective retribution' had turned out to be an empty promise.

In 1983 and 1984, the United States had lost citizens and soldiers as a result of suicide terror attacks launched by Iranian-inspired fundamentalists in Lebanon. During that time, the single most devastating terrorist act had been the bombing of October 23, 1983, when a terrorist truck-bomber had reduced to rubble the Marine Battalion Landing Team at Beirut International Airport. In less than five minutes, 241 Americans had perished. U.S. intelligence officials had gathered conclusive evidence – through the collection of electronic intercepts – that the governments of both Iran and Syria had sponsored the bombing of the Marine barracks. Yet despite Reagan's tough talk there had been no retaliation or retribution.

Between January 1, 1980, and December 1, 1988, more than 400 Americans had died in terrorist attacks. With the dead from Flight 103, the terrorists could tally more than 600 dead Americans. Clearly, the terrorists were unafraid of the U.S. and its leader's angry talk of retaliation. It was just talk, after all.

As Reagan enjoyed his last Christmas as president in the warm sunshine of southern California, there was precious little he could do about the problem that had troubled him so deeply for the past eight years. He had been elected president with dozens of Americans held hostage by terrorists in Iran. And now he was leaving the Oval Office with hundreds dead by a terrorist's hand in the improbable hills of southern Scotland.

Reagan had failed in his war against terrorism, but not for lack of will, and certainly not for lack of support from those government bureaucrats at whom he was always railing. In the Pentagon and at the CIA, hundreds of dedicated men and women had spent tens and thousands of hours planning ways to strike back at terrorists. Precise information on terrorists was extraordinarily hard to come by, however, and opportunities to act were few and far between. Still, there had been rare successes. In October 1985, U.S. Air Force jets forced an Egyptian jet bearing the hijackers of the cruise ship *Achille Lauro* out of the sky over southern Italy. Thanks to Italian perfidy, however, Abu Abbas, the mastermind of the hijacking, had been allowed to slip away into the night across to Yugoslavia and back to the impenetrable chaos that was Lebanon. In another rare bright moment for the U.S., in September 1987, FBI agents working with operatives from the CIA and the Drug Enforcement Administration had lured a Lebanese terrorist onto a boat in international waters off Cyprus with the offer of a drug deal. Fawaz Younis, a used-car dealer and two-bit hijacker, had been brought to the U.S. and tried before a district court judge. Instead of the drug deal he hoped would make him rich, Fawaz Younis got a thirty-year sentence in an American prison.

There were not many other happy events to recount, however.

Lockerbie could have a profound effect on U.S. policy against terrorists, some government officials believed. The passengers on Flight 103 had not been soldiers, stationed at a foolishly exposed Marine barracks in the madness of Beirut. They had been ordinary Americans on their way home to see their families for the holidays. On Christmas night, the investigators in Lockerbie and Langley were still only assuming that they were correct, that a bomb had blown the Pan Am jet out of the sky. If that were so, it would mean even greater pressure on Reagan's successor to act. And that, the officials thought, was not necessarily a bad thing.

Meanwhile, at his spacious oceanfront home in Kennebunkport, Maine, George Bush had enjoyed a typical Christmas with his own family – with children, grandchildren and guests in abundance. So far, Bush had been given no evidence that the Pan Am plane had been blown up by terrorists. The investigators themselves could not give him any, yet.

On the twenty-sixth that changed. Now there was proof.

CHAPTER 8

Secure phones rang in the State Department and at the CIA and FBI with the news. The investigators' assumptions were correct, and they had the evidence to prove it: A bomb had blown up the Pan Am jumbo. A terrorist had reached across oceans and brought his war into the homes of hundreds of ordinary families. The bomb that had blown up the jet had been meant expressly for them, and the proof, for once, was irrefutable. This time, with luck, the investigators had a chance to show conclusively who was responsible for the bombing and how it had been carried out.

For many of the American investigators, it had seemed a strange way to launch what would become the world's largest counterterrorism investigation. Crawling on hands and knees through the dripping Scottish countryside seemed an odd way to catch criminals.

Others among the investigators thought differently. Tom Thurman and Walter Korsgaard knew that this investigation, like all the others in which they had been involved, would have to be built from the ground up, starting with the tiniest bit of evidence. And they had been confident from the start that they would find it. Since his arrival in Lockerbie early on the morning of December 22, Korsgaard had kept his slides and photographs to himself, to discourage speculation about a bomb. Wearing his battered FAA cap, Korsgaard moved from one search area to another, staying in touch with the helicopters through the Raynet operators. John Boyd and Superintendent Stuart Henderson had never handled an aircraft-bombing case before, but they knew all about evidence, and about how carelessness could screw up an investigation. Henderson, in charge of the day-to-day work of the investigators, reported to John Orr, the senior investigating officer. Orr, a police officer for twenty-four of his forty-three years, had attended the Scottish police college; having obtained a postgraduate diploma in forensic medicine from the University of Glasgow, he had a special appreciation for the finer points of investigative work. Relying on air-disaster experts such as Korsgaard and his British counterparts from the AAIB, Boyd and Orr instructed all the searchers each day on the importance of care and thoroughness. Korsgaard remembered one speech from the very first days after the crash. The searchers were told: 'If it's not a rock and it's not growing, pick it up and put it in a bag.'

And that's precisely what they did. On Christmas Day, a searcher crisscrossing a field in Tundergarth found a piece of metal that looked exactly like one of Korsgaard's much-travelled slides. Other pieces would be found later, but this was the first, and it was proof positive of a bomb. Forensic specialists from the British Defence Ministry's Royal Armaments Research and Development Establishment would test this and other parts of the luggage carrier that held the bomb.

The laboratory, located at Fort Halstead, in Kent, would confirm the experts' eyeball appraisal. Fort Halstead is probably the most sophisticated crime lab in the world. Unlike the FBI crime lab, which is itself world-renowned, the British facility affords working conditions rivalled only by those of NASA or the most well-endowed R&D labs in Europe, Japan and the U.S. At Fort Halstead, for instance, static electricity on most testing benches is reduced to zero – a phenomenally expensive proposition. 'We're very good on the forensics,' an FBI investigator close to the Lockerbie investigation said. 'But the Brits are very, *very* good.' For the kind of analysis done on the baggage container, the vast resources of Fort Halstead were probably unnecessary. The baggage container fragments very nearly spoke for themselves. Only a bomb could have shredded the metal in that way. If there was any doubt, the traces of explosives residue the forensic team would pick up in the next few days erased it immediately. Call it Exhibit A.

The only thing was, none of the investigators wanted to disclose their find. If those responsible for blowing up Flight 103 didn't know that evidence of a bomb had been found, it would give the investigators more time to make their inquiries without spooking them. 'As long as those who were responsible thought we didn't know it was a terrorist bombing,' said the FBI's Oliver Revell, 'they might make some mistakes and not flee or take some other evasive action.' That hope lasted all of several hours. On the afternoon of the twenty-sixth, L. Paul Bremer, the State Department's ambassador-at-large from the Office for Combatting Terrorism, received a call from his opposite number in the British Foreign Office. He was told of conclusive evidence that a bomb had been found. Within the hour, Revell received a similar call at his office at home. Before Mills had sat down to dinner with his family or Bremer had even packed his briefcase to leave for the day, CNN was moving a story from London confirming that a bomb had blown up Flight 103. The story was thin on details, but word had begun to leak.

Earlier on the twenty-sixth, officials at the National Security Agency in Fort Meade had begun a concerted effort to mine through volumes of intercepted communications from around the globe in the hope of shedding more light on the terrorists' planning of the attack. If the detectives in Frankfurt, London and Lockerbie were focusing on the minutiae of the case – which suitcase held the bomb and how it had been smuggled on the plane – the intelligence community could help with some of the larger questions. Who had authorized the attack? Who had paid for it? Which terrorist group had carried it out?

When it was mentioned at all in public, the National Security Agency was almost always described with the adjective 'supersecret'. Although it is probably the largest employer in the state of Maryland, with a payroll estimated at somewhere between 20,000 and 50,000 people, the NSA *is* the most secret and secretive of U.S. spy agencies. Surrounded by ten-foot-high fences with rows of razor-sharp concertina wire on top, the NSA compound is protected by guard dogs, electrified gates and what must be the world's most expensive and extensive computer security system. The place is big. In its joint headquarters-operations building alone are nearly 8 million feet of telephone wire, a cooling tower capable of handling 11 million gallons of water a day and a hallway that is reliably described as the single longest unobstructed corridor in the nation. At 980 feet, the C corridor at NSA extends farther than three football fields.

All those resources and people have a purpose. According to a General Accounting Office report cited by James Bamford in *The Puzzle Palace*, the definitive work on the NSA, the agency classifies between 50 million and 100 million documents a year. This adds up to about 40 tons of material a day, or roughly 200 a week.

Thus, when NSA officials decided after the crash in Lockerbie to begin mining its storehouse of intercepts, it was no small undertaking. From its array of ground-, sea-, air- and space-based collection systems, intercepts were routinely forwarded to the NSA's Office of Telecommunications and Computer Services, known as the T organization. This office then parcelled out the

113

intercepts to analysts, linguists and codebreakers in the Office of Signals Intelligence Operations, which is run by the deputy director of operations. The DDO is comprised of three signals-intelligence-analysis groups and two support groups. Of the three SIGINT-analysis groups, the A group monitors the Soviet Union; B, Communist Asia; and G all other parts of the world. Within the G group are five offices, four divisions and fourteen branches. It is within this last group that the ALLO (all others) section is located, and it has numerous suboffices. ALLO-34 is the one responsible for the Middle East.

If the NSA had anything useful to tell the Lockerbie investigators, it would almost certainly come from the files of ALLO-34. And if the FBI, the CIA or any other U.S. intelligence agency wanted to know what was in the ALLO-34 files that might be relevant to Lockerbie, they would have to make the request through a 'consumer staff liaison group' known as PO5, within the Office of Signals Intelligence Operations.

Anticipating the calls to PO5, NSA managers had already authorized operators of the agency's massive computers to begin searching for key words the bombers might have used in planning the bombing of the 103.

At the counterterrorism centre in Langley, and among Ambassador Bremer's small staff in Foggy Bottom, the evidence didn't change much. They had the most complete databases on terrorist organizations, and they were pretty far along in the research. The word from London and Lockerbie on December 26 only made them intensify their efforts to find out which terrorist group might have targeted the 103. There were plenty of mad bombers with track records.

As their profiles grew in length in the DESIST computers in Washington, there was an eerie sameness to them. Sponsors, objectives, targets: all were more or

114

less the same. At the top of the list of terrorist organizations, those with the technical capability to blow airplanes out of the sky, most received financial backing from Libya, Syria or Iran or some combination. All were opposed to the 'Zionist enemy', committed to the 'armed struggle' that would result in its destruction, and absolutely enraged by the admittedly dim prospect of peace raised by Yasir Arafat's on-again, off-again bid for rapprochement with Jerusalem.

Two weeks before the crash of Flight 103, in a meeting with American Jews and Swedish officials in Stockholm, Arafat had announced that the Palestine Liberation Organization had publicly accepted the existence of Israel and 'rejected and condemned terrorism'. It was big news, coming a year after the start of the *intifada*, the Palestinian uprising in the West Bank and the Gaza Strip. But it was difficult to believe, in light of the PLO's past record on terrorism. Just weeks before Arafat's declaration in Stockholm, the Reagan administration had announced it would deny the PLO chairman a U.S. visa to address the United Nations General Assembly in New York because he 'knows of, condones and lends support to' terrorist acts.

Now, all of a sudden, Arafat was a man of 'peace'. Or almost, anyway.

Privately, State Department officials professed to be heartened by the Arafat remarks in Stockholm. Publicly, however, they said that his statements were still too ambiguous for the U.S. to open a dialogue with the PLO. Translation: Try again, Yasir. As a child, Arafat had changed his name from Mohammed to Yasir, which in Arabic can mean 'easy'. Over the next few weeks, Arafat's attempts to get the language right would be anything but. In November, the Palestine National Council, the Palestinian parliament-in-exile, had met in Algiers and declared an independent Palestinian state, but without specifying its borders. On December 12, the State Department – having sent

115

messages to Arafat through the Swiss, the Saudis, the British and the Egyptians – reiterated that Arafat still had not said the magic words renouncing terrorism unambiguously and recognizing Israel's right to exist. Later that day, the Swedish foreign minister, Sten Andersson, a highly respected diplomat who had been trying for months to midwife the U.S. – PLO dialogue, sent Secretary of State George Shultz three paragraphs of a speech Arafat would deliver the next day before the United Nations General Assembly in Geneva. Barred from the United States, the itinerant Arafat would say his piece in Switzerland.

This time, what the PLO chairman said was better but still not good enough. Arafat delivered the speech, but without the promised words. Still the U.S. was not persuaded. On December 14, one week before the crash in Lockerbie, with Andersson virtually whispering in his ear, Arafat, in yet another clarification press conference, uttered precisely the right combination of words on terrorism and Israel's right to exist. He recognized, he said, 'the right of all parties concerned in the Middle East conflict to exist in peace and security . . . including the state of Palestine, Israel and other neighbours.' The PLO, Arafat insisted, 'totally and absolutely renounces all forms of terrorism.' In Washington, a State Department spokesman announced that Arafat had finally gotten it right. The U.S. would open a diplomatic dialogue with the PLO, the spokesperson said. The American ambassador to Tunisia, Robert Pelletreau, Jr., was designated the only 'authorized channel' for the talks. Across the Middle East, Yasir Arafat's legions of enemies were in high dudgeon: the Americans had meddled again where they had no business; somehow, they would pay for their arrogance.

In Washington, the intelligence analysts assigned to the investigation into the bombing of the Pan Am jet paid scant attention to Arafat's shenanigans in Switzerland.

On December 26, when it became known publicly that a bomb had destroyed the plane, government authorities in Washington and London denied a link between the nascent PLO dialogue and the bombing of Flight 103. No matter how sophisticated a terrorist organization and how clever its operatives, the government officials said, it would have been impossible for any terrorist group to plan and execute a bombing in the two short weeks it took Arafat to get his syntax straightened out. What the officials did not say, however, is that Arafat had been involved in a dialogue of some sort with the Americans since at least March 1988 and that more than a few people, including Arafat's most virulent enemies, knew about his efforts.

There was no shortage of people who wanted to disrupt the new dialogue, notwithstanding the only slender chance that it would result in a resolution of the Arab-Israeli conflict. And there was no shortage of people who wanted to undermine Arafat and smite the United States. The only thing curtailing the list of terrorist organizations on the list of suspects assembled by State, CIA and FBI intelligence analysts was the lack of technical know-how on the part of the terrorists. Bombs and timers are a tricky business, and not every terrorist organization has someone who knows how to use them with skill. The intelligence analysts figured that only a handful of terrorist groups could have carried out the bombing of Flight 103, and they were probably a bit too generous in their assessment of some of the groups' abilities at that.

The analysts listed the Japanese Red Army, for instance, although the Red Army had for a while been regarded as something of a joke, even among other terrorist organizations. Its few remaining members were somewhat long in the tooth, and even though they were based primarily in Lebanon, they would seem to have had no precise motive for bombing the Pan Am jet. It is true they did have some ability to plant

117

bombs and explosives, but even that seemed to have declined radically in recent years. At 6:45 A.M., on April 12, 1988, a state trooper spotted an Oriental man loitering near a car at the Vince Lombardi Rest Area of the New Jersey Turnpike, just across the Hudson River from Manhattan. According to police and federal prosecutors, the place was well known as a busy trafficking spot for drugs and guns, and the state police tried to watch it carefully. The Oriental man, looking dishevelled and distracted, was thus a figure of some interest on this morning when the trooper drove by. From outside the car, the trooper could see several containers in a travel bag. They were labelled 'Gunpowder'. On the floor of the backseat were three industrial fire extinguishers from which the hoses had been removed. The trooper asked the Oriental man his name. It turned out he was Yu Kikumura, an aging bookstore owner from Athens and a member, it would turn out, of the Japanese Red Army. Police would allege, and prosecutors would later prove, that on April 14, the second anniversary of the U.S. bombing of Libya, Kikumura intended to blow up at least three targets in New York City. According to the prosecution, pinholes in a map Kikumura was carrying showed that his targets were a U.S. Navy-Marine recruiting station in lower Manhattan, the United Nations complex on the East River and a third place in the busy garment district not far from Madison Square Garden. The bombs, had they gone off, certainly would have killed a lot of people. But law enforcement officials who reviewed the case afterwards said Kikumura was so clumsy in his preparations that it was only a matter of luck that he had not been arrested sooner. If the Japanese Red Army couldn't pull off a bombing on the ground, what were the odds they could have blown up Pan Am Flight 103? Understandably, the JRA was not very high on the list of suspects for the disaster in Lockerbie.

There were other terrorist organizations that were,

however. The analysts had to look not only into which groups were capable of blowing up an American airplane but also into which ones had the motivation. The Arab 15 May Organization was one such group. It had taken its name from the founding date of the state of Israel. In the late 1970s, 15 May had split from the Popular Front for the Liberation of Palestine, making clear its disdain for moderate Palestinians and other Arabs who favoured a negotiated settlement of the Palestinian issue. The organization had been founded by, and continues today under the direction of, Hussein al-Umari, one of the Middle East's most clever and committed practitioners of terrorism. He had assumed the nom de guerre Abu Ibrahim, and there was certainly no more accomplished bomber in the terror business than he. Because his specialty through the 1980s appeared to be airplane bombings, he was at the very top of the list of suspects for the bombing of the *Maid of the Seas*.

His grim accomplishments were considerable. On August 11, 1982, a slender young man named Mohammed Rashid planted a time-delay bomb on a Pan Am flight from Tokyo to Hawaii. On the approach to the international airport in Honolulu, the bomb exploded, killing one person and injuring fourteen others. Two weeks later, Ibrahim's terrorists tried again. On August 25, 1982, a cleaning woman discovered an unexploded bomb beneath a seat of a Pan Am jet in Rio de Janeiro. The bomb was compact and cunningly made, but had it exploded, it would probably not have disabled the aircraft. Police and intelligence agencies said they believed the explosive device had been planted by one of Abu Ibrahim's bomb-makers, but no one was ever arrested.

In late 1983, after Israel had begun withdrawing its troops from Lebanon, 15 May embarked on its most ambitious and alarming campaign ever. Five years later, immediately after the crash of Flight 103, intelligence officials in Washington were wondering whether the 15

May operation had culminated in the tragedy in Lockerbie. According to Western intelligence sources, Abu Ibrahim's plan in late 1983 was to target five airliners at once. It is unclear whether the intelligence agencies ever determined the exact combination of targets, but they are known to have included Pan Am, British Airways and El Al aircraft. Sometime just before December 1983, intelligence officials said, Abu Ibrahim had altered five suitcases to conceal small but potent explosives packages wired to a timer, a barometer and a miniaturized energy cell. The bombs could be activated in such a way that the person carrying them aboard could get off the plane after the first leg of a flight, and the explosion, triggered by the barometer, would occur on the second. One of Abu Ibrahim's operatives, Mohammed Rashid, was assigned the job of getting the suitcases aboard the planes, which, evidently, had already been targeted. The operation is thought to have begun in mid-December, and somehow – no one will say exactly how – several intelligence services, including the CIA, learned of it. It started in Athens. Rashid had given one of the five suitcases to a British woman he knew there. She was going to Tel Aviv on a business trip, and intelligence officials familiar with the episode said she had no idea the bag Rashid gave her had a bomb in it; when she found out, she was horrified. Fortunately, the bomb failed to go off. But the CIA, and apparently some other Western intelligence service, alerted Greek police to the plot. Authorities in Athens knew nothing of it and rushed to investigate. However, several examinations of the woman's suitcase by a police bomb expert failed to detect either the explosives or the triggering device. Abu Ibrahim's design was that good.

Then specialists from the CIA examined the bag, and they did find the bomb. Rashid, who had been placed under surveillance, was immediately arrested and interrogated by authorities in Athens. The police there refused to tell the Americans anything about the interrogation and accused the CIA of running secret operations on Greek soil. Worse, the Greeks soon released Rashid, and other intelligence services that had been aware of the operation blamed the Americans for blowing the investigation. Somehow, at some point after Rashid's interrogation in Athens, a Jordanian man who had been informing on Ibrahim's organization for one of the intelligence services was identified as the source. Rashid simply vanished, but intelligence officials later confirmed that the Jordanian was killed by Ibrahim. As to the five suitcases, the one in Athens was disabled, but the other four disappeared for a time. Two were later discovered by El Al security personnel before being loaded on two Israel-bound flights. Another bomb was detected nearly a year later, just before the suitcase in which it was hidden was to be loaded onto a Pan Am flight from Rome's Leonardo da Vinci Airport to Kennedy Airport in New York. The fifth bomb is believed to be missing still, and among several intelligence officials alerted to the crash of Flight 103, it sprung to mind immediately.

Intelligence officials believed 15 May was still planning aircraft bombings in late 1988, although Ibrahim had lost one of his best men by then. In 1986, U.S. intelligence officials say, Rashid may have struck again, planting a bomb on a TWA flight from Rome to Athens. It had exploded over the Mediterranean, and four Americans, including a mother and her small daughter, had been sucked out of a hole in the side of the plane: they had fallen to their deaths. A few months after that, Rashid had been arrested as he crossed the border from Yugoslavia to Greece, and he was being held now in an Athens prison. Greek authorities had so far refused American requests to extradite him to stand trial for the aircraft bombing in Hawaii. Rashid thus could have had nothing to do with the Lockerbie bombing. But Abu Ibrahim had other lieutenants like him. And there was still that fifth suitcase bomb that remained unaccounted for. For those reasons, 15 May had to be right near the top of the list of suspects.

But there were others.

The Abu Nidal organization had conducted more than a dozen terrorist attacks in Europe in 1985, and the State Department continued to describe it as 'the most dangerous terrorist organization in existence.' Abu Nidal's real name was Sabri Khalil al-Banna, and his hatred for Arafat was implacable. A squat man with brooding eyes and a fast-retreating hairline, he had been born in Jaffa, in what was once Arab Palestine. In 1967 he had joined Arafat's al-Fatah guerrilla movement; he broke with Arafat after the October 1973 Arab-Israeli war to form his own, more militant Fatah Revolutionary Council. Arafat had decided to focus terrorist operations 'only' within Israel and the occupied territories; Abu Nidal wanted to widen the scope of terror, targeting Jews all over the world as well as pro-Arafat Palestinians and moderate Arab states. Abu Nidal didn't like Arafat's retreat from international terrorism; he vowed publicly to kill Arafat. Even those who trucked with Arafat tempted fate. Austrian chancellor Bruno Kreisky and Italian prime minister Bettino Craxi learned that well. After friendly overtures by those governments to the unkempt PLO leader, Abu Nidal's terrorists attacked airports in Rome and Vienna with machine guns and hand grenades.

Within days after the crash of Flight 103, some U.S. intelligence officials said they were certain that Abu Nidal 'had his hands all over this'. It was almost as if it bore his trademark, one official said; 'Wanton destruction without after-the-fact signature.'

Within the Abu Nidal organization, there was one man the intelligence analysts focused on in particular. Where terror and bombings were involved, 'the Professor' always had to be considered a suspect. Between 1983 and 1985, intelligence officials say, Samir Kadar helped organize a rocket-propelled grenade attack on the U.S. embassy in Rome, a grenade and machine-gun attack on an Italian synagogue, and the attempted assassination of Jordan's ambassador to Italy. In 1986, Kadar, just thirty-eight at the time, outdid himself. The attack on the El Al ticket counter in Rome's Leonardo da Vinci Airport was his finest hour. He murdered twelve people, including an eleven-year-old American school-girl who died in her father's arms; sixty others were seriously injured.

Whether the Professor was still around in December 1988 was anyone's guess, however. The young man who called the U.S. embassy in Helsinki warning of a bomb attack on a Pan Am jet departing from Frankfurt had mentioned Kadar by his pseudonym, Finnish police say. But Kadar, a handsome, muscular man with wavy hair and clear, dark eyes, was well known to many in the tight-knit Palestinian community in Scandinavia. In October 1986, he had married a Finnish woman he had met in the Café de Paris, a fashionable bistro across from the U.S. embassy on Rome's via Veneto. Kadar and Arja Saloranta had set up house-keeping in a pleasant three-room apartment in a suburb of Stockholm. Thoughtfully, he had adopted his wife's surname as his own. In April 1988, Arja Saloranta, who knew nothing of her new husband's real occupation, had borne the Professor a son. They had named him Omar.

Not long after, the Professor disappeared.

Was Samra Mahayoun, the man who called the Helsinki embassy, simply using Kadar's name to give his wacky story the patina of plausibility? The intelligence officials would have to find out. Unfortunately, they had precious little to go on. The last time anyone had seen Kadar was on the afternoon of July 9, in an auto-rental agency in Athens. Using a Libyan passport as identification, Kadar had picked up a blue Opel Ascona. On the afternoon of July 11, when Kadar was supposed to return the Opel, another car, a metallic-green Nissan, exploded in a grimy corner of the Athens waterfront. Kadar never returned the Opel, and Greek police thought he may have died in the explosion; they did not know for sure. They had found three pairs of men's shoes in the charred Nissan, but the fingertips of only two men. The police believed Kadar and his colleagues were part of a larger operation. Four hours after the Nissan exploded, an Abu Nidal gunman attacked the ferryboat *City of Poros* in Piraeus harbour. The police believed Kadar planned to use the Nissan either to attack the ferry when it docked or as a threat to hijack the ferry and demand the release of two Abu Nidal operatives imprisoned in Greece. After the Nissan blew up unexpectedly, the lone gunman attacked on his own; he killed nine people before he managed to kill himself accidentally with one of his own hand grenades. Had Kadar escaped from this monumental screwup? U.S. intelligence officials had reason to believe so. In Stockholm in the summer of 1988, Swedish detectives discovered a cache of weapons in an apartment and some inconclusive evidence that the Professor might have been living there. It was just possible that the young man who called the embassy in Helsinki knew what he was talking about. They would have to go back and check.

In the meantime, Kadar or no Kadar, the Abu Nidal organization remained on the intelligence officials' short list of suspects for the bombing of the 103, even though they were aware that Abu Nidal may have been much too busy to bomb an American airplane. When the 103 crashed in Lockerbie, he had been preoccupied with murdering as many of the grumblers in his own organization as he could, according to allegations of dissident group members later made public by the PLO. Even before the *intifada* had erupted, in December 1987, some members had begun to object to Abu Nidal's leadership. One group leader, Abdulrahman Issa, would

124

later call Abu Nidal a 'living example of schizophrenia'. But they objected more to his obsession with random violence, such as the attack on the *City of Poros* and another shortly afterwards on a country club in Khartoum. What did such violence achieve, the dissidents asked, except to discredit the Palestinian cause in the eyes of the world? Abu Nidal didn't like questions like that one bit.

So he decided to do something about it. According to *The New York Times*, Issa and other dissidents recounted how Abu Nidal invited most of the senior members to his house near Tripoli. Let us iron out our differences, Abu Nidal said. When the others arrived, however, there was no talking; according to Issa and others, Abu Nidal killed everyone instead. After the shooting, he buried the bodies in the foundation of his house. 'Right there,' Issa said in a statement made available by the PLO. 'Abu Nidal and his hirelings poured the cement on their bodies themselves.' About twenty senior members were murdered, 150 members in all, the reports stated. Right around the time he would have had to plan the bombing of Pan Am Flight 103, intelligence officials say, Abu Nidal was murdering two more of his top men. So pleased was he with his handiwork that he decided to add a new room onto his house where the two commanders died. Today, according to statements by Issa and others, their bodies lie encased in the concrete foundation of the new addition. Although some intelligence officials discount the allegations, and although no evidence has been disclosed of bodies buried in concrete, terrorism analysts at the CIA and the Pentagon agree that the Abu Nidal organization was wracked by internal dissent.

Other groups on the intelligence analysts' list of candidates for the bombing of the 103 fit the definition of 'usual suspects', and they certainly had to be rounded up, so to speak. The governments of Iran and Libya, the fanatics of Hezbollah: it was no secret that any one of them would take delight in the bombing of an American jet and, with or without assistance from other terrorists, might have carried it out.

The organization most suspected was one the world had not heard much about, however. But those familiar with the grisly business of terrorism inside and out knew plenty about the group. And when they thought back to the events of a pleasant autumn day in Germany just seven weeks before, they catapulted the little-known group to the number-one position on their list.

CHAPTER 9

Among the counterterrorism experts at the CIA, the State Department and the FBI, the one name that kept popping up most in regard to the bombing of Flight 103 was the Popular Front for the Liberation of Palestine – General Command. There were two reasons for this. Like the 15 May Organization, the PFLP-GC had a considerable track record of airplane bombings. But more important, less than two months before the Lockerbie explosion, several PFLP-GC members had been arrested in Frankfurt, the point of departure for the first leg of Flight 103, with bombs and timers of the type that would be useful only for blowing up planes in the air.

Popular Front for the Liberation of Palestine – General Command is not exactly the kind of name that comes trippingly off the tongue, but that was just fine with Ahmed Jibril, its founder, chief factotum and star fund-raiser. With his comfortable paunch and colourful sports clothes, Jibril looked more like a hardworking shopkeeper content to keep a few steps ahead of the bill collector than the bloody-minded terrorist officials of a dozen intelligence services said he was. The Israelis, to whom Jibril was anathema, considered him one of their most ruthless adversaries. But take Jibril at his own word. He cheerfully confessed to the use of terror tactics; if that's what it took to blot Israel from the map of the Middle East, so be it. As to those who supported the Jewish state, particularly the United States, Jibril had this to say, at a noisy press conference in Tripoli, in February 1986: 'There will be no safety for any traveller on an Israeli or U.S. airliner.' In a twinkling, Jibril had stated not only his vendetta but the means by which he would carry it out. Airplane bombings were his thing.

Over the course of nearly two decades, Ahmed Jibril had concluded that there was no more effective means of expressing his hatred for Israel than by blowing up planes. By such tactics, he seemed to believe, he could best achieve his dream: the elimination of the state of Israel. Even in the years Jibril had been forced to assume a low profile, the Israelis said, they considered him their most deadly nemesis, willing to wait for years, if that's what it took, to strike. With his seemingly unlimited patience and implacable will, he gave Israel and her allies no quarter, ever.

Within the DESIST computers in the U.S. intelligence community, there was a long file on Jibril. Born in 1937 in the Arab village of Yazur, near Jaffa, Jibril had left Palestine with his family in 1948 and settled in Quneitra, Syria. At nineteen, Jibril had joined the Syrian army and graduated from military college in Damascus. A good soldier, he rose quickly and attained the rank of captain in the engineering corps. According to intelligence files, Jibril had a specialty: he was a demolitions expert, and a damned good one. But he was also a troublemaker. He was eventually drummed out of the Syrian army for what were described as 'revolutionary activities'. Jibril decamped to Cairo, where he began what would become his life's work. He rejoined the Syrian military after the split-up between Egypt and Syria in 1961. After the Egyptians created the Palestine Liberation Organization in 1964, Syria mounted provocations against Israel. But not wanting to incur Israeli retaliation, Syria 'discharged' scores of top officers, including Jibril, to form their own 'independent' units to attack Israel. With a number of other Palestinian officers, he established an underground organization called the National Front for the Liberation of Palestine.

The organization had a policy platform consisting of exactly one plank: Destroy Israel.

Oddly enough for a man who earned his living killing people, Jibril always felt underappreciated. From the Golan Heights, which overlook Israel's northern border, Jibril led a number of daring attacks and made something of a name for himself. In December 1967, hard on the heels of their embarrassing defeat in the Arab–Israeli War, Jibril was among several Palestinian leaders who decided to join forces with George Habash in a larger, more powerful organization, the Popular Front for the Liberation of Palestine. His followers referred to Habash as al-Hakim, 'the physician' or 'the wise man'. Jibril thought he was a show-stealer.

Jibril lasted less than a year with Habash. Although the PFLP quickly established itself as one of the most violent Palestinian terror groups, Jibril in effect accused Habash of being soft. Specialists who have studied the Palestinian movement believe the explanation for Jibril's split with Habash is more simple. Jibril didn't want to be second banana to anyone.

Once again he decamped. This time Jibril set up shop in Damascus, with a branch office in Beirut. The name of his new organization, the Popular Front for the Liberation of Palestine – General Command, got the message across, separating the less vigorous from the real fighters. It also reflected Jibril's belief that for the Palestinian cause to be successful, it would have to have conventional military capabilities beyond the occasional terrorism spectaculars that dominated television newscasts for a day or two and then vanished almost without a trace, without having changed anything.

But the real reason for his new organization was Jibril's own monumental ego. He installed his wife, Samira (who had assumed her own nom de guerre, Um-Fares), as leader of the PFLP-GC's women's division. And after the Israeli invasion of Lebanon in 1982, he installed his two sons, Jihad and Khaled, in positions of greater influence in the organization. Today, Jihad is the head of the GC military camp at Ein Taksur and is in charge of training new recruits. Khaled, responsible for the GC's 'special operations', spends much of his time in Libya, studying in Qaddafi's military training schools.

Although Syria has been his most generous sponsor and ally, Libya has also supported Jibril. In fact, in 1977, PFLP-GC pilots flew bombing missions in Libyan bombers as part of Qaddafi's war with Egypt. Throughout the years, Qaddafi has provided weapons and millions of dollars to Jibril; this assistance has enabled the aging Palestinian terrorist to retain a certain amount of independence from Syria. Qaddafi had also allowed use of Libyan embassies to support Jibril. In 1980, for example, American intelligence discovered that a PFLP-GC member was accredited as a Libyan diplomat in London.

Outsiders remained a threat, however. Abu Abbas, the mastermind of the *Achille Lauro* hijacking, joined Jibril in 1968 as his overall chief of operations, but he left in 1976, after numerous disputes with Jibril. In the violent contest between the Palestinian people and their Israeli adversaries, Abu Abbas reportedly said later, Ahmed Jibril wanted the spotlight all to himself. He would share it with no one.

Jibril was an unreconstituted rejectionist. As far as he was concerned, there was simply no room for an Israel in the world, and certainly not in the land of his birth. The emblem of the PFLP-GC bore a map of Palestine crossed by two rifles equipped with bayonets. Under the map was the PFLP-GC name, spelled out in Arabic: Al-Jabha ash-Sha'bi li-Tahrir Filastin – Al-Qiyada al'Amma (Popular Front for the Liberation of Palestine – General Command). On each side of the logo, in case the point should be lost, were two Palestinian flags.

From his earliest days, Jibril had been a proponent of high-tech terrorism. His was the first Palestinian terrorist organization whose operatives used walkie-talkies to communicate with superiors beyond the terrorist site. They were also the first to wear booby-trapped belts on missions into Israel, to use if they were captured. Drawing on his training as an engineer, Jibril became something of an inventor in Damascus, where he still holds several patents.

Perhaps that background explains his early fascination with airplane bombings. According to Israeli intelligence files, it is almost certain that Jibril, in 1970, was responsible for the very first plane bombing carried out with a barometer-triggered explosive. That was also the first time Western intelligence agencies got a look at the handiwork of one of Jibril's bomb-makers, a technical wizard named Merwad Abd Rezak Mufti Kreeshat, also known as Marwan Kreeshat. Police are still unsure how Kreeshat or another of Jibril's men got the bomb on board. But they know everything that happened afterwards.

On February 21, 1970, fifteen minutes after Swissair Flight 330 left Zurich for Tel Aviv, Kreeshat's bomb exploded in the rear baggage hold of the plane. The Swissair jet was at only 14,000 feet, and pilot Armand Étienne was confident he could bring the plane down safely.

'I suspect there has been an explosion in the aft compartment,' Étienne radioed the tower in Zurich. His voice was calm. Smoke was soon filling the plane.

'I cannot see anything,' Étienne radioed. And seconds later: 'We are crashing. Good-bye, everybody. Good-bye.'

The plane came down in a forest in the Swiss canton of Aargau. All forty-seven passengers and crew died. Although it detonated sooner than planned, Kreeshat's bomb had been murderously effective.

That same day, Ahmed Jibril's terrorists struck again. Once more, the police and intelligence agencies of the West would assemble a long and thorough file, and again it would be passed on to counterterrorism intelligence officers in Washington. Fortunately, the second attempt by Jibril was a failure. The bomb, placed aboard an Austrian Airlines flight from Frankfurt to Vienna and on to Israel, exploded at 10,000 feet, ripping a two-foot hole in the plane's baggage hold. Amazingly, the pilot was able to make an emergency landing at Frankfurt, and none of the thirty-eight passengers and crew was hurt. Israeli and European investigators later determined that the bombs on both the Austrian Airlines and the Swissair flights had been concealed in transistor radios assembled in East Germany. Packed in airmail parcels bearing addresses in Jerusalem, the bombs apparently had been mailed from a downtown Frankfurt post office.

Barometer-triggered bombs had made their debut in the no-holds-barred war of the terrorists.

Jibril added a new wrinkle two years later. He began using unwitting passengers to plant his bombs on planes. This time Italian and Israeli police investigated, and their findings were added to the growing files on Jibril in the offices of intelligence services around the globe. On August 16, 1972, a bomb exploded on an El Al flight from Rome to Tel Aviv, blowing a hole in the floor of the passenger compartment and cracking the rear door. Intelligence officials concluded later that the bomb had been made by Jibril's bomb-maker in chief, Marwan Kreeshat. Because the plane had been delayed on departure, the bomb exploded at only 14,700 feet – and not at a higher altitude, where the plane would have been pulled apart much more quickly. The pilot was able to return safely to Rome, where police surrounded the plane. A quick inspection showed that the bomb had been placed in a record player, which had been checked aboard by two young British women.

The women, among the 140 passengers and crew back safe on the ground, were questioned by police and El Al security officers. TNT residue and the remnants of a timing device had been found along with the wreckage of the record player. The women, both eighteen, had received it as a going-away gift from two men with whom they had shared an apartment briefly during their stay in Rome. The women burst into tears when they were told about the bomb.

One had a photograph of the two men. It had been taken as a souvenir of their stay in Rome. Interpol immediately circulated the photo, which showed two handsome young Arabs. On August 19, three days after the bomb went off, two Rome policemen on via Veneto spotted the two men, and Ahmed Zaid, twenty-four, from Iraq, and Adnan Mohammed Ali Hasham, twenty-nine, from Jordan, quickly told all. They had met with Kreeshat in Yugoslavia, they said. He had given them the bomb there. The handsome young men were then packed off to jail.

As usual, nothing happened to Jibril. He went back to planning more terrorist raids.

In the DESIST files on Jibril was a wealth of information that had nothing to do with airplane bombings but plenty to do with his ruthlessness and zeal. On May 22, 1972, he had dispatched a terrorist gang from a training camp in Lebanon across the border into northern Israel near the small kibbutz of Avivim. Only 500 yards inside Israel, Jibril's commandos had set up their weapons and, in the early-morning darkness, had hidden in the underbrush. When an Israeli schoolbus had come within 100 feet of them a short while later, the terrorists had fired bazooka shells at the bus, creating an inferno that killed twelve children and wounded twenty-two others. In April 1974, three of Jibril's terrorists crossed into northern Israel from Lebanon again, this time at the town of Qiryat Shemona. The attack occurred just before dawn, at an apartment building on the edge of the village, and Jibril's men went from room to room, methodically emptying a short burst of their machine guns at anyone who moved. By the time the sun came up, eighteen Israelis, mostly children and women, had died. An Israeli assault force killed the three terrorists before they could slip back into Lebanon. Two months later, Jibril's terrorists came across the border again, in an attempted raid on a school nursery at Kibbutz Shamir, where 250 children lived. It was their most brazen attempt to date. Unexpectedly, they encountered three women, whom they shot in the head. The gunshots alerted civilian guards, who forced the terrorists into a farm shed, where they killed them in a gun battle.

One incident in particular spoke volumes about Jibril. During the 1982 Israeli invasion of Lebanon, Jibril's men captured three Israeli reservists, including a polite young bank officer named Chesai Shai. Shai had been commanding the last tank in a convoy that had run into a Syrian ambush at a place called Sultan Ya'acub in southern Lebanon. Their tank disabled, Shai and his men had dived for cover. Shai's men were gravely wounded. Shai himself, after hiding in underbrush, attempted to make his way back to Israel, more than fifteen miles away. A Syrian soldier demanded Shai's identification somewhere along the way and Shai, who spoke fluent Arabic, tried to bluff him. He almost got away with it, but the soldier looked down and despite the nighttime darkness noticed that Shai's shoes were not the kind Syrian forces are issued with. Challenged for identity papers, Shai said he didn't have any and finally admitted that he was an Israeli soldier. He was thrown into the back of a car. Before he knew it, Shai found himself in Damascus, bound, gagged and shackled in a tiny, windowless room.

Through the Red Cross and the Austrian government, Israeli authorities made inquiries about Shai in Damascus. The Syrians denied knowing anything. In fact, they said, an Israeli who fit Shai's description was buried in a graveyard in Damascus. Jibril too issued a statement denying he had Shai in his possession.

For eighteen months, Jibril ordered Shai held in

solitary confinement. The Israelis, however, were convinced Shai was alive and that Jibril had him. To pressure him, Israeli commandos kidnapped a favourite nephew of Jibril's in Lebanon. Release Shai, the Israelis said, and we'll let your nephew go. Jibril didn't even respond. The implied message: He wouldn't be pressured.

By this time, Jibril had moved Shai from solitary confinement and ordered him placed with other Syrian prisoners. During his year and a half in solitary confinement, Shai had tried to kill himself, but that had had nothing to do with Jibril's moving him in with the other prisoners. When Shai was questioned by Syrian authorities along with the other prisoners, he refused to answer questions. Jibril, who was looking on during the interrogation, stood up dismissively and, without making any eye contact with Shai, instructed the Syrian officers: 'Tell him he is still missing. Anything could happen to him, his family doesn't know. He could still return a cripple.'

The message was clear. Shai was Jibril's prisoner, and he would do with him what he liked.

A year later, Jibril finally decided to make use of Shai and the two other Israeli reservists. Through Austrian and Red Cross intermediaries, he told the Israelis he would trade them for a number of Palestinian prisoners in Israeli jails. The Israelis agreed in principle. They had made a similar deal with Jabril in 1979. The only question now was how many prisoners Jibril would demand in exchange for the three Israelis' freedom.

Jibril did not conduct the negotiations this time. In the 1979 prisoner swap, he had arranged for the release of a man named Hafez Dalkamouni. In the years since, Dalkamouni had risen in the PFLP-GC to become one of Jibril's key aides. This time Dalkamouni would handle the negotiations with the Israelis, and he would prove an even more difficult adversary than Jibril.

Because he was confident that the Israelis would cave

in, he was ultimately successful in getting them to release some of the most vicious terrorists in their prisons. He insisted, for instance, on the release of Kozo Okamoto, the one surviving member of the Japanese Red Army group that had carried out the 1972 massacre at the Lod airport, in which twenty-seven people had been machine-gunned to death. Okamoto was one of 400 prisoners serving life terms for murdering Israelis. Dalkamouni wanted all of them freed. Before it was over, the Israelis, amazingly, agreed. For the release of Chesai Shai and the two other reservists, Israel would free 1,150 prisoners from its jails.

But still it was not enough. Although only 300 of the prisoners were members of the PFLP-GC, Jibril, through Dalkamouni, insisted that every one receive a letter before his release.

'Dear militant brothers and comrades,' the letter read, 'the Popular Front for the Liberation of Palestine – General Command's members, cadres and leadership relay their revolutionary compliments to every militant in his name, highly appreciate your struggles, admire your long-standing patience, your sufferings and pains inside the prisons, [and] would like to convey news of your impending liberation and release.'

While he was rubbing the Israelis' nose in it, Jibril might as well do the same to his terrorist confreres, especially the hated Arafat.

And still Jibril was not satisfied. Before Shai and the other two soldiers were freed the terms of the swap called for the mothers of the three men to travel to a run-down house south of Jaffa, where they would pose for a photograph. This, Jibril informed them, was the home in which he had been born, in the tiny village of Yazur, in 1937. The Israelis had no proof that this was so, but the photograph was taken anyway and forwarded to Jibril.

Finally, on May 20, 1985, in Geneva, the exchange was completed.

The following year, the Israelis tried to exact revenge. In February, they intercepted a small executive plane as it flew from Tripoli to Damascus, forcing it to land in Tel Aviv. Israeli soldiers, operating on information provided by Mossad, Israel's intelligence service, boarded the plane expecting to find Ahmed Jibril and George Habash aboard. But Israeli intelligence in Libya was not 'real-time', that is, right up to the minute, and evidently Jibril had changed his travel plans right before the plane left. After twelve hours, the Israeli soldiers let the plane go.

In another instance, Israeli officials, having learned that Jibril was visiting a training camp in Lebanon, ordered jets in for a strike. The bombs hit their target, but it turned out the intelligence was wrong. Jibril had not been there after all.

For Jibril, the high point of his campaign against Israel came in November 1987, when two of his men used motorized hang gliders to fly from Lebanon to an Israeli army base on the northern border town of Qiryat Shemona, where they killed six Israeli soldiers and wounded seven others. The operation had Jibril's high-tech stamp on it. The hang-glider pilots wore helmets wired with radio transmitters that allowed them to talk to each other and to their base back in Syria. Besides their automatic weapons fitted with silencers, they had infrared binoculars for night vision. The spectacular hang-glider attack spread a deepening sense of gloom across northern Israel. One of the two attackers, a muscular fighter named Khaled Aker, emptied eight magazines from his automatic rifle and threw five hand grenades before he was killed by the soldiers' return fire. The second man died when his hang glider crashed.

In Damascus, Jibril issued a statement praising the 'heroic struggle'.

The hang-glider attack had a bigger impact than even Jibril could have imagined. According to many

Middle East observers, it was one of several important events leading to the uprising of the Palestinians in the West Bank and the Gaza Strip a month later. According to Israeli officials, Jibril had planned a spectacular series of attacks on Israeli targets in Europe to show that he could deliver for Palestinians just as well as Arafat. The hang-glider attack outshone everything else, however.

For all his bold 'successes', Ahmed Jibril had not been able to cultivate a wide following among Palestinians in the occupied territories. In Damascus, he had a comfortable home and an office with a fax machine. About forty miles outside the city, he had an extensive training camp for his men. Among his commandos, he was revered as both a fighter and an inspired and dedicated leader of the Palestinian cause. No matter how busy he might be in Damascus, or jetting off to Tripoli or Teheran, Jibril spent a great deal of time with his fighters, and they regarded him as a father figure. Before each of their missions, he blessed them. And he made sure the families of those injured or killed were provided for.

Among many of the Palestinians he strove to woo, though, Ahmed Jibril ws not trusted. Not only did he live in Syria and have his base of operations there, he received financial and logistical support from Syria and its president, Hafez al-Assad. His terrorists had been found with Syrian passports and Syrian-issue weapons. Jibril's main point of contact was believed to be with Syrian air force intelligence. Many Palestinians evidently did not feel comfortable with close ties to that nation. During the 1976 Syrian siege of the refugee camp at Tel Zatar, southeast of Beirut, thousands of Palestinians had died.

Oddly enough, despite his string of aircraft bombings, hang-glider attacks and prisoner exchanges with the Israelis, Jibril had never achieved the kind of international notoriety he evidently craved. Certainly, Abu

Nidal, Abu Jihad, who was assassinated by Israeli agents in Tunis in April 1988, and Abu Abbas were much better known to the world.

Whether that was the reason Jibril decided to wage the Palestinian struggle in Europe is unclear. Certainly the targets in Europe were softer and more susceptible to terrorist attack. And if the right deal were struck, some of the governments there might even leave him alone. Jibril had no idea how right he would be.

Had it not been for events half a continent away in October 1988, however, Ahmed Jibril might still be consigned to the middle ranks of the Middle East's more dangerous fanatics, a clear and present danger to Israelis and moderate Palestinians who live in the region, but hardly anyone ordinary citizens of Europe or the United States needed to worry about.

CHAPTER 10

The men of the Bundeskriminalamt (BKA), the German federal police, are not known for their fondness for surprises. Yet for the past several weeks they had been hit with one unpleasant surprise after another. They had been patient, and their patience had been rewarded with embarrassment. It was time to bring things to an end and find out exactly what the hell was going on. Operation Autumn Leaves must be concluded.

About seven weeks before, in early September 1988, BKA technicians had installed taps on phones in a number of apartments frequented by the mysterious characters they were watching. One such place was a flat at 16 Isarstrasse in the pleasant town of Neuss. A green-grocer named Hashem Abassi lived there with his wife, Somaia, and their thirteen-month-old-son. Abassi was of interest to the police only because of his houseguest. The man was travelling with a Syrian passport under the name Hafez Mohammed Hussein. His acquaintances would tell the police afterwards that everyone simply called him Hussein. The police knew him by the same name. In accordance with the German law requiring all foreigners living in the country to register with the authorities, Abassi's houseguest had presented himself in January 1988 to the local police in Neuss, and that was the name he had given.

In fact, Hafez Hussein was really Hafez Dalkamouni. Somaia Abassi was Dalkamouni's sister, so he and Hashem Abassi were brothers-in-law.

Dalkamouni was a terrorist of considerable accomplishments, each paid for at an extraordinarily high price. He had been born in 1945 in the Arab village of Yafia, not far from Nazareth. In his teens he had left Israel, landed in Jordan, and he hadn't returned to the land of his birth until 1969, when he intended to blow the place up. Dalkamouni's homecoming was a disaster. He and a small band of terrorists under his command crossed the Jordan River sometime in the middle of the night. Their aim was to blow up power lines in Galilee. Unfortunately for Dalkamouni, the explosive device he was carrying went off prematurely in a farm storage shed near Beit Qeshet, on the Israeli–Jordanian border. The men with Dalkamouni left him for dead. According to one eyewitness, the Israeli security officers who came to investigate the next morning found a dazed and bleeding Dalkamouni lying on the ground, shouting 'Vengeance, vengeance'. The Israelis carted Dalkamouni off to a military hospital, where what was left of the lower part of his left leg was amputated. Then he was tried and convicted of plotting terrorist acts on Israeli soil and sentenced to a life term in an Israeli prison. Dalkamouni spent ten years there, until Ahmed Jibril arranged for him to get out in 1979.

Nine years later, the one-legged bomber had turned up in West Germany, where he was giving the officers of the BKA fits.

According to U.S. officials, West German authorities had kept Dalkamouni under surveillance intermittently since at least January 1988, but they had not shown a lot of concern about his activities. As far as German authorities knew, Dalkamouni was buying weapons in their country to ship them out, to Lebanon and Syria. That, apparently, was fine with them. Since the bombing of the Pan Am jet, some intelligence officials have said that German authorities had an effective quid pro quo with Dalkamouni, and perhaps with others affiliated with terrorist organizations: We will leave you alone if you leave Germans and German targets alone.

The record of West German dealings with terrorists and terrorist states is not an encouraging one. At the same time Dalkamouni was wandering around the country, for instance, the German company Imhausen-Chemie GmbH was assisting the Libyan government of Colonel Muammar al-Qaddafi in the construction of a plant that intelligence officials had identified conclusively as a facility for the production of chemical weapons. It was shown afterwards that officials in the German chancellor's office, as well as senior German intelligence officials, knew of Imhausen's activities in Libya, but nothing was done to stop the company. According to a senior U.S. official, the attitude in Bonn was simply that construction of the plant 'was good for German business.'

Senior German police and intelligence officials heatedly denied that any deal had been cut, implicitly or explicitly, with any terrorist. Even if that is so, it is still awfully difficult to put a charitable interpretation on the bizarre and tragic series of events leading up to the bombing of the Pan Am jet in Lockerbie. In August 1987, as a train carrying U.S. troops was passing the village of Hedemünden in Lower Saxony, a bomb went off. No one was hurt and no one was arrested, but officials in Bonn said much later that evidence was developed linking the bombing to Dalkamouni and several other suspected members of the PFLP-GC. Early in 1988, Israeli intelligence officials warned their counterparts in Germany that they had reason to believe Jibril's men were planning to strike again on German soil. This time the warning was quite specific. On February 2, a BKA officer duly noted in the agency log: 'We had a warning [from Israel]. PFLP-GC conducted tests and training for purposes of destroying [American military] railroads [in West Germany].'

Twelve weeks later, on April 26, as another U.S.

troop train was passing through Hedemünden, another bomb went off. Miraculously, once again, no one was hurt, although the locomotive sustained extensive damage. Despite the warnings, there is no evidence that German authorities stepped up surveillance on Dalkamouni.

In the summer there were several more warnings. On July 3, the USS *Vincennes* shot down the Iranian airbus in the Persian Gulf. Even before the *Vincennes* had fired the two missiles at the plane, the U.S. fleet in the gulf had been on alert for some kind of Iranian-inspired attack: Shortly afterwards, Israeli intelligence intercepted several messages between Jibril's headquarters in Damascus and the Sheikh Abdullah Barracks, the headquarters of Iran's Revolutionary Guards in Lebanon. On the basis of the intercepts, Israel's Mossad warned West German authorities, and others as well, of an emerging new alliance between Jibril, the Revolutionary Guards and the Iranian-backed Hezbollah movement based in Lebanon. The odds of an attack now seemed greater than ever.

In West Germany and elsewhere in Europe, American military installations were put on a higher state of alert. Immediately after the *Vincennes* shot down the Iranian airbus in July, according to Israeli intelligence sources, Mossad issued a specific warning to the U.S. and to West Germany and other European nations that Jibril or Iran might launch a retaliatory attack against an American airliner. But the Germans did not appear to take any additional precautions. Hafez Dalkamouni continued to move about in Germany, and German intelligence agents continued to watch him on an intermittent basis and make some notes in their notebooks. In August the Israelis alerted Bonn again. An Israeli handball team from the town of Ramat Gan was touring Germany, and Israeli intelligence officials had been tipped that the team could be the target of some type of terrorist operation. No attempt was made.

143

From across the street, BKA agents saw Dalkamouni move into the flat on October 5, having arrived from a PFLP-GC safe house in Yugoslavia. Within days Dalkamouni had his first visitor. Ahmed Abassi, the greengrocer's younger brother, had come from Sweden for a few days. Ahmed was fluent in English and German, and Dalkamouni was not. For several days the two men were observed going nearly everywhere together, Abassi serving as Dalkamouni's translator. Agents followed Dalkamouni as he travelled to Berlin on October 7 and to Frankfurt on October 9.

Soon more visitors arrived. The apartment at 16 Isarstrasse was filling up. With the BKA agents at their posts, a white Volvo with Swedish licence plates pulled up in front of the building, and three men got out. All appeared to be of Arab origin. The three men unloaded packages from the Volvo and carried them inside. Then they carried other packages from the apartment back to the car. It appeared the three wouldn't be staying long after all. The BKA men were stumped.

Something about Dalkamouni's activities made police officials nervous: perhaps it was the accretion of warnings from abroad, the two train bombings on German soil, or simply the fact that, for all their casual surveillance of the one-legged terrorist, they still had no clear idea what he was up to. One bright morning in late September, they suddenly had additional reason to find out. All hell, it seemed, was breaking loose.

On the morning of September 21, Hans Tietmayer left his home in fashionable Bad Godesberg, near Bonn, as he usually did. The morning was crisp but pleasant; his driver was waiting. It would be a busy day. Tietmayer was the state secretary in the Finance Ministry, and he had been placed in charge of preparations for a conference of the International Monetary Fund that was to meet in Bonn starting on September 24. There were still plenty of last-minute details to be attended to.

So preoccupied was Herr Tietmayer that he failed to

notice the two men in ski masks standing just beyond the edge of his property, in a small wooded area. He was just approaching his car when the men opened fire. Fortunately for Tietmayer, the men with the guns didn't quite know what they were doing and his driver did. A Kalashnikov rifle jammed and was left in the woods; that probably saved Tietmayer's life. The men in the masks continued firing with shotguns, but they missed Tietmayer and did only superficial damage to his car as the driver sped away. The driver went straight to the nearest poice station, and only much later did Herr Tietmayer return to the Finance Ministry to attend to those pressing last-minute details.

As BKA and other police officials descended on Bad Godesberg to investigate, a man with an uncertain accent called a news bureau in Bonn to claim responsibility. Investigators suspected the Red Army Faction, the small band of fanatic successors to the Baader–Meinhof gang. Andreas Baader and Ulrike Meinhof had killed themselves in prison a decade or so earlier, committed to the end to their loopy vision of a radical Marxist-Leninist state. By the late 1980s, the Red Army Faction had come to number maybe twenty or thirty people and had become more narrowly focused on activities directed against NATO. Their attacks, however, had been fewer with each passing year. An attack on Tietmayer, although aimed at disrupting the IMF conference, would have been perfectly within their scope.

But another organization claimed responsibility instead. The caller to the news bureau said that the attack on Tietmayer had been the work of heroic commandos of the Khaled Aker Brigade. Khaled Aker was the PFLP-GC commando who had died in the spectacular hang-glider attack near Qiryat Shemona almost a year earlier. After Jibril himself, there was probably no more revered or respected member of the PFLP-GC. All of a sudden, it seemed, Bonn investigators were awaking to the obvious. They simply had to find out what Dalkamouni and his associates in Germany were up to. Thus was Operation Autumn Leaves begun.

More than seventy agents of the BKA, assisted by officials of the BfV (Bundesamt für Verfassungsschutz), the West German interior intelligence agency, and the BND (Bundesnachrichtendienst), the agency responsible for intelligence gathering beyond German borders, were assigned to the investigation. Suspects, including Dalkamouni, were placed under round-the-clock surveillance and videotaped – some officials say the BfV made hundreds of hours of tapes. More wiretaps were installed. Before the operation was over, German agents would track more than a dozen people in six federal states. What they saw and heard made them very nervous indeed.

On October 13, BKA agents watched as yet another visitor arrived at 16 Isarstrasse. A hasty check showed that the man had just arrived in Frankfurt from Amman, Jordan. He had flown in with his wife. From his visa application, BKA agents got the man's name: Marwan Kreeshat. Interpol took almost no time at all to identify Kreeshat as Jibril's bomb-maker.

Dalkamouni was clearly plotting something, but what?

On October 16, BKA agents followed Dalkamouni as he drove to the town of Hockenheim. There two men loaded his car with plastic bags and boxes. One bag in particular caught the agents' attention. As they recorded later in a BKA surveillance log, it contained 'an unrecognizable brown mass'. Dalkamouni, they noticed, took care to place the bag away from the others 'on the car's hat rack'.

A bomb-maker, and now some brown stuff in a bag. Strange.

The next evening, the agents watched as Dalkamouni visited someone in jail in Cologne. It appeared to be a personal matter.

On October 19, BKA technicians listened in as Dalkamouni made a number of phone calls from Hashem Abassi's apartment. First he called King's Take-Away, a takeout restaurant in Nicosia, Cyprus; he spoke with a man named Amer. With the sounds of kitchen bustle behind him, Amer said that he had arranged for a German visa and that it would be valid as of the twentieth. He could leave anytime, he said. He was waiting now only for Dalkamouni to give him the word. Scottish investigators later said that Dalkamouni also called Jibril from West Germany, using a sophisticated telephone-relay system in Cyprus. Cyprus was becoming a mighty interesting place.

The police already knew who Amer was. His real name was Amer Dajani. From computerized consular records, they confirmed that his German visa was valid not for October 20, but for October 24. What was going on?

As the BKA technicians listened, Dalkamouni dialled again. This time it was Damascus.

First he spoke with a man named Abed. In a few days, Dalkamouni told Abed, 'everything would be ready'. Then another man, Safi, got on the phone in Dalkamouni's place. The police would later figure out, if they didn't know already, that Safi wa actually Marwan Kreeshat. Safi told Abed that he had 'made some changes in the medicine' and that it was 'better and stronger than before'. Dalkamouni then got back on the phone, had another brief chat with Abed and concluded by saying, according to the BKA, that 'things are under way'.

When Dalkamouni was finished with his phone calls, he left the flat, followed by BKA surveillance agents. Agents watched him as he went about purchasing 'electronic devices' in Düsseldorf. Later that same day, at 8:10 P.M., in a remote corner of the restaurant in the train station in Giessen, they watched as Dalkamouni fell into conversation with a bearded man in a grey

147

sweater and a floppy jacket. Later, in a report, one of the surveillance agents would describe the man as having 'noticeably large ears'. After about twenty minutes in the restaurant, the two men strolled out onto the station's pedestrian overpass and continued talking. At 8:50 P.M., the strange man with the big ears left in a BMW. The police had no idea what the two men had said to each other. They couldn't get close enough to hear.

Over the next two days, BKA men followed Dalkamouni as he made more phone calls, arranged to rent an apartment in Frankfurt, visited another apartment near the Frankfurt zoo, met a stranger at Goetheplatz and went shopping with Kreeshat for additional electronic items. Dalkamouni went back to the apartment near the zoo several times. The address was 28 Sandweg; it was across the street from a synagogue. A man was living in the apartment, but the BKA agents didn't know who he was. They had never seen or heard of him before. They had no records on him, as far as they knew. The agents were getting increasingly nervous. Should they make the arrests now or wait?

A few more days, they decided. If Dalkamouni was going to plant a bomb somewhere, they still didn't know what the target was.

Later in the day on October 23, BKA technicians listened in as Dalkamouni, back in Neuss, got a call from Damascus. The call was from a man named Abu Hassan Jomah. 'The things are almost ready,' Jomah told Dalkamouni. He would be arriving in Germany very shortly.

The next day Dalkamouni and Kreeshat took another shopping trip. At the Huma-Markt department store in Neuss, they bought three mechanical alarm clocks and a digital clock. Then they went to Kaufhalle, another department store, where they picked up sixteen 1.5-volt batteries and some switches, screws and glue. In a phone call later that day to Amman, Kreeshat said that he 'had just begun work' and that it would take 'two or three days until he returned.'

The agents were going nuts. They had no doubt now that a terrorist operation of some type was about to take place. In an internal log, a BKA officer noted that 'the purchase of the materials under the clear supervision of a PFLP-GC member designated as an explosives expert leads to the conclusion that the participants intend to produce an explosive device which, on the basis of the telephone taps, would be operational within the next few days.' But they still didn't know anything about the target. If they moved too quickly, they would certainly arrest Dalkamouni and the others. But other members of the terrorist organization, whom they knew nothing about, would still be free to complete the operation.

Where, the BKA wanted to know, was Amer, the man awaiting Dalkamouni's instructions in the kitchen of the Cypriot stakeout place? Had he already arrived? And who else might be involved? Previous experience had shown the Germans that terrorist operations were often organized by one cell and carried out independently by other cells of the same organization. If that were so in this instance, Amer Dajani's arrival could be a sign that an attack was imminent. The police could not hold back any longer. In a sobering conclusion, a BKA agent noted in the internal agency log that the 'course of events is becoming increasingly unclear and, as far as the BfV and BND are concerned, uncontrollable.'

Senior officials of the BND, BfV and BKA met late in the day on October 25, and the decision was finalized. It was time for Autumn Leaves to fall.

At 7:45 A.M. on October 26, the order went out from BKA headquarters. Within minutes, police with guns drawn began their moves. Before the day was out, they would raid twelve apartments and five businesses in locations all across Germany. Two teams of BKA agents had been assigned to Dalkamouni and Kreeshat, one

149

comprised of heavily armed soldiers from the elite SEK commando unit. Dalkamouni and Kreeshat were the prime targets of the operation, and the BKA didn't want anything to go wrong at the last minute.

As BKA men watched, Dalkamouni and Kreeshat strolled out of 16 Isarstrasse and got into a silver-green Ford Taurus with licence plate AA-RJ736, registered to an address in the city of Aachen. With two cars of BKA agents behind them, Dalkamouni and Kreeshat drove carefully into the centre of Neuss, parked on a side street near a shopping mall and locked the car. Hobbling on the prosthesis that had given him trouble ever since he had been fitted for it in the Israeli prison hospital almost twenty years before, Dalkamouni walked a block with Kreeshat to a bank of public telephones. As Kreeshat spoke to an unidentified party, Dalkamouni waited outside.

The BKA agents waited nervously for Kreeshat to complete the call. Then they moved in.

A dozen agents surrounded Dalkamouni and Kreeshat, who made no effort to resist. Inside the Ford, the agents found blank Syrian and Spanish passports. There was also a Toshiba radio–cassette player under a blanket. While some of the BKA men placed Dalkamouni and Kreeshat under arrest, others went back to Hashem Abassi's flat. There they found a stopwatch, batteries, a detonator, two types of fuses (time-delay and barometric), radio components, soldering irons and several more Syrian passports in among Dalkamouni's personal effects. One of the passports was an official government passport, blank; another, also blank, had been issued by the Syrian Ministry of Religious Affairs.

Elsewhere, Autumn Leaves was being rolled up in the orderly and efficient fashion for which the BKA was known. At 28 Sandweg in Frankfurt, the BKA agents hit paydirt. The second-floor flat there, in a neighbourhood where many Arabs and migrant workers lived, had been under continuous surveillance since Dalkamouni had visited several days before. Some neighbours had run into the cops on the surveillance detail and wondered what was going on. Horst Hoos, who owned a butcher shop almost directly across the street from the address, had stumbled across the surveillance teams on more than one occasion.

'One time, there was a vehicle, a car, blocking my exit,' the butcher recalled months afterwards. 'So I was forced to go over and ask it to move. I noticed that the people were armed and had night binoculars, so I thought straightaway that they must be police officers.'

On the afternoon of October 26, the commotion in front of Horst Hoos's butcher shop was incredible. Police vans, bomb-sniffing dogs, flashing lights: the street was almost impassable. Inside the apartment, the BKA men were agog. They had found a small arsenal: a bazooka, American-made; five Hungarian-made automatic rifles and a sixth assembled from a grab bag of parts, as well as twenty fully loaded clips of ammunition. There were also a grenade launcher, a carbine and thirty hand grenades. Besides that there was a variety-store assortment of explosives: five kilograms of Czech-made Semtex, nearly six kilos of commercial-grade TNT, and fourteen sticks of dynamite that police would later trace to a Soviet-bloc manufacturer. Alexander Prechtel, the spokesman for the German federal prosecutor's office that handled most major terrorism cases, told news reporters, 'This is the largest weapons and explosives cache of terrorists we have ever found in the Federal Republic.'

The BKA men couldn't believe their eyes.

Neighbours recalled later that the police had waited until there was someone home at the apartment before they threatened to break down the door. 'They must have watched him coming home,' said a woman who

151

lived a few doors away. 'When he was about five minutes in the apartment, they just arrested him and took him outside. It must have been some foreigner.'

Over the next twelve hours, BKA agents picked up another thirteen suspects in Neuss, Frankfurt, Hamburg, Mannheim and Berlin. All had been seen meeting or talking with Dalkamouni during the Autumn Leaves surveillance. A total of thirty-four people suspected of being connected to the PFLP-GC had been placed under surveillance during the course of the operation, but arrest warrants had been issued only for the sixteen men picked up on October 26 and for one other man who was believed to be somewhere outside the Federal Republic.

In jail, the mystery man arrested at 28 Sandweg was identified as Abdel Fattah Ghadanfar, a forty-seven-year-old Palestinian. Ghadanfar, it turned out, was known to police in at least five countries by at least as many aliases. In Britain police knew him as Ronald John Bartle. In Spain he had three names: Gelabert Coma, Clement Navarro Rabasco and Luis Canal Rodriguez. In France he went by François Seris. Besides his native Arabic, Ghadanfar was fluent in English and Spanish, and he could understand French. In any language, after the BKA picked him up, he was plenty willing to talk.

'I am here on behalf of the PFLP-GC,' Abdel Ghadanfar told investigators proudly. He said that he received his orders from Dalkamouni and that he had rented the apartment at 28 Sandweg ten months before. For much of that time, however, Ghadanfar had been living in Damascus, he told the investigators; he had returned from Damascus just a month earlier, via Belgrade.

Ghadanfar said that Dalkamouni, his boss, was the head of the PFLP-GC's new 'foreign division', which had been founded by Ahmed Jibril approximately a year earlier. The mission of the foreign division,

Ghadanfar said, was to represent students of Ahmed Jibril's organization who were living abroad.

But what would 'students' want with high-powered weapons? Ghadanfar was asked.

Ghadanfar said that Dalkamouni had brought the weapons to 28 Sandweg and that he, Ghadanfar, had stored them in a suitcase under the bed. Later, the police would determine that Ghadanfar was one of Jibril's key money men and that he had funnelled money from Syria to West Germany and set up a series of bank accounts that would make the money extremely difficult to trace. It would be used to pay Jibril's operatives in Europe.

On the evening of October 26, however, BKA agents were more interested in talking about guns than about money. They also wanted to learn what kind of operation Dalkamouni had been planning with Marwan Kreeshat's bombs.

Dalkamouni, sitting in a cell not far from Ghadanfar, refused to talk.

German news organizations carried congratulatory accounts of the arrests by the BKA that had 'prevented a major terrorist operation on German soil'. The Ministry of the Interior issued a brief statement praising the 'exemplary work of our security forces'. More soberly, in an internal BKA memo, a supervisor made this notation: 'Cannot say what [the] precise target was, but we can say with high probability that attacks were not intended [against] the Federal Republic of Germany.'

Later on the evening of the twenty-sixth, two of the sixteen arrested were released; evidently, they had simply been caught up in the sweep and had nothing to do with any terrorist operation. The police seemed to have solid evidence on many of the others, although there were some peculiar details. For one of those arrested, Ramzi Diab, there was almost no information on the arrest documents: no address, nothing about employment or a previous criminal record. The only information the BKA provided for Diab was his year of birth, 1959, and the city in which he was arrested, Frankfurt. The identification papers he produced for the police were bogus. Under questioning by the BKA, Diab adamantly denied knowing Dalkamouni or being a member of the PFLP-GC. Asked repeatedly by a BKA officer whether he had been involved in planning a terrorist act, Diab replied: 'I have to remark that I know neither Mr. Dalkamouni nor anything of an arrangement for a criminal act.'

That was a lie. BKA officers produced surveillance photographs they had taken of Diab and Dalkamouni. One showed the two men standing by a bench in Goetheplatz in Frankfurt. Another showed Diab and Dalkamouni in conversation as they walked down a street together. Suddenly Diab's memory returned, at least partially. Oh yes, he told the BKA agents, he *had* met Mr. Dalkamouni for the very first time at a hamburger stand just ten days before. Dalkamouni had walked up to him, Diab recalled, and introduced himself. 'He asked me if I could help him out in Germany,' Diab remembered. '[He] said he was dealing in cars.'

In fact, Ramzi Diab's name was Salah Kwikas, and he, like Dalkamouni, was a terrorist of some note. Israeli commandos had captured Diab on a terrorist mission inside Israel in the early 1980s, and he had been among the 1,150 Israeli prisoners released in the 1985 exchange Dalkamouni had negotiated for Chesai Shai and the two other Israeli reservists.

That kind of background, not to mention the phony identification papers and his flimsy story about how he had come to meet Dalkamouni, would seem to dictate holding Diab for further questioning. But that is not what happened, investigators in Lockerbie and Washington found out.

On the afternoon of October 27, in a courtroom in

154

Düsseldorf (the jurisdiction encompassing the town of Neuss), security officers paraded Diab, Dalkamouni, Ghadanfar and the other eleven men still in custody before Judge Christian Rinne. The judge, who has since been transferred from the criminal division to the civil bench, let all but three of the men go. The judge's reason: lack of evidence. Even though many of those arrested provided explanations – some of them highly implausible – for their activities, evidence of their link to terrorism was indisputable. Nevertheless, eleven suspects were released on their own recognizance. Within seventy-two hours of their leaving the courthouse, six of them had vanished from West Germany, and later could be found nowhere in Europe.

One of those released was Adnan Younis, a one-eyed pizza-maker who preferred the name Abu Tarek. Born in 1954, Younis had been a member of the PFLP-GC for several years. He had come to the attention of German police most recently in December 1986, when a plot to send booby-trapped pens to Jewish leaders in Germany had come unravelled. The pens, filled with explosives and wired with detonators, were to have been mailed to two Jewish community centres, but an Egyptian man with whom Younis had stored the pens got nervous and told West Berlin police. Somehow, Younis, who had been arrested in connection with the terrorist pen plot, was back running his pizzeria in Berlin. It was a difficult job. In the early 1980s, while training in one of Jibril's camps in Lebanon, Younis had mishandled some explosives. In the blast he had lost one hand, disfigured another and lost an eye. Despite the BKA documentation of Younis's involvement with Dalkamouni, the judge found no evidence to hold him.

At the end of the day, then, only Dalkamouni, Ghadanfar and Kreeshat remained in the custody of the police, charged with violations of the war-weapons control law and with formation of and membership in a terrorist organization. (Another man, Martin Kadourah, was not immediately arrested. But he soon surrendered in Yugoslavia, where he had been visiting, and police in Belgrade returned him to Germany, where he was detained for several days by officers of the BKA, questioned extensively and then released.) Of these three men remaining behind bars, one would get his freedom quickly.

Marwan Kreeshat's career as a bomb-maker spanned at least eighteen years, going back to the Swissair jet crash in 1970 that killed forty-seven people, and he was a bona fide terrorist. After his arrest with Dalkamouni, Kreeshat would not talk to investigators or even sign his name to a routine police identification form. But after several requests from an Arabic-speaking BKA agent, however, Kreeshat began providing the names of senior officials of the PFLP-GC. According to one official, he told the investigators that he had overheard Jibril talking about a 'planned attack on an American club in Germany'. And on the day of their arrest, Kreeshat said Dalkamouni instructed him, 'Wait four or five days, and you will be told everything on target.'

Kreeshat admitted to BKA officers that he was familiar with explosives. But he denied again and again that he knew anything about Dalkamouni's targets. The officers pressed him, but Kreeshat was adamant. He knew nothing.

At one point in the interrogation, Kreeshat asked to make a phone call. The authorities agreed, and on November 5, a German office placed a call for Kreeshat to Jordan. That was odd. BND agents would say later that the call had been placed to an official in the Jordanian intelligence community. But the BND would give no details of the person's identity or the conversation. Was Kreeshat working for a Jordanian spy agency? And if he was, would he be foolish enough to call it directly and blow his cover? What was going on?

Four days after the phone call to Jordan, a German prosecutor asked the court to delay the proceedings against Kreeshat. The prosecutor asked for the continuance so that Kreeshat's arrest documents could be supplemented with more information. The judge denied the request.

'[Kreeshat's] contacts with the other accused were limited and on the level of friendship,' the judge ruled. 'He did not know anything [about] planning or preparing for an attack. We lack the required urgent suspicion to justify further . . . custody.'

Set free, Kreeshat, like his colleagues, simply vanished.

Then things really became unpleasant.

In Lockerbie, London and Washington, for the investigators assigned to the bombing of Pan Am Flight 103, which was now an official murder investigation involving 270 deaths, the bad news from Germany came in small doses, at least at first. In the days after Christmas, the investigators complained, they could not get an accurate list of the people Judge Rinne had released several weeks earlier. What had become of famous German efficiency? Investigators in Lockerbie complained of sloppy translations of some police documents and did little to discourage the impression that the sloppiness was deliberate. In Washington, intelligence officials with knowledge of the investigation said plainly that once they did pry loose the list of those arrested in October from the authorities in Bonn, they believed it was almost certainly not accurate.

What did the Germans have to hide, anyway?

At the nuts-and-bolts level of the police investigation, many officials believed the Germans were unhelpful to the point of irresponsibility. According to some, German authorities would not even concede the *possibility* that the bomb that had blown up the *Maid of the Seas* might have been placed on board during the loading of the first leg of Flight 103 in Frankfurt. Questioned about the probability of links between the people arrested in October and the bombing of the Pan Am jet, German authorities were almost deliberately obtuse. 'There is just no evidence,' prosecutor Achim Thiele said in his cramped office on the seventh floor of the Frankfurt court building months after the bombing. 'It is all speculation and, I will grant you, some rather strange coincidences.'

A few days after the release of most of those arrested in October, another German prosecutor, Kurt Rebmann, opened his own investigation into the possible existence of a PFLP-GC terrorist operation and its possible links to the bombing of Pan Am Flight 103. But it is well known that Rebmann and Thiele are rivals professionally, and the dual investigations seem to have had the effect of tying BKA investigators further into knots.

More important to the understanding of the German role in the investigation of the Lockerbie bombing is the background of Jibril's organization, its ambitious new plans for terrorist operations outside the Middle East and the strange acquiescence to its presence in Germany by the Bonn government.

In his interrogation by BKA officers, Abdel Ghadanfar referred to Jibril's new 'foreign division'. Israeli intelligence officials refer to his 'Western apparatus'. Whatever its name, the relatively new European operation had very little to do with helping students, except inasmuch as the students are useful for the spread of his terrorist campaign. The only exchange students here, Western intelligence officials say, were terrorists committed to their own fanatical cause. And Hafez Dalkamouni was their tutor.

Dalkamouni, for several reasons, was an inspired

choice. Since 1979 he had been travelling regularly to East Germany for treatment of his bad leg. From there, he could travel easily to Yugoslavia, West Germany and Scandinavia. Israeli intelligence officials believed that Dalkamouni and perhaps other Jibril agents had been recruiting Palestinians and even Shiites in Europe as far back as 1986. Rejuvenated by the influx of the hundreds of terrorists and operatives whose release Dalkamouni had negotiated a year earlier, Ahmed Jibril had begun establishing a network of supporters, 'sleepers' and safe houses in Eastern and Western Europe, intelligence officials said. Despite the enmity among the many factions of the Palestine Liberation Organization, particularly between Arafat and Jibril, it continued to pay the salaries and finance the activities of all its members, Israeli officials said. In Europe, according to the Israelis, Jibril's new network of operatives was paid out of the same PLO funds that Arafat, George Habash and his other enemies were drawing on.

According to Western intelligence officials, many of the Palestinians in Jibril's European network came from Israel, Jordan, Lebanon and Syria. Some of the Shiites recruited by Jibril and his people may have been simply fleeing the civil war in Lebanon, but his European operations nevertheless provided a convenient base of support. Many of his new recruits were invited, all expenses paid, to Syria, where they were trained in espionage and terrorist activities. Then they would return to Europe, enrol in universities there, or seek political asylum and remain as permanent residents. By early 1988, intelligence officials said, Jibril had people in Frankfurt, Stockholm, Bonn, Berlin, Copenhagen, Rome and Barcelona and in Yugoslavia.

Israeli and Western intelligence officials say that one of Dalkamouni's primary responsibilities in Europe was to purchase weapons and arrange for their shipment to the Middle East, where they would be used against

Israel. There is some evidence to suggest, according to those officials, that German authorities were willing to wink at Dalkamouni's activities as long as he and his people did not target people and property inside the Federal Republic.

But was he doing more than simply buying weapons and shipping them out of West Germany? How many people were working for Dalkamouni and Jibril in Europe? What were their intentions?

Clearly, even after the arrests on October 26, some German officials had serious concerns. In an internal BKA log from sometime soon after that date, an officer wrote: 'On the basis of arrest of Dalkamouni, we can presume that at least [the] central organization of a group has been destroyed. We cannot assume that all involved people have been arrested.'

In turning a blind eye to Dalkamouni's actions for so long, German authorities had allowed a bloody terrorist organization to establish operations in the very heart of Europe. Some of Jibril's operatives were later found to have taken reconnaissance photographs on Jewish, Israeli and American targets there. If it turned out that Jibril's new European organization was responsible for the murder of 270 innocent people in a tiny Scottish village, and that some European governments had effectively given Jibril a free pass to operate, there would be absolute hell to pay. In East Germany, which had provided support for Qaddafi and for other terrorists, and in Yugoslavia, which had provided shelter for 'Carlos the Jackal' – a notorious international terrorist and killer – and at least a dozen other murderers, Jibril and Dalkamouni had no trouble with access. In other places in Europe, the arrangements were more complicated, but Jibril's people nevertheless continued to operate there.

In West Germany, some people did have doubts about Ahmed Jibril's terrorist network, the extent of its support base and the goals it hoped to achieve. In

Lockerbie, as Christmas came and went, the investigators had no inkling of the extent of Jibril's network in Europe. The only thing they knew for sure was that Pan Am Flight 103 had been brought down by a bomb, and they had to find out who was responsible.

CHAPTER 11

Outside the U.S. embassy in London on the afternoon of December 27, a thin drizzle chilled the empty trees of Grosvenor Square. Theoretically, the embassy was still on a quiet holiday footing; as a practical matter, it was bedlam. At 3:45, a phone rang in the American Citizens Services section. Consular operations involving Pan Am Flight 103 were being moved from the embassy's cramped task-force rooms to the more accommodating quarters of Citizens Services. From there, consular officials would try to assist families of the victims with a host of problems most had never dreamed of. Flying bodies across the Atlantic? Who knew about such things? On this afternoon the call to Citizens Services represented a small milestone. It was Lockerbie on the line. The Scottish authorities – the police investigators under the direction of John Boyd, and the morticians reporting to Captain Tony Balfour of the RAF – would be releasing the first five bodies from the wreckage later that day. Within a few hours, the coffins would leave Lockerbie for Edinburgh to begin the long journey back to the States. The families there had to be alerted.

Which bodies were being shipped back? the families inquired. The consular officials in London didn't know. And for some reason no one in Lockerbie could tell them. The families of those who died on Flight 103 were aghast. And then outraged.

The first news stories asserting that a bomb had blown up the 103 had broken a day earlier. In the States

162

and Britain the families of the victims wanted to know if it was true. From the officials they asked, they got insincere denials. And from the news media they got more speculation. But worst of all, a week after their loved ones had died in the nighttime sky over Lockerbie, they still had no word on when they could recover the bodies and at least give them a proper burial. It was outrageous.

There were all sort of complaints. Why should families in their grief be further subjected to lies, diplomatic denials, sluggish Scottish detectives and a host of impossible questions by investigators and news reporters? A day after Christmas, a rabbi consoling some of the victims' families had called the State Department to raise concerns about the treatment of the remains of the Jewish victims. Orthodox Jewish law prohibits autopsies, except in instances where such a procedure could yield information that might save another person's life. That was of course not the case here, yet a day later, British officials had told Jewish relatives that autopsies were being performed on all the victims before their identities were established. No exceptions. That's what Scottish law required, and the law would not be waived for religious or any other reasons. That seemed strange. Everyone knew what had caused the victims to die: they had been in a plane that had blown apart at 31,000 feet, and then they had fallen to earth. Why were the damn autopsies so important?

That afternoon in Lockerbie, Angus Kennedy, the tough Glasgow cop John Boyd had brought to the village to keep the news media in line and, more important, the families of the victims informed, called a meeting of some seventy family members who were in Lockerbie waiting to claim the bodies of their loved ones. To many of the family members, Kennedy was about the only person in the world making any sense, even when he didn't have many answers for them. His grief for the victims and concern for the families was evident to anyone who talked with him. In Lockerbie, however, his was a lousy job. On the afternoon of December 27, he told the families that despite the best efforts of the searchers, only 240 bodies had been found so far. The bodies of the other nineteen passengers on the 103, he conceded, might never be recovered. He could not even say for certain how many would ever be identified. Some were just too horribly mangled. His remarks sent another shock wave through the families of the victims. Lockerbie was a nightmare.

Sadly, it would get worse.

Ordinarily, the week between Christmas and New Year's is one of the slowest in the government and the news business. Washington, for all intents and purposes, shuts down. On December 28, however, more than a hundred reporters from around the world jammed the briefing room at FBI headquarters on Pennsylvania Avenue. Hours before, Scotland Yard had announced that explosives residue had been found in the wreckage of Flight 103. FBI director William Sessions would now deliver the official response of the U.S. government. A former prosecutor and federal judge, he did it in typically lawyerly fashion. The FBI's authority to investigate the incident, he told the reporters, was based on Title 18, U.S. Code 32, which relates to 'interference with or destruction of United States' aircraft travelling in foreign or interstate commerce.'

Time and again, in response to the reporters' questions, Sessions said there was no evidence that passengers on Flight 103 had been victims of a terrorist attack. 'I want to make it very clear,' Sessions said, 'that we have no suspicions that [the incident was] criminal or that it [was] terroristic.'

But mere confirmation that a bomb had blown up the 103 rocked the families of many of the victims as if it were the explosion itself. It is difficult, even now, for some of the victims' families to explain the effect of Sessions's announcement. It is one thing to accept the loss of a loved one in an accident. Everyone who has read about and seen TV coverage of air disasters knows that they are terribly tragic events but they happen. It is quite another thing to come to terms with the loss of a family member who has been murdered. Truly, the victims of the 103 were innocents. Understanding that, however, only deepened the pain and, for some, fuelled a sense of rage and a yearning for revenge.

In late December, Bruce Smith, the veteran Pan Am pilot, was still at home waiting to claim the body of his wife, Ingrid. It had been recovered by December 24 and identified conclusively by December 28. Bruce Smith wanted to know why the Scottish authorities would not admit that the body had been found, so he could arrange for funeral services and burial. He telephoned the police every day, he remembered. On December 29, a detective asked him about the half-moon–shaped pendant Ingrid wore around her neck, the one Bruce wore the other half of. Smith recalled the conversation with the detective:

'Have you found her?' Smith asked.

'Well, no, but she's on the "possibly identified" list,' the detective told him.

'How long has she been on that list?' Smith asked.

'I can't tell you,' was the reply.

Smith had had enough. On New Year's Day he gave an interview to British television excoriating the Scottish detectives. A sergeant called him the same day, as Smith put it, to 'explain things'. Smith would have none of it. If Ingrid's body were not released within twenty-four hours, he told the authorities in Lockerbie, he would file a writ of habeas corpus. He was fed up.

In contrast, Diane Maslowski's family suffered quietly at home in Haddonfield, New Jersey. Christmas had been a blur of tears. Suzi, Diane's younger sister,

165

was determined not to allow her parents to fall apart. After a good friend of hers in high school had died, the friend's family was virtually destroyed. 'I think [that] was my biggest fear when this whole thing happened,' Suzi Maslowski said. 'I see those people in town, and they're oblivious to the world. That was my biggest fear, that it would happen to my parents.' She remembered that it was touch-and-go with her parents for the first few days after the crash. Then the fog lifted. 'I knew my dad was going to be all right when he started yelling at me for being in the shower too long,' Suzi recalled, 'and I thought to myself. "Thank God, he's going to be okay." ' On December 27, there was a memorial service for Diane at Christ Church in Haddonfield, and it seemed as if the entire town turned out. Five days after that, on New Year's Day, a Scottish detective telephoned. The man said that Diane's body had been recovered and identified. 'He was very courteous, very polite,' Diane's father, Stan, recalled. The Maslowskis decided it was time to get their daughter.

They left for London the next day. At Diane's apartment in Chelsea, the plants were all dead. Diane had been a plant lover. 'It was a very traumatic experience,' her mother, Norma, said. 'I would use another word, but I don't know what would better describe my feelings. I could almost sense her presence there.'

For the Maslowskis, as for all the other families and friends of those who had died, the ordeal was just beginning. Toward the end of January, two FBI agents came to visit the family in Haddonfield. They wanted to know whom Diane had been dating in London, and whether she had taken a taxi to the airport. The investigators needed to find out such things, and in many cases there was no other way except asking the survivors.

Like the Maslowskis, Suruchi Rattan's family, what was left of it, also suffered quietly. Her father, Shachi, and her uncle, Sudhakar Dixit, had returned to London from Lockerbie on Christmas night. In Lockerbie they had gone to the temporary morgue, where they identified Suruchi and Anmol, her little brother. The children's grandparents also had been identified. Only Shachi Rattan's wife, Garima, had not yet been found. In London, a relative had called Rattan and Dixit. The bouquet of flowers addressed to the 'little girl in the red dress' was making news around the world. Suruchi's father decided he had to go back to Lockerbie to see it. 'It has to be her,' he remembered thinking after being told of the bouquet and the note. 'Truly speaking, I did not have any doubt that it was her.' Back in Lockerbie, Suruchi's father and uncle looked through scores of dripping bouquets and ink-smeared notes before they found the right one. They took several photographs. And then they left.

Among the families of the American victims, many wondered why the FBI wasn't leading the investigation. After all, the dead were mostly Americans.

In fact, the Bureau was more deeply involved in the investigation of the case than in that of any previous international terrorist action. It was not only that Buck Revell was determined that there would not be 'another Zia'. It was not just that the Bureau this time refused to be stonewalled by diplomats determined to avoid unpleasantness. It was a combination of uncommonly smooth relations with Scottish and English authorities and a quiet but intense determination on the part of a whole range of U.S. officials in several very different agencies that the crime would not go unpunished. This time, the consensus was, terrorists had gone too far.

The Scots were the lead investigators, simply because Scotland is where the plane had blown up and where the 270 people had lost their lives. But everyone from John Boyd to the most senior officials in Whitehall recognized the extent of the American interests in the case. At some level, perhaps because Boyd had an easy manner or because authorities in Lockerbie and London recognized that the U.S. intelligence community would have to be deeply involved in the hunt for the terrorists, a decision was made not to consider yet such matters as a location for the trial of the Pan Am bombers if they were convicted and captured. 'It was,' said Lord Peter Fraser, who as lord advocate of Scotland would prosecute any case against the terrorists in court, 'simply a decision that we would cross that bridge when we came to it, that the most important thing was investigating as thoroughly and effectively as possible and worrying about the rest of it all at a later date.'

FBI director Sessions was careful always to talk of 'furnishing assistance' to the Scots. In effect, although John Boyd and John Orr were issuing the orders in Lockerbie, the American investigators were in the case up to their hips.

According to several senior FBI officials and others outside the Bureau who know Sessions well, for him the investigation was a crystal-clear example of the FBI's unique role in American law enforcement. At the press conference on December 28, he said as little as possible so as not to jeopardize the proceedings. For the moment, the less said, the better the chance of a successful outcome. The inquiry into the bombing of Pan Am 103 was a kind of special challenge for him personally.

When William Casey died, as details of the Reagan administration's worst scandal, the Iran-contra affair, were being revealed, the president was advised to appoint a new CIA director who could shore up the Agency's credibility. Reagan had chosen William H. Webster, the dapper former district court and appeals court judge from Missouri who had assumed the directorship of the FBI some years earlier, when the Bureau had needed its own shoring up after its abuse by senior officials of the Nixon administration. With very few exceptions, particularly in the area of minority hiring and the elimination of racial bias within the Bureau,

Webster was generally credited with having done a superb job. He had moved the FBI into whole new areas of responsibility, and he had been absolutely intolerant of sloppy police procedures or abuse of investigatory authority. The result had been a dramatic enhancement of the Bureau's reputation, and not only in Washington. In moving Webster to the CIA, Ronald Reagan had hoped he could work the same spell there.

But who to replace Webster?

Embarrassed by Iran-contra and diminished by his own personal legal troubles, Attorney General Edwin Meese had begun looking for a Webster clone. But for many reasons Meese was an ineffective salesman. Through the autumn of 1987, he shopped the FBI directorship to a number of current and former federal judges, and none would bite. After several such rejections, he asked Sessions.

In late October 1987, sitting in his empty chambers in the handsome federal courthouse in downtown San Antonio, just a few blocks from the Alamo, Sessions explained why he had said yes. Most of his law books had been boxed away, the oak bookshelves behind the desk were bare, and the judge was waiting for someone in Washington to call and tell him when he should show up to be sworn in. Why had he taken the FBI job? There would be a new administration in just over a year's time, and in the dark days of the investigations into Iran-contra in late 1987, very few of the so-called political experts were willing to give any odds at all that it would be George Bush and the Republican team. From his vantage point in 1987 – Sessions would have to sell his comfortable house in Alamo Heights in order to take a job several of his colleagues had already turned down; he had no real reason to expect that the job would be his for very long – what would motivate him to move to Washington to run the FBI?

He pondered the question for less than a minute, and then said simply: 'Because it is an opportunity to serve.'

Not many people can get away with such a line. It was too hokey by half, its author too much the Boy Scout. And yet that, in a very real way, is Judge Sessions. And it probably explains why, in a place such as Washington, which chews up and spits out wise and well-meaning souls indiscriminately, there soon began a bit of a whispering campaign against Sessions. He wasn't smart enough, he wasn't aggressive enough, the line went; he was something of an empty suit. This was heard even in the corridors of the FBI.

But few people in Washington really knew William Steele Sessions. They probably didn't know, for instance, that although he had had polio at sixteen, he had worked hard since to become a highly proficient mountain climber: he had scaled Mount Everest not once but twice. And if Washington insiders knew something about a court case he had tried in the early 1980s, they had failed to draw the proper lessons from it. In 1979, U.S. District Judge John H. Wood, Jr., had been shot in the back as he had left his home to preside over a drug-smuggling case. Wood had not been just a colleague of Sessions's on the bench but a dear friend as well. Three years later, after FBI agents from the San Antonio field office had arrested four men for Wood's murder, Sessions was sitting on the bench. Defence lawyers had argued vigorously that because of his friendship with Wood, Sessions should recuse himself from the trial. Sessions had refused, saying that every defendant deserved the full respect of the court. The defence attorneys had appealed his ruling, and it had been kicked all the way up to the Supreme Court.

The high court had sided with Sessions.

After his conviction for murdering Wood in return for a payment of $250,000, Charles Harrelson had stood before Sessions in the John H. Wood, Jr., Federal Courthouse, awaiting sentencing. But first Harrelson had a few things to say. He had accused the prosecution of using 'Gestapo tactics'. He had accused Sessions himself of 'unspeakable evil'. 'I think the court should consider charges against itself for rape and murder,' Harrelson had railed. 'You have killed the Constitution of the United States, and you have had carnal knowledge of every person in the United States.'

Sessions had listened patiently. And when Harrelson had completed his screed, Judge Sessions, who for months had been living with his wife and three sons under a round-the-clock guard by U.S. marshals, had quietly sentenced Charles Harrelson to two consecutive life terms in prison. That pretty much summed up Judge Sessions's approach to law and order: Be honest, be fair, and give no quarter.

In December 1988, with just thirteen months on the job, the FBI director was unwilling to see the Lockerbie investigation hamstrung or compromised in any way. Whatever the investigators needed, they should have.

A long cab ride from FBI headquarters on Pennsylvania Avenue, in a grubby waterfront district known as Buzzard Point, was the Washington Metropolitan Field Office of the FBI. This field office, bristling with a dozen or more strange-looking communications antennae, was housed on the upper floors of a grim government building surrounded by puddled empty lots and street after street of squat buildings of uncertain integrity. It was unique within the FBI. In the Buzzard Point office were two counterintelligence divisions (the guys who watched the other side's spies) and a special squad known as C-3. Normally, there were seven special agents assigned to C-3, and the squad had had its share of successes. It was a team of C-3 agents who had arrested the terrorist Fawaz Younis in the Mediterranean in September 1987 on a boat in international waters off Cyprus. C-3 agents had also had a hand in the arrest of Mohammed Ali Hamadei, the hijacker of TWA Flight 847 in 1985, who had killed U.S. Navy diver Robert Dean Stethem. Hamadei had been prosecuted in West Germany and sentenced to life in prison.

171

In the days between the crash of 103 and Christmas, Special Agent Douglas Gow, who was in charge of the Washington Field Office at the time, anticipated trouble. Like Buck Revell and Director Sessions, he sensed that it was no ordinary air disaster. 'Something of that magnitude,' Gow remembered thinking, 'and you have to suspect foul play.'

Holiday or no, he put the agents of C-3 on alert. They would have to stay close to the phones. If Gow needed them, he would alert his assistant special agent in charge of C-3.

Besides C-3, Gow had some other unusual resources to draw on. The FBI's international response team was also based in the Washington Field Office. These were special agents fluent in foreign languages who could be moved at a moment's notice to question suspects or witnesses anywhere in the world. Then there was another team of agents who handled hostage-taking cases overseas, and another ad hoc group of computer wizards who could jury-rig a state-of-the-art system to meet the needs of almost every investigation, no matter how complicated. Gow told all of them to be prepared to move on very short notice.

Already some of his people were in Lockerbie, assisting with the investigation by the Scots and the recovery of bodies and debris. On December 28, Judge Sessions ordered Gow to pull out the stops. A Lockerbie task force would be set up. The investigation would be given a code name: SCOTBOM.

In Room 11610, a depressing, windowless office just down the hall from Gow's suite, SCOTBOM was launched. The Scots' HOLMES computer system would be installed here in a day or two. But Gow also wanted a separate FBI computer system just for the Lockerbie investigation. 'We have the computer jockey in house who could do it,' Gow said. 'Headquarters uses the Washington Field Office all the time as a test bed for some of their newer technical setups.' In Lockerbie, senior investigator John Orr assigned detectives Andrew Jackson, Bob House and Vance Graham to Buzzard Point. Ian Stewart of New Scotland Yard was also dispatched to Washington. Besides the hundreds of FBI agents working on the case in the States and the scores of agents working on it overseas, Gow assigned one of his own men permanently to Lockerbie. Hal Hendershot, a good-natured guy who had worked as a certified public accountant before joining the Bureau, was told to report to Lockerbie by New Year's Day. He was a bachelor, so leaving was no great problem. He just didn't know when he would be coming back.

The determination of Sessions and Gow was reinforced by George Bush. Having confounded the expectations of the political pros of a year before, when Sessions had agreed to come to Washington, the president-elect was outraged by the bombing of the 103. Just before New Year's, as he concluded a quail-hunting trip in Texas, Bush said the United States would 'seek hard' and 'punish severely' those responsible for downing the *Maid of the Seas*.

'The most imprudent thing a responsible official could do is to discuss what kind of action would be taken [against those responsible],' Bush told reporters. 'But when I say punish severely, that's what I mean.'

In Lockerbie, New Year's Day, like Christmas, came and went. No one paid much attention. For John Boyd, the wrenching grief and the bitter recriminations of the victims' families weighed heavily. The laws of evidence in Scotland were strict, however, much more so even than in the States. Boyd rationalized his actions: in time, perhaps, the families would somehow come to terms with their loss, but if he failed to assemble the evidence that could lead to those responsible for bringing down the 103, the families would surely have reason to hate him forever. If that meant holding bodies and belong-

173

ings a few more days to be absolutely certain they were not relevant to the investigation, Boyd would do so.

Nonetheless, more bodies were being released to family members with each passing day. The day after New Year's, Michael Bernstein's body was flown from London to Washington, and other bodies were to be shipped in the next few days. There was one tragic mix-up, however. Scottish police had mistakenly released the body of Karen Hunt, the pretty and ebullient college student returning from a semester in London loaded with gifts, to the family of Mary Johnson, a victim from Wayland, Massachusetts.

On January 8, the Johnson family was just about to bury their daughter when FBI agents found them and explained that there had been an error. A medical examiner in New York had discovered it the day before, when Karen Hunt's parents had asked him to verify that the body sent to them was that of their daughter; they didn't recognize the clothing and jewelry that had been returned with the body. A forensic investigation had shown that the corpse returned to the Hunt family was not Karen. FBI agents, alerted to the problem, tried quickly to resolve it. There were calls to Lockerbie and a check of medical records. They soon found the answer.

Did Karen wear an anklet? one of the FBI agents asked the Hunts.

Yes, they said, her younger sister had made it in camp and given it to Karen. They knew the answer. Somehow, the medical examiners in Lockerbie had switched Karen Hunt's body with Mary Johnson's.

A few days later, the bodies were exchanged. Karen was buried on January 12. The family would not get Karen's anklet back for another two months; when they did, it was in pieces.

For all the trauma they had gone through, though, Bob and Peggy Hunt were grateful for the assistance. The FBI agents had sorted things out promptly and professionally, they said. 'They did all they could to help.'

Despite that mistake and the anger and bitterness of many families, John Boyd was convinced that he was doing the right thing by being so cautious. About the search for clues he was obsessive. And very nervous.

In a vast hangar at the Ministry of Defence's Central Armaments Depot in the village of Longtown, where the grieving families of victims were never allowed, technicians from the British Air Accident Investigations Board had begun reassembling the *Maid of the Seas.* Workmen from Lockerbie had knocked out the old stone wall bounding Jimmie Wilson's field, where the plane's cockpit had come to rest. An enormous truck had come to haul the cockpit away, and now it sat at one end of the hangar at Longtown. Slowly, more pieces of the plane were coming in from Blue Band Motors, and the AAIB techs were carefully trying to figure out where they all went and, more important, which ones were missing.

John Boyd went down for a look one day and was amazed by what he saw. 'They literally put the nose at one end and [pieces of] the tail at the other,' Boyd recalled, 'and started assembling the pieces in between. It was, quite simply, a jigsaw puzzle.'

Only there were still so many pieces missing. So vast was the hangar at Longtown that the AAIB people in their jumpsuits were using bicycles to get from one end to the other. How many pieces of the plane must still be found, Boyd wondered, to fill up such a space?

Boyd's nervousness was understandable, and the FAA's Walter Korsgaard tried to reassure him. In all his years investigating air crashes, Korsgaard had never seen debris spread over such a large area. But neither, he told Boyd, had he seen such a massive investigation organized so quickly and effectively.

In early January, Korsgaard himself found out just

175

how thorough the searchers were. On the fourth, a helicopter had dropped him in yet another search area, and he was walking behind a line of soldiers and police officers as they made their way painstakingly across a new section of boggy field. A strong wind was beating, and suddenly Korsgaard noticed that his right ear was very cold. He wore a hearing aid behind each ear, and in the helicopter he had worn a radio headset on over his FAA cap to communicate with the pilot. When Korsgaard discovered that his right hearing aid was gone, he began retracing his steps. 'The ground was just bog,' he recalled, 'and the tall grass was just soaked in water.' He soon gave up. The hearing aid was lost forever, he figured.

At Boyd's nightly briefing for the searchers, however, Korsgaard decided to mention it. 'If any of you tomorrow sees a sheep hearing better out of his right ear than his left,' he said, holding up his remaining hearing aid, 'look in his ear, because this little thing might be there.'

For days after Korsgaard had given up his hearing aid for lost, he was going through bags of debris collected by the searchers. There were hundreds of bags in the field still waiting to be emptied. Korsgaard and the Scottish police officer with him set to the task. The first bag contained the same dispiriting stuff he had been looking at for days: torn clothes, sodden books, bits of luggage. The second bag promised more of the same, and then, Korsgaard recalled months later, 'there it was, the hearing aid, and it still worked. . . . It just proves [the searchers] were doing an incredibly good job.'

Elsewhere in Lockerbie on January 4, a memorial service was held for the victims of the 103. Dryfesdale Parish Church was jammed, and the crowd spilled out the double front doors into the ancient cemetery with its massive headstones, some leaning and broken, some inscriptions made indecipherable by age. Inside, organist Alistair McEwen led the faithful in hymn after hymn. There was a reading of Psalm 23, another from Corinthians. Charles Price II, American ambassador in London, read the story of Lazarus from the gospel of St. John. And then the Right Reverend Professor James Whyte, moderator of the General Assembly of the Church of Scotland, addressed the gathering of family and friends of the deceased. Outside on the High Steet, there was still debris from the crash of the 103. In Sherwood Crescent, where Maurice and Dora Henry's house had vanished with several others, and up in Rosebank, where Ella Ramsden's house was shattered, the wounds of the 103 were raw.

The Right Reverend Whyte, one of a dozen churchmen of several faiths on the altar of the church, spoke about those wounds, and about those who had caused them. 'It is not only pain and grief that we feel at this catastrophe,' he said quietly, 'it is also indignation. For this was not an unforeseeable natural disaster, such as an earthquake. Nor was it the result of human error or carelessness. This, we know now, was an act of human wickedness. That such carnage of the young and of the innocent should have been willed by men in cold and calculated evil,' the clergyman said, 'is horror upon horror.'

No one needed to remind the searchers in the field of that.

In Tundergarth, June Wilson had watched as the young men of the Royal Highland Fusiliers traipsed daily across fields and through rough gullies. These were the soldiers who had arrived by bus from Edinburgh in such splendid physical condition that John Boyd had assigned them the roughest terrain to search. Day after day, June Wilson watched them as they started out, their heads high and their chests out. In the afternoons, the light dying, they would return, having spent the intervening hours picking up bits and pieces of bodies. They were, almost literally, deflated. And they would leave Lockerbie, Wilson recalled, 'like old men'.

But Boyd and the other investigators were not content to rely only on the sharp eyes of the searchers in the field. By early January, they had already arranged for reconnaissance satellites and aerial infrared photography over the whole search area, all 845 soggy, hilly square miles of it. A French commercial satellite had already delivered a batch of photographs, and British technicians were working to improve their clarity with enhanced computer-imaging techniques. The satellite, known as SPOT, could 'see' large objects obscured by tree cover or other obstacles, but it was not good enough.

On January 15, Boyd took his first day off since the crash of the 103. It was a Sunday, and Ross, his grandson, was to be christened. It was a brief ceremony, and Boyd barely remembers it. His thoughts were elsewhere. Looking at his new grandchild, he recalled, he thought of the fact that nine of the victims on Flight 103 were age five or under; the two youngest were just two months old. The whole day, Boyd says, 'was very emotional'.

The next day it was back to work. If the French satellite couldn't help, the Americans had several that could. By January 17, spy satellites operated by NASA and the Pentagon were repositioned over southern Scotland to provide higher-resolution images of the search area. In George Bush's formulation, they were 'seeking hard' for clues to the killers of Pan Am 103. But the clues would be slow in coming.

As more of the *Maid of the Seas* found its way from the fields of Lockerbie into the searcher's clear plastic bags and then to the Blue Band garage on Bridge Street and, finally, to the yawning hangar in Longtown, the AAIB specialists were beginning to reassemble much of the fuselage. From the dim corners of the hangar, it looked as if the plane were rising again like a spooky phoenix. But there were still so many holes.

There was enough to come to some tentative conclusions, though. As Boyd recalled it, the men 'came to a fifty-foot section [of the fuselage] that was missing, and from that we began to figure where the bomb was.' Actually, the AAIB technicians and their FAA counterparts, had come to their own conclusions independent of the reconstruction work in Longtown. One look at the cockpit lying in Jimmie Wilson's field was enough to give most of them their first clue. The nose, the cockpit and the forward cabin had been blown clean off the 747, and this suggested strongly that the bomb had been placed forward of the wing.

Captain McQuarrie's plane had vanished so quickly and quietly that some of the technical experts, once they saw the cockpit lying on its side in Tundergarth, were willing to venture a more specific guess as to the bomb's location. The explosion had occurred in the forward luggage hold, as seemed likely from the severed cockpit. If the bomber had been devilishly clever, or just plain lucky he could have disabled all of the aircraft's electronic and navigational systems at the same time.

The nerve centre of the Boeing 747, known as the lower E&E bay, is bolted to the aircraft's bulkhead. Station 41 houses an electrical substation big enough to power a small town just about the size of Lockerbie. From generators on the 747's four engines, station 41 feeds power to nearly every electrical and electronic system on the aircraft. Autopilot, communications equipment, navigational aids and even the equipment that causes oxygen masks to drop down in emergencies are powered by station 41.

Having station 41 disabled by a bomb almost certainly would have left MacQuarrie and his crew no time to punch out the international Mayday code, 7700, or to alert air controller Alan Topp at the Prestwick control centre by radio. The bomb had to have been forward.

But which side had it been on? The answer to that question could tell the investigators whether the bomb had been loaded in Frankfurt, London or even San Francisco or Los Angeles, where the *Maid of the Seas* had begun her journey.

From FBI headquarters in Washington, orders had gone out to the field offices in Los Angeles and San Francisco. Agents there were assigned to question baggage handlers and security personnel from Pan Am and its subsidiary security firm. From the Washington Field Office of the FBI, Doug Gow had dispatched agents to do the same thing in London and Frankfurt. Working through Darrell Mills's legal-attaché office at the embassy, the FBI agents teamed up with detectives from Scotland Yard and London's Metropolitan Police. In Frankfurt, Dave Barham, the FBI's legal attaché in West Germany, arranged for the agents from Buzzard Point to conduct interviews with officers of the BKA and other German police agencies. Detectives from Lockerbie, reporting directly to John Boyd and John Orr, also participated in the interviews. Everyone had to be questioned.

At Longtown, the investigators proceeded cautiously. In the right inboard engine, AAIB technicians found plenty of baggage debris. A search of the two left-side engines yielded no such debris. The bomb, the technicians concluded, must have been placed on the right side of the plane: when it had gone off, it had blown a hole in the fuselage and the bags had been sucked into the nearest engine. That meant the bomb had almost certainly been sneaked aboard at Heathrow. Iran Air was at Heathrow, and several passengers who were to have boarded there had missed the flight. Investigators at Heathrow doubled their efforts.

The Heathrow theory made sense on another level. If a barometer had triggered the bomb, as some investigators suspected, Heathrow was the likely place to try to get it aboard. 'If it were a barometric device,' one official said, 'it would have to trigger only once.' Placing a bomb on the 103 anywhere else, if it were barometer-triggered, meant it would have to trigger more than once. 'Much too complicated,' said a U.S. official briefed on the AAIB findings.

As good and careful as they were, however, the techs from the AAIB took a wrong turn in the early days of the inquiry at Longtown. Even though they had found baggage debris in the turbines of the right-side engine, the bomb still could have been on the left side of the plane, some U.S. officials argued. The 747 has no cargo door on the left side of the fuselage, but it does have one on the right. And the cargo door can be one of the weaker parts of the plane. FAA officials working with the AAIB experts suggested the possibility that the bomb had been on the left side of the plane, but according to several knowledgeable authorities, the AAIB rejected it, at least for a while

Evidently, further reconstruction of the fuselage in Longtown, and probably a few more consultations with the FAA and other authorities, persuaded the AAIB. Searchers working from Korsgaard's slides and photographs retrieved enough pieces of metal bent by the blast that the AAIB technicians were able to make an amazingly complete reconstruction. The bomb, they concluded, had been placed on the left side after all. It had exploded just below the big blue P in the Pan Am logo. More careful analysis would narrow the location even more. The bomb, AAIB investigators concluded, had been stored in cargo bay 14L.

So much for the London theory. There were almost no bags from Heathrow in 14L.

CHAPTER 12

In his news conference with reporters on December 28, in which he had announced that a bomb had blown up Flight 103, Judge Sessions had actually said very little. That was by design. He had not said that FBI agents from every field office were working the investigation, that holiday vacations had been cancelled for many, or a great many other things for that matter. What Sessions had taken special pains to avoid was any discussion of Frankfurt.

Heathrow leads would have to be checked, but already the investigators had begun to focus more heavily on the German connection. After the first leg of Flight 103, Frankfurt to London, 49 of a total of 125 passengers had transferred from a Boeing 727 to the 747 bound for New York. FBI special agents in the U.S. were interviewing families of every one of the 192 Americans who had been on board Flight 103 when it had exploded, and detectives from several other countries were busy tracking down the families of the non-American passengers. Detectives and FBI agents were instructed to pay special attention to the forty-nine people who had boarded in Frankfurt. Had one of them carried the bomb aboard without knowing it?

Like John Boyd, Judge Sessions and Buck Revell wanted to keep a close hold on the Frankfurt connection. The less those responsible knew about the investigation, especially in the days immediately after the bombing, the better the chance of picking up their trail. The bombers of Pan Am 103 had taken precautions and gone to ground after the plane crashed in Lockerbie, the investigators were certain of that. But if they could focus quietly on the passengers who had boarded in Frankfurt, they might still have a chance to develop a few leads without alerting the terrorists. A bit of surprise was something a good detective looked for in any investigation. 'You always want to get a jump on the bad guy,' one FBI agent said, 'without him knowing.' Unfortunately, it was not to be.

On New Year's Eve, *The Times* of London carried a front-page account of the Lockerbie investigation. The headline fairly shouted:

DISASTER BOMB WAS 'PLACED ON BOARD JUMBO IN FRANKFURT'

The *Times* story got widespread pickup in Europe and in the States. That surprised no one. At the FBI, the investigators assigned to SCOTBOM were aware of the facts in the story. An internal document dated December 31, 1988, concluded that the bomb that had brought down the *Maid of the Seas* had 'entered the Pan Am system at Frankfurt'. But FBI officials were dismayed by the disclosures. Now they hoped they could contain the damage by issuing statements declaring the account 'premature'. To give the investigators even half a chance to get a lead on the bombers, it was decided to try a little damage control. In Washington, that often meant a Sunday-morning talk show.

On that Sunday, January 1, William Sessions hit two of the three networks, ABC and NBC. On NBC's *Meet the Press*, moderator John Dancy pressed Sessions about the inquiry.

'Do we know where the bomb was put aboard the plane?' he asked.

'No,' Sessions replied. 'We do not.'

'Do we know what caused the bombing?' Dancy asked.

183

'No,' Sessions answered again. 'We do not.'

Although he expressed 'optimism' that the terrorists would be found, Sessions told Dancy, 'We do not have real leads.'

If it failed to provide great television, Sessions's *Meet the Press* performance did something else: it gave the investigators a bit of breathing space. If the terrorists thought they were that slow off the mark, maybe, just maybe, they would be a little careless. It was worth a shot anyway.

Unbeknownst to the investigators and the intelligence officials beavering away on the 103 inquiry, a Pandora's box had already been opened. The same day Sessions was doing his *Meet the Press* routine, West German Interior Ministry spokesman Michael Andreas Butz was convening a news conference to respond to the *Times* account of the day before. 'There is no indication,' Butz declared stiffly, 'that the explosives could have been put on board at Frankfurt airport.' In fact, he added ominously, 'there is evidence which is contradictory.'

What did the Germans know that the Americans and the Scots didn't?

Butz went on to assert, with some vehemence, that German agents had determined that the 'Disaster Bomb' had been smuggled aboard the 103 in London. The German agents had proof of it, Butz said. Smarting from the accusation that sloppy West German security had allowed this terrible act of terrorism, which had resulted in 270 deaths, Germany would begin to strike at the British with a vengeance. In a matter of days, news stories began to leak from Bonn and Frankfurt that security at Heathrow was far worse than at Frankfurt.

British authorities were outraged. For days and weeks, as the families of those killed on the 103 watched this ugly game of diplomatic Ping-Pong, Britain and Germany fought a nasty proxy war through their TV networks and newspapers. Clearly, the feud was based on more than a technical dispute among forensic specialists. Some went so far as to assert that the bitterness of the dispute showed the extent to which the age-old cultural animosities between the two nations had still not abated after two world wars.

There was probably something to that. But it was also true that security in London and Frankfurt had been more than a little spotty, and in throwing mudballs at each other through the obliging news media, British and German authorities evidently hoped to keep that fact a secret. The secret would not keep for very long, though.

Even before the fires had been extinguished in Lockerbie, late in the night on December 21, rumours of spies had begun sprouting like weeds. Over the next few days and weeks, they would get only worse.

It was known to senior investigators in Lockerbie in the first few hours after the crash that several U.S. intelligence officers had been among the passengers on board. That was fact. It soon became surrounded by lies. The untruths about spies were the result of several things. The presence of intelligence officers on the plane soon became bound up with the cancelled cheques retrieved by the Dodd boys up in Tundergarth, with the real or apparent presence of drugs among the luggage, and simply, as Angus Kennedy put it, with the 'surreal nature' of the tragedy.

There were some unfortunate moments. One reporter, quoting a Tundergarth farmer, told a story about a mysterious 'white helicopter', operated by agents of the CIA, which darted from hill to dale around Lockerbie like a dragonfly. The farmer, Chris Graham, said that he never spoke with the reporter. From the helicopter story, others grew. There were allegations that some police officers tampered with luggage, that evidence was withheld in some way to protect the operations the intelligence officers were involved in, that the intelligence officers themselves might have been up to no good. It was all nonsense. But such stories fed off themselves.

The Dodd boys were told what the cancelled cheques they had found were, and they simply accepted that as fact. Others, for some reason, would not. And so stories persisted about huge sums of cash claimed variously to have come from drug deals, hostage-rescue operations or money laundering. Too simple was the explanation that the cheques, which were of no value, were being returned from one bank to another to settle credit-card accounts. But what of the strange orange bag the Dodd boys had seen scooped up by a helicopter? Perhaps it was the drugs everyone seemed to be talking about? Or maybe the missing CIA papers? The orange bag, it turned out, was mail, plain and simple. But again, that didn't keep people from saying otherwise. Rubbish, both stories.

Other stories were more difficult to evaluate, however. What could be said for certain about the presence of the intelligence officers on Flight 103 was that Matthew Gannon and Charles McKee had come from the most dangerous part of the Middle East earlier that day and that, with at least two diplomatic security officers, Daniel O'Connor and Ronald LaRiviere, they had been involved in some of the most sensitive work of the United States in that troubled region.

What was it they were doing? The authorities involved in the Lockerbie investigation, from the CIA and FBI to the Scottish police and British Home Office, will not comment on what they know about the work of the four men in the Middle East. What is clear, contrary to other reports, is that the bomb that blew up the *Maid of the Seas* over Lockerbie was not targeted at any of the four men. The investigators looked at that theory very carefully. And when Dan O'Connor's American Tourister suitcase turned up unexpectedly at Kennedy

Airport in New York a couple of days after the crash, some investigators, believing that it held the answer, pressed hard to pursue that line of inquiry too. After all, his bags and those of the other men had been transferred from the Cyprus Airways flights to the 103 in London, and they had all wound up in baggage container 14L, the one that had contained the bomb. Further checking in Longtown, however, showed that the bomb must have been eighteen to twenty-four inches from the floor of the container. That was too high for interline bags in 14L. And except for Dan O'Connor's bag, the bags of all the men had been recovered. There was nothing, then, to support a theory that the 103 had been blown up to murder the intelligence officers. Their presence on the doomed plane was coincidence, tragic but understandable. At this time of year and with the relatively small number of flights from the Middle East to Europe to the U.S., it would have been strange had some U.S. officials not been on the plane. In fact, the American ambassador to Lebanon at the time, John McCarthy, had been scheduled on the flight, but had changed his reservations two weeks earlier because of pressing diplomatic business.

For every lead that had to be followed by the FBI and the Scottish detectives, these were the kinds of unhappy but understandable answers they came up with: Some people missed a scheduled flight to disaster, and others made the connection and perished.

As to the intelligence officers on the 103, what was true was that at least two of them were involved in an operation that so far has remained secret. Like nearly everything else about the Lockerbie investigation, the story came not from supersecret spy sources, but from the plodding detective work of the searchers in the forests and fields around Lockerbie.

On January 6, a team had been dispatched from Lockerbie to the far northern end of the search area designated by John Boyd and John Orr. There were already some 200 civilian volunteers searching fields all the way to the edge of the North Sea. Like the searchers closer to Lockerbie, the volunteers farther north found themselves working in miserable, cold and wet conditions. It was a depressing business, but they were reported to be doing a good job. One person remembers that they had picked everything up, even the little airline-issue packets of cellophane-wrapped crackers; in Northumberland, the searchers had collected more than seventy of them. Soon after January 6, according to two officials involved in the search in Northumberland, word came that an army officer had recovered what looked like diplomatic papers. It remains unclear whether these were the much-talked-of papers in the plastic container with the red seal on the outside. What is known is that the officer had been assigned to look for wreckage and debris on the Otterburn firing range, a practice bombing range for the RAF. According to the two officials, the papers the army officer recovered from the Otterburn range referred unambiguously to the American hostages in Lebanon; appended to at least one sheaf of the papers was a roughly sketched map of a city, possibly Beirut, indicating buildings of some sort. The two officials emphasized that the reference to the hostages was clear.

According to U.S. officials familiar with the activities of Matthew Gannon and Charles McKee, the 'hostage issue' was their primary responsibility in Beirut. According to Pentagon officials, McKee in particular had a special mission. In the autumn of 1986, when the Defense Intelligence Agency had requested a volunteer for an intelligence-gathering assignment in Beirut, McKee had jumped at the chance. His officially nonexistent unit within the Pentagon, the Intelligence Support Activity, had backed McKee's decision, and by January 1987, he had been in Beirut. Just over a year after that, however, Marine Lieutenant Colonel William Richard Higgins, in Lebanon as part of a United Nations peacekeeping mission, was abducted by armed men. Pentagon officials familiar with McKee's assignment in Beirut say that he was responsible for gathering any and all information on American hostages in Lebanon. But because of the special status senior Pentagon officials accorded to Higgins – an unarmed peacekeeper in Lebanon who, unlike the other Americans who had been abducted, was there with the distinct and prior .approval of his government – McKee had paid special attention to intelligence that might conceivably have something to do with his fellow soldier.

With the starkly reduced U.S. presence in Lebanon in the late 1980s, American officials said, Matt Gannon and Chuck McKee comprised the heart and soul of an admittedly modest effort to achieve the release of the hostages. Details of their activities in Beirut have been impossible to confirm with specificity, but the few U.S. officials willing to discuss the subject even in general terms said that the efforts of Gannon and McKee to gain the release of the hostages were still in an 'early phase' and that when Flight 103 crashed in Lockerbie there was no expectation of a release anytime soon.

In the largest sense, what is important about the efforts of the two men in Beirut was that even in the dying days of his presidency, having been deeply embarrassed and seen his administration badly wounded by the disclosures of the Iran-contra scandal, Ronald Reagan had not been willing to give up on the hostages. Among the many terrible tragedies of the Lockerbie disaster was this: With the deaths of Matthew Gannon and Charles McKee, the terrorists unknowingly had struck yet another blow at the West. According to one senior Pentagon official familiar with the issue, these two deaths set back U.S. efforts to achieve the hostages' release 'by at least a year, and almost certainly, much longer'.

By this time, other information was also beginning to

tumble out. On January 6, Reuters in London, attributing its account to 'West German security sources', reported that an airport worker at Heathrow had planted the bomb in the forward luggage hold of the 103. According to the sources quoted by Reuters, investigators had arrived at the Heathrow link because of the 'fact' that the bomb that had blown up the 103 weighed 'at least sixty-six pounds'. Luggage restrictions limited carry-on bags to seventy pounds, but the sources cited in the Reuters account said that the bomb was loaded aboard by an airport worker. What the sources evidently didn't say is why the airport worker couldn't have been in Frankfurt instead of London.

Charges and countercharges continued to fly.

In Washington, administration officials were not at all pleased by the unseemly bickering between the British and the Germans. At the end of Pennsylvania Avenue on the Capitol grounds, just a brisk ten-minute walk from FBI headquarters, George Bush would be sworn in as the next president, and Ronald Reagan would depart on *Air Force Two* for the West Coast. Despite the change in administrations, U.S. officials say, there was barely a hiccup in the course of the 103 investigation being conducted on the U.S. side of the Atlantic.

'It was a friendly takeover,' Buck Revell recalled months later. 'And besides, the case was well along when there was a change of administration.'

In Lockerbie as well, things were progressing, but it was slow going, and for many of the families of the victims, every day seemed to pass excruciatingly slowly. More bodies were being released by the medical examiners, and the searchers in the fields had fallen into a rhythm. In the hangar at Longtown, the *Maid of the Seas*, like Humpty-Dumpty, was being slowly put back together again.

The feuding between Bonn and London was a real problem, though. If the murderers responsible for downing the 103 were ever to be caught, German and British cooperation would be essential.

Whether the Germans were prepared to admit it or not, the investigators in Britain and Washington were convinced that Frankfurt was the key. But that answer only led to more questions. Had one of the forty-nine passengers brought the bomb aboard in carry-on luggage? That could be ruled out now because of what was known about where the bomb had gone off. Next question: Had the bomb been among luggage checked at Frankfurt by a passenger or in a bag shunted through to the 103 from a connecting flight, an interline bag? The investigators already knew that a number of interline bags had been loaded on the first leg of the 103 in Frankfurt. Investigators would determine that baggage carrier 14L had held luggage checked only in Frankfurt, and another six to eight pieces that had been interlined from connecting flights.

Frankfurt Main Airport was itself a nightmare for the investigators. Opened with great fanfare by the Nazis in 1936, by December 1988, it was home to 89 international airlines and 170 charter operations. It accommodated 700 flights daily, and more than 23 million passengers passed through the airport each year, coming and going from places in Africa, the Middle East, the Mediterranean, the Soviet bloc and Scandinavia. It was literally the busiest airport in all of Europe.

Where to start asking questions in such a place?

Dave Barham had been the FBI's legal attaché in Bonn for nearly six years, and he was due to return to the States in another six months. Two of his three children had been born in Germany, and he and his family had greatly enjoyed their stay there. Like Darrell Mills in London, however, Barham was unhappy if he wasn't busy; he too made a point of knowing as many of the police officers on his turf as he could find time to meet. He liked them, respected them as fellow professionals, and he knew he could call on them, as they could on him, when the need arose. If ever there was need, it was now.

There had been many U.S. military personnel among the 125 people who had boarded Flight 103 in Frankfurt. Stationed in West Germany, they had been heading home for the holidays. Some, like Oliver Revell's son and daughter-in-law, had been coming home for good. Others were just on holiday leave. Initially, Barham had had no indication that Frankfurt would figure prominently in the Lockerbie investigation. After the crash in Scotland, his opposite number at the BKA had asked if the Bureau could help in identifying victims, talk with relatives of the deceased still in Germany and assist in going through clothing, birth records and so on. Doug Gow had sent several C-3 agents from Buzzard Point to help Barham, and men from the U.S. Army Criminal Investigative Division also had been assigned to the inquiry. With the BKA and detectives from Lockerbie, the task force had set up shop in drab but convenient offices just off the autobahn connecting Mannheim and Heidelberg. Detectives from Scotland Yard had a separate liaison with the BKA in Meckenheim. Although Meckenheim was technically a field office, it worked all international terrorism cases for the agency. Oddly enough, BKA headquarters in Wiesbaden handled only domestic terrorism cases, and those involved mostly some new outrage by the Red Army Faction.

The German end of the investigation into the bombing proved a bit awkward at times. Responding to the investigators' questions, a relative of one of the 125 people who'd boarded in Frankfurt would often find himself facing three detectives: an FBI man, a BKA man and an investigator from Lockerbie with a funny burr in his voice.

By early January, there was nothing funny about the 103 inquiry, however. There was the feuding between the Germans and the British, and American and Scottish investigators wanted to know more about the men who had been swept up in the Autumn Leaves operation back in October. Where were they now? It was, American and Scottish officials say, like pulling teeth.

Oliver Revell had been in Germany in the first week of December, and he had been given a briefing on Autumn Leaves. He had learned about the Toshiba radio–cassette player the BKA men had found under a blanket in the backseat of Dalkamouni's Ford Taurus. But it was not until October 29, three days after the BKA men had picked up Dalkamouni and Kreeshat, a known bomb-maker whom police had seen purchasing suspicious materials, that anyone had thought to take a closer look at the Toshiba. And only then did they find the bomb.

It was a diabolically clever device, and Revell had been given a photo of it. Someone with a macabre sense of humour must have purchased the Toshiba product specially. He had literally gone out of his way to get the Bombeat model RTF53D, an odd choice indeed. The Bombeat, according to several sources, is not sold in Europe; it can be purchased only in northern Africa and the Middle East. There were signs that the back of the Bombeat had been tampered with, but specialists who examined the grey and unextraordinary-looking device reported 'no outward sign that the radio was abnormal'. Inside was another thing.

The Bombeat measured just ten by seven by two inches. The model found in Dalkamouni's car had two sources of power, the standard batteries used to power the radio and cassette player, and four 1.5-volt batteries used to power a bomb. The bomb itself was a marvel: 300 grams of Semtex sheet explosive that had been shaped into a cylinder, wrapped with aluminium foil and decorated with a Toshiba label. Semtex is a most unusual product. Czech-made, it can be rolled like dough, moulded like putty or folded like paper. It is nearly impossible to detect by most conventional means. The Bombeat bomb had one standard electric detonator and two activating devices. In the parlance of explosives experts, it was a 'two-stop bomb'. It was state-of-the-art.

Thanks to the miracles of advanced microcircuitry, terrorists in the business of confecting and concealing bombs have moved far beyond the days of the dry-cell battery, some crude wiring and a bulky alarm clock. The Bombeat retrieved from Dalkamouni's car showed just how far they had come. The first activator was a barometer concealed cleverly beneath the motor that drove the cassette player. The other was a simple 'ice-cube' timer that would activate when it dissolved. There was also an electric fuse, placed snugly in among the electronic guts of the Bombeat, and someone had wired all the elements together very neatly.

In other words, when the BKA men found it in Dalkamouni's car, the bomb was armed and ready to blow.

But activating the bomb was tricky business. The electric fuse was wired in such a way that it would set the bomb off only after it had been charged continuously for at least thirty-five minutes. Any less and the bomb wouldn't go off. The fuse would be triggered when the barometer had been pressurized to a preset point for thirty-five minutes. At that instant, the barometer would close an electric circuit, activating the bomb's timer, which could be set for any predetermined time, either minutes or hours. The reason for the thirty-five-minute delay was to fool aircraft security equipment, the kind that subjects checked luggage to low-pressure tests precisely to discover such explosives; that equipment tests the luggage only for short periods of time, however. The barometer was wired to the fuse in the Bombeat so that it could undergo numerous pressure tests, but if none was longer than thirty-five minutes, the fuse wouldn't trigger the bomb.

In explaining all this to U.S. officials in early December, West German police had not been particularly stingy. The bomb was a frightening piece of

194

business, they told Revell, designed for one thing and one thing only: to blow up an airplane at altitude. The Germans had taken precautions to alert the appropriate authorities. The bomb had been found and examined on October 29. For some reason, however, it would take more than a week for German police to alert airlines and airports to the bomb threat. On November 8, they finally disseminated a packet of information, along with copies of the same photograph they would later give Revell, to airlines and airport security personnel in Frankfurt. Other packets of information on the Bombeat were made available to Interpol. And airline authorities in the United States and the United Kingdom were alerted.

On November 18, the FAA issued a security advisory to American air carriers flying overseas. The Toshiba Bombeat was described in detail, and the FAA warned that the device was 'nearly impossible to detect through normal inspection procedures'.

On November 22, the British Ministry of Transport issued a warning on the Toshiba Bombeat, but only to domestic air carriers in the United Kingdom.

On December 19, the Ministry of Transport issued a second advisory on the Bombeat. From its offices at 2 Marsham Street came a 'restricted' notice to all U.K. airports and airlines, as well as to El Al, Air-India, all U.S. international carriers and South African Airways. The six-point advisory warned again that 'the explosive device will be very difficult to discover'. Key things to look for were that the radio-cassette player would not work when turned on and when X-rayed would appear to have more wiring than was normal (although the advisory conceded that 'this is not a significant indicator'). Over the signature of J. Jack, principal aviation security advisor, the warning was typed up and paper-clipped to a colour photograph of the Bombeat retrieved from Dalkamouni's car on October 26. Then secretaries dropped the whole business in the mail.

Pan Am security officials got their copy four weeks later, nearly a month after the fireball in Lockerbie.

As far as the Germans were concerned, however, they had done their job. They had disseminated the information and the photographs of the Bombeat as soon as they could, they said; everyone had been alerted.

In early December in Germany, Revell had been impressed. But when he had asked what had become of the men picked up in Operation Autumn Leaves, the men who had evidently been intent on blowing up an airplane, he had gotten very little information. In early December, there had been no reason to press.

In early January, there was every reason to do so. According to a classified State Department cable sent from the U.S. embassy in Bonn to Foggy Bottom that month, the Germans believed that neither the Americans nor anyone else needed to know what had become of the suspects arrested in the Autumn Leaves investigations. The Germans, one FBI official said later, 'seemed to believe that if they stuck their heads in the sand, the problem would go away'. If that was truly their view, they were dead wrong.

Frustrated on one level, Lockerbie investigators tried others. According to informed U.S. officials in Washington, Dave Barham's office was instructed to find out whatever it could about the arrests of Dalkamouni and company and, most important, where those who had been released had gone. The massive CIA station at the Bonn embassy was instructed to do the same.

By late January, Lockerbie investigators had demanded a list of the names of the seventeen Autumn Leaves arrestees. They got back a list of twelve names. American officials placed a series of requests with German authorities to review their intelligence files on PFLP-GC operations and personnel inside West Germany. The answer was no. Finally, American and Scottish detectives asked that they be allowed to interview

196

Hafez Dalkamouni and Abdel Ghadanfar, the only two of the seventeen still in custody. The Germans refused.

According to one senior official in the Lockerbie inquiry, the German response to nearly every request was not even a straignt no, 'just something a bit screwy'. The BKA insisted that all questions of potential suspects be submitted in writing. Then they sent the questions back. Not specific enough, the BKA said, according to the official. Besides the problems with sloppy and sometimes unusable translations, which some investigators suspected were deliberate, the BKA insisted on occasion that the Scots and the Americans lacked sufficient 'evidences' against the PFLP-GC.

Months afterwards, German authorities would continue to toe this line. 'Our BKA so far has not found any links between the GC and Lockerbie,' prosecutor Achim Thiele told a reporter. That interview took place not in January but in *June*.

Within weeks of the crash in Lockerbie, CIA agents had met with intelligence operatives of more than thirty countries, according to informed U.S. officials. Middle Eastern countries were especially important. If the terrorists' trail could be picked up, investigators were almost certain it would lead back to Iran, Syria or Libya.

Making their rounds, U.S. intelligence officials met with representatives of the intelligence services of Egypt, Saudi Arabia, Israel, Morocco, Tunisia, Pakistan and Jordan. Of those countries, Israel, for obvious reasons, had the most complete files on Ahmed Jibril, Abu Nidal and the terrorist organizations on the CIA's list of suspects. The Israelis did not have a smoking gun for the Lockerbie investigators, but they gave their best guess as to who might have been responsible, and they offered to press contacts in their own extensive intelligence network.

Meetings with Arab intelligence services produced the usual pleasantries, but little else, according to U.S.

officials. Egyptian representatives said they would turn over whatever information they had, but nothing ever materialized. Saudi officials, many of whom had been trained by American intelligence agents and antiterrorist commandos, also offered to help. But over the next year they failed to generate any useful information.

As was not the case in their visits to European intelligence services, the CIA representatives in the Middle East made their rounds without FBI agents. It just seemed more simple that way. In much of the Arab world, cooperation with Americans had to be sub rosa because of U.S. support for Israel. In the mid-1980s, for instance, the FBI had begun to expand its activities more aggressively beyond U.S. borders and extend its network of legal attachés abroad. The Middle East was deemed a vital area, but no Arab government wanted a legal attaché stationed permanently in its country.

If the Arab countries couldn't or wouldn't help, then Yasir Arafat, a man without a country, would. In a meeting in Tunis on New Year's Eve with the PLO chairman and Hakim Belaaoui, the PLO's delegate to Tunisia, U.S. ambassador Robert Pelletreau, Jr., asked if Arafat could provide any information on the bombing of Flight 103. Arafat was ecstatic. Not only was the U.S. now talking with him through proper diplomatic channels, it was asking for *his* help! Of course he would help. Not only would the PLO chairman assist in the investigation of the Pan Am bombing, he would assemble a 'hit squad' to hunt down and assassinate the killers, he said. Reporters wrote stories. 'According to PLO sources,' one major U.S. newspaper said, 'the PLO had shared intelligence on terrorism with several Western European governments on the assumption that much of the information would be passed on to the United States.'

In fact, according to knowledgeable U.S. officials, the PLO never provided any useful information. On January 9, Arafat held a news conference, however, and professed to have the answer investigators were looking for. The bombing of Flight 103, he said, was the work of 'Israel's Mossad and other antagonistic organizations determined to carry out operations in order to abort all the peace efforts in the Middle East.' The PLO, Arafat assured everyone, was conducting a 'full-scale investigation'. Unfortunately, it was all nonsense. Had Arafat decided to be genuinely helpful, it is likely he could have saved the Lockerbie investigators a lot of time and effort.

Sometimes, when just about everything else has failed, including the strange games of the spy services and the foolishness of the politicians, good old-fashioned detective work can't be beat. In fact, if the history of terrorism in the late twentieth century shows anything, it is that nuts-and-bolts detective work results in successful investigations more often than do spy games, high-tech trickery or anything else. It was painstaking police work that had unmasked the Professor, Samir Kadar, in Greece. It was two ordinary foot patrolmen who had collared Ahmed Jibril's two would-be plane bombers in Rome. And it was a New Jersey state trooper who had arrested Yu Kikumura, the bumbling Japanese Red Army terrorist, after the trooper had spotted boxes labelled 'Gunpowder' on the backseat of Kikumura's car in a turnpike rest stop.

In April 1986, diligence prevailed again. A young Irish woman had been attempting to board a 747 from London to Tel Aviv on April 16, when sharp-eyed El Al security officers detained her. There had been no explicit warnings, no specific intelligence that led them to stop Ann Murphy. They had simply questioned her, hadn't liked her answers and had held her up until they could figure out what was going on. Miss Murphy had answered the El Al men politely. She was going to Israel, she'd said. Her fiancé, a Jordanian named Nezar Hindawi, would meet her there the next day. Miss

Murphy was expecting, and Nezar Hindawi was the father. Before leaving, Hindawi had kindly packed her bag. It was a new one, a trolley bag. Although they had no reason to doubt Ann Murphy's story, she'd fit the 'profile' of an unwitting accomplice to a terrorist bombing: a single woman given a bag to carry by someone not boarding the plane. The promise of marriage also worried the El Al security officers: they had encountered similar 'promises' before. A terrorist, it seemed, would stop at nothing, even blowing up a woman carrying his unborn child. Ann Murphy had already cleared British security. With nothing but their worries to go on, the El Al officers had searched Miss Murphy's luggage twice with X-ray scanners and several times by hand before they had finally found what they were looking for. The bomb had been cleverly concealed in the construction of the trolley bag. An electronic calculator, thrown in among clothing, had been converted so that it would activate the bomb. The patience, diligence and determination of the security men had prevented the almost certain deaths of nearly 300 people that day. The value of that kind of police work could hardly be overstated.

The lesson of past terrorist investigations was not lost on the investigators in Lockerbie. It was John Boyd, within hours of the December 21 crash, who recalled the Air-India tragedy of June 1985, in which a Boeing 747 had fallen into the sea off the Irish coast with 329 passengers. Sikh terrorists had placed a bomb on board in Vancouver, but because every clue to the case had been in hundreds of feet of water, police had never been able to get enough evidence to prosecute anyone for the crime.

No, John Boyd and the investigators in Lockerbie didn't need any lectures on the importance of good police work. While CIA agents trolled the globe for clues to the bombers of the *Maid of the Seas* and expensive spy satellites whirred high in the sky over Lockerbie, soldiers and police officers continued crawling through the freezing mud and wet grass looking for the kinds of evidence on which a prosecution would have to be built, block by block. It is hard to explain, even by those most closely bound up in the investigation in Lockerbie, but the nature of the crime and the depth of the loss suffered by the victims' families and the tiny village made the searchers almost fanatical in their zeal. It was mind-numbing, back-breaking work: scuttling through forests, clambering up and down inclines, looking for clues.

Hal Hendershot, the FBI agent assigned to the Lockerbie investigation on a permanent basis, had quickly made himself well liked. He was supposed to serve more as a liaison among John Boyd and John Orr in Lockerbie, Darrell Mills in London and Doug Gow at Buzzard Point, but he insisted on going on the search teams regularly, usually once a week. He also became something of a dominoes player. Dominoes were an addictive habit among many in Lockerbie, and Hendershot soon caught the bug. In his first match, he lost to an Irishman. But then he got the hang of the game.

The investigators didn't have much time for such games. Under the direction of Boyd and Orr, they were in the fields every day. In early February their efforts began to produce significant results.

Covering more than 800 miserable square miles, the searchers in Lockerbie had turned up pieces of a grey radio-cassette player almost identical to the Bombeat. Three little pieces, but they had found them. Soon they would also turn up pieces of a hard-sided Samsonite suitcase, which the forensic wizards at Fort Halstead determined conclusively was the bag that had carried the bomb onto the 103. The suitcase would puzzle the investigators for a while, but finally they had enough to tell the world what they knew.

In a crowded news conference in Lockerbie on February 16, John Orr stood up and announced the findings.

Things were proceeding swiftly, he said: 'There is total coordination and cooperation between the many agencies engaged in this widespread investigation.' The Scots didn't need any more headaches than they already had: there was just no percentage in embarrassing the Germans at a press conference.

On the other side of the Atlantic that same day, however, Orr's statement was given the lie. In Montreal, a special meeting of the United Nations aviation group had been convened, and British transport minister Paul Channon had called his own press conference to announce the discovery of the radio-cassette player bomb; the findings of the investigators in Longtown, who had determined that the device had been placed in baggage container 14L forward on the 103; and the further conclusions of the experts at Fort Halstead, who were reassembling the baggage container itself. It was a phenomenal piece of detective work, and the reporters followed Channon's prepared statement closely as he praised the investigators' efforts.

In the prepared text, Channon's original statement read thus: 'The reconstruction of the baggage container suggests that the explosive device may have been among the baggage from the Frankfurt flight.' In another, larger typeface, two lines had been inserted before that sentence: 'It has not yet been firmly established where the bag which contained the device was originally loaded, but . . .' The night before Channon's statement, Bonn's minister of transport, Jürgen Warnke, had asked that there be no reference made to Frankfurt. The most he had been able to get from Channon was the hasty two-line insert.

It was strange that no one asked any questions about it.

For all the foolishness and wasted time they put up with in the Middle East, the U.S. intelligence officials finally hit paydirt in the early part of February, and in the most surprising way imaginable. Marwan Kreeshat had surfaced, they were told. And he was talking.

After he had been released from jail by Judge Rinne in West Germany, Kreeshat had fled to Jordan. Perhaps he was an informant for Jordanian intelligence after all, as his phone call from the jail in Frankfurt had suggested.

Kreeshat's release had provoked a storm of dissent from some of the BKA agents involved in Operation Autumn Leaves. But now Jordanian officials were telling U.S. intelligence agents that the little bomb-maker had actually been working for them all along. Ahmed Jibril had long been a threat to King Hussein, the Jordanian officials explained; he had sent terrorist teams from Syria across the border into Jordan, where they had launched attacks on both Jordanian and Israeli targets. A moderate who had secretly held talks with Israeli government leaders since at least the late 1960s, the diminutive Hashemite potentate had survived at least two dozen assassination attempts. In 1970, Palestinian guerrillas had attempted to overthrow him, but he had put down the rebellion at bloody cost. Although roughly sixty percent of Jordan is Palestinian by birth, Hussein had won the enmity of the more radical elements of the Palestinian community.

It was only natural, the Jordanians told U.S. intelligence officers at a meeting in the Middle East, that he would try to protect himself by maintaining an informant in their camps. Kreeshat, they said, was the man.

And this is what the man said: He had made five bombs in Germany, not one.

At least that's what the Jordanians told the U.S. officials.

Were they absolutely sure? the Americans demanded.

A short time later, in response to interrogatories prepared by U.S. intelligence officials, the Jordanians provided a statement by Kreeshat. It was in Arabic. At CIA headquarters in Langley, translators ripped into it.

Kreeshat was certain he had made five bombs, the statement said; in fact, the bombs were probably still in Hashem Abassi's flat at 16 Isarstrasse in Neuss.

As big a surprise as this was, the Jordanians delivered an even bigger one: They had already passed along this same information from Kreeshat to the German foreign-intelligence service, the BND, they said. The Germans, supposedly full partners in the Pan Am investigation with the Scots and the Americans, had kept quiet about this. In the fun-house world of foreign intelligence, with its trapdoors and trick mirrors, this was no great sin. As a matter of practice, intelligence services share only what they have to. In this world, there is no higher demand than that of protecting sources and methods of acquiring information. But this source, this man Kreeshat, was talking about bombs here. And there was every reason to believe that one of his bombs might have caused the death of 270 innocent people. If Kreeshat's bombs could provide a clue, the Lockerbie investigators had a right to know about it. For one thing, if they weren't found, they could be used to blow up another plane and murder still more innocent people.

Suddenly the Germans' strange reticence with Buck Revell in early December looked much more suspicious. At the FBI, there was fury. And still greater pressure on the investigators in Germany to find out what was going on. The Germans would simply have to go back to search Abassi's flat, the Lockerbie investigators decided, that's all there was to it.

The only thing was, Abassi had moved. And when the FBI and the Scots pressed the Germans in late February to take another look at him, they learned to their astonishment that the BKA already had. Acting on the reports from the Jordanians, on January 31 BKA specialists from Meckenheim had returned to 16 Isarstrasse. Abassi and his wife, Somaia, and their baby had moved to the town of Ratingen, and he had stored some of their belongings in the basement of his greengrocer's shop at 14 Neumarkt, in Neuss. In the bitter cold, the BKA men had gone from Abassi's former flat in Neuss to his current one in Ratingen to the basement of his shop in Neuss – and then to six more places they thought Abassi or someone else might have hidden Marwan Kreeshat's bombs. The men from Meckenheim had found nothing.

The Lockerbie investigators were astounded. In one meeting with American officials, a BKA officer admitted that the BND had maintained secret dealings with some element of the Jordanian intelligence community and received regular reports on Kreeshat. Was that true? And even if it wasn't, how had the BKA agents missed finding Kreeshat's other bombs?

Go back and search the flat, the Lockerbie investigators insisted once more.

No, came the response from the BKA. They had searched twice now, and there were no bombs at Hashem Abassi's home or business. The Germans didn't like to be told how to conduct their affairs, and their impatience this second time was barely disguised.

From the Germans' perspective, the Americans and the Scots were exceeding the limits of diplomatic propriety. Even Buck Revell could understand their resentment. 'Essentially, it was their case,' he said. 'It's in their territory. They [had] not made the connection to Pan Am 103, so we were being obnoxious. We [were] essentially interfering in what was, to them, an internal investigation.' But the stakes were also too high to let diplomatic niceties foul things up.

Others in the new administration of George Bush wanted to force the issue, but cooler heads prevailed. The FBI decided to pursue another tack. They requested once again a list of those picked up in the Autumn Leaves arrests in October. They also asked once again to review any intelligence the German authorities had on PFLP-GC activities in Germany and anything they might have gotten from any of those arrested, especially Dalkamouni and Ghadanfar, under interrogation. Having placed those requests, for the second time, through proper channels, the Bureau waited patiently for a response.

And waited. And waited.

Finally, in the middle of March, the German answer: No. No files, and what little the Bureau did get it had reason to doubt. As a senior U.S. intelligence official put it, 'It was half-assed, and we just didn't believe it, God damn it.'

In the State Department and the FBI, some officials saw a deliberate pattern of deception by the Germans. Their continued refusal to look for Kreeshat's missing bombs could mean only one thing, a cover-up by certain elements of the German intelligence community. But which one? And why?

At the end of World War II, the Allied powers faced a dilemma: How to guarantee German security without arousing its bellicosity; how, as historian Thomas Schwartz put it, 'to reconcile the West's need for Germany with her fear of it'? Specifically, this meant that a new Germany would have to be organized to prevent the emergence of Nazi-style army groups. It was the last great question of the postwar Western alliance and the rebuilding of Europe, and it was a devilishly tricky one. In the end, it was decided that the powers of government would be broken down among semiautonomous *Länder*, or states. If that meant a certain amount of confusion among government agencies, that was a small price to pay.

In a 'Police Letter' of April 14, 1949, the Allied military governors of Germany authorized the creation of a new agency under the chancellor's office to collect and distribute information relating to state security. Modelled on Britain's internal security service, MI-5, the Verfassungsschutz (Protection of the Constitution) was to be separate from the police authorities and have no powers of arrest or search and seizure. By September 1950, the agency would evolve into the Bundesamt für Verfassungsschutz, or BfV, which would report directly to the Interior Ministry. Five years later, the cabinet of Chancellor Konrad Adenauer authorized the formal establishment of a foreign intelligence-gathering service, the Bundesnachrichtendienst, or BND. With the BfV and the intelligence units of the renascent German military, the BND would form the West German intelligence community.

Authorities familiar with the operations of the West German security and intelligence agencies credit them with stunning successes against terrorists, in spite of the fact that lines of responsibility for operational and intelligence-gathering matters often seem unclear. Its first mission was to keep tabs on Communists and extreme right-wing groups, for instance, but the BfV soon expanded its portfolio. In 1972, new legislation authorized BfV agents to conduct surveillance of aliens and engage in the 'collection and evaluation of information, intelligence and other data' against people or activities deemed detrimental to free and democratic order. Although still a domestic intelligence-gathering service, the BfV was further authorized to investigate 'security-endangering' or intelligence-gathering operations in Germany by a foreign power and any other activities conducted within Germany that could jeopardize the 'foreign-affairs interests' of the Federal Republic. The lines, in short, were beginning to blur.

When might the activities of more than 1,000 BfV agents compromise or complicate those of more than 7,000 BND operatives? And what of the BKA, the federal police agency whose authorities and responsibilities overlapped not only those of the BfV but also those of the security and police agencies of the individual states within the Federal Republic? With regard to terrorists travelling in and out of Germany, which agency would be responsible?

It was complicated, but the German agencies also worked well together. In the investigation of the April 1986 bombing of the La Belle discotheque in Hamburg, U.S. officials with knowledge of the case say, the BfV and BND cooperated in exemplary fashion. Immediately after the bombing, in which an American soldier and a Turkish woman were killed, German and U.S. officials suspected Libya's Colonel Qaddafi. The BND has enormous signal-intelligence-gathering capabilities, and knowledgeable officials say it had cracked the Libyan cipher code years before. On March 25, 1986, the BND intercepted a cable sent from Tripoli to eight Libyan People's Bureaus, as Libyan embassies are called. One of the cables went to the People's Bureau in East Berlin, and BND technicians in Pullau picked it up in its entirety. That information was passed along directly to the National Security Agency in Fort Meade. The BND had done its job, and it would continue to monitor the airwaves. After the bombing, the BfV picked up the ball. Agents from its foreign surveillance section increased their stakeouts of Libyan diplomats in West Germany, and, it is believed, their efforts helped confirm the Libyan involvement in the bombing. Citing the evidence collected by the German and U.S. intelligence communities, President Reagan authorized the U.S. bombing raid on Libya that narrowly missed killing Qaddafi. Unfortunately, Reagan's disclosures infuriated German authorities, who believed it was unnecessary to divulge the BND's electronic intercepts and the agency's obvious success in breaking the Libyan code.

Despite such successes, German and U.S. officials say, the legacy of World War II on the intelligence and law enforcement communities is such that the relationships among agencies are still fraught with secrecy and some confusion. Simply because of the way the security and police agencies evolved after their creation at the end of the war, information is still highly compartmentalized, and too often one agency does not know exactly what the other is doing.

Trying to make sense of it all in early 1989, many U.S. officials involved in the Lockerbie investigation didn't quite know what to think. Perhaps the deadlock on the German end was simply the result of a bureaucratic spat, with one agency withholding information from another. 'Whether [the BKA] received it or misinterpreted it, [or] didn't realize what they had, or [whether] it was garbled,' Buck Revell said, 'I don't know.' Such things certainly happened in the U.S. With the FBI, CIA and Defense Intelligence Agency at the Pentagon, there were crossed wires and missed signals more often than most people cared to admit. One of the more tragic breakdowns in communications occurred in Beirut in 1983, when Special Forces training teams there were alerted to a terrorist threat against Marine barracks near the airport. Somehow the information never filtered up to the Marine command. On October 23, a suicide truck-bomber demolished the barracks, and 241 Marines died.

Formally to accuse the Germans of obstructing the Pan Am inquiry would have been foolish. The Germans were critical to the investigation. And if it degenerated into a shouting match between Bonn and Washington, the Americans could wave good-bye to any future hopes of German cooperation on a wide range of matters. Besides, there was probably another way. Officials at the FBI and the CIA believed they had access to the same intelligence the BND was getting, and they were firmly convinced that Marwan Kreeshat had built more than one bomb. They just couldn't understand why the normally efficient Germans couldn't find them.

'We thought that perhaps they had seized them and not known what they had,' Revell recalled. 'Or that the material had been spirited away, or something of this nature. We were just trying to make sure that they had properly, carefully inventoried what they did have and [determined] whether there had been any collection of other devices that might have been the repository for other explosives during the search.'

Needless to say, the Germans didn't appreciate the Americans' concern. With frosty glances all around, the investigation into the bombing of Pan Am 103 began to falter.

CHAPTER 13

All this while, however, another avenue of investigation had been going forward as well.

The fact that the Lockerbie investigators could rule out the U.S. intelligence officers as the passengers who unknowingly might have carried a bomb on board the plane or had a bomb slipped into their luggage by a terrorist had freed up more resources for the Frankfurt end of the inquiry. The conclusions drawn by technical experts in Longtown relating to baggage carrier 14L had made the Frankfurt connection the most plausible theory, but certainly not the only one. The existence of the Dalkamouni network and the Autumn Leaves arrests in October had bolstered the theory further still. Oddly enough, although investigators had gone back over the telephone threat received in Helsinki on December 5, it still seemed like nonsense. The caller had specified that a Pan Am flight from Frankfurt would be targeted sometime in December. He had been interviewed and reinterviewed by police, intelligence and security officials. He knew nothing, they concluded. But his reference to the Professor, Abu Nidal's master bombmaker, Samir Kadar, led some Lockerbie investigators to an alternative theory: Perhaps Dalkamouni was the red herring. After all, his network had been broken up, and his operatives were scattered and in hiding. How could such a group carry out a bombing seven weeks after the Autumn Leaves arrests? The Professor, on the other hand, had shown he could do almost anything. After the metallic-green Nissan had exploded on the Athens docks in July 1988, a growing number of intelligence officials believed he had planted his fingerprints in the car and simply vanished to cover his tracks. Perhaps Kadar had murdered the 270 in Lockerbie after all.

Few investigators subscribed to the Abu Nidal theory by late February 1989, but all knew they would not make the case one way or the other simply by spinning webs. They needed to know how the bomb had gotten on the plane, and who had put it there. In Frankfurt, this meant looking at the 125 passengers who had boarded Flight 103 to London there. Almost immediately, the U.S. military personnel who had boarded were ruled out as suspects, although sacks of holiday mail from U.S. military personnel had been loaded into the cargo hold of the Boeing 727 without being examined or X-rayed at all. There had been considerable confusion, even among the investigators, about the total number of pieces of luggage loaded in Frankfurt. Pan Am's figures showed that seventy bags loaded in Frankfurt wound up in the *Maid of the Seas*. Further checking by the investigators, however, would show that only a fraction of the luggage loaded in Frankfurt had been closely examined. According to the airline's figures, cited by sources knowledgeable about the investigation, security personnel in Frankfurt X-rayed a total of ten suitcases, three garment bags and one box. The rest, the sources said, were unexamined.

In February and March 1989, the closer the Lockerbie investigators looked at their Frankfurt leads, the more unsettling things they found. Pan Am security at Frankfurt Main Airport was a mess, they discovered; there was just no other word for it.

Increased terrorism in the spring of 1986 had cut deeply into the business of almost every international air carrier; business on some Pan Am routes had fallen by half. To improve security and reassure travellers, Pan Am had established its own security operation that year. Alert Management Systems, Inc., would be financed, in part, by a surcharge of $5 per ticket on each transatlantic flight. But after the Lockerbie crash even some Alert officials said the operation was more for show than genuine security. When Alert began operations at New York's Kennedy Airport, for instance, its personnel paraded dogs in front of the Pan Am checkout counter. But they were not bomb-sniffing dogs, as many people seemed to think; they were, according to Fred Ford, Alert's first president, 'your well-behaved German shepherds'.

Pan Am did more. It contracted with a consulting firm, Ktalav Promotion and Investment Ltd., to review its operations at Frankfurt Main and twenty-four other airports around the globe. Isaac Yeffet, a former chief of security for El Al, universally acknowledged as having the most thorough security system, conducted the Pan Am review for KPI. In a confidential report to the airline, Yeffet wrote that 'Pan Am is highly vulnerable to most forms of terrorist attack' and that 'a bomb would have a good chance of getting through security' at the Frankfurt airport. Yeffet could hardly have been more blunt. His report concluded, in part, by saying: 'The fact that no major disaster has occurred to date is merely providential.' And more specifically: 'It appears, therefore, that Pan Am is almost totally vulnerable to a mid-air explosion through explosive charges concealed in the cargo.'

What Pan Am did with Yeffet's report was to file it away. And Alert's Fred Ford, complaining that security was inadequate, was dismissed. He returned to his previous position as vice-president of Pan Am's general aviation division.

Since the crash of the *Maid of the Seas*, Pan Am has received a great deal of criticism for ignoring the KPI findings. Some of it has been unfair. The fact is that precautions such as those taken by El Al, in which passengers are often required to purchase tickets in person weeks in advance and complete detailed questionnaires, are unrealistic for most commercial carriers, in the U.S. or any other Western country. Another fact is that most travellers would simply not put up with such onerous security precautions.

Those two facts aside, the Lockerbie investigators – and later, the Federal Aviation Administration – would find security lapses in Pan Am's Frankfurt operations that were difficult to countenance.

On the afternoon of December 21 at Frankfurt Main Airport, Alert's chief of security was Ulrich Weber, a flamboyant twenty-nine-year-old with a modest criminal record, a fondness for late-night partying and a none too scrupulous record of hiring staff. One Alert employee, Sabine Fuchs, admitted to having no background in the business and receiving no training. Ulrich Weber nevertheless put Fuchs to work as a screener, interviewing passengers to see if they might be carrying bombs, guns and the like on board Pan Am jets. Fuchs's background? She had previously worked as a hairdresser, and a good one at that, she said. Another employee, Simone Keller, also had no training and no background in the security business. Why did she get the job? she was asked. 'Mr. Weber told me I had wonderful blue eyes.'

The problems at Frankfurt went far beyond Ulrich Weber and his cast of incompetents. In court documents, a Pan Am security supervisor alleged that Weber had backdated a warning about the bomb threat Samra Mahayoun had telephoned to the U.S. embassy in Helsinki on December 5. Alan James Berwick, a senior Pan Am security official based in London, had got to Helsinki immediately after the call and had been advised by Finnish security officials that it was nonsense. To be on the safe side, however, Berwick had issued a confidential memorandum instructing Alert personnel to place 'special emphasis on the handling of interline baggage' at Frankfurt.

On the night of December 21, after the crash, Weber called an Alert employee named Oliver Koch at home, according to an affidavit given later by Koch. According to court documents, Weber said that Koch, who was in charge of training Alert personnel responsible for screening passengers, was to report for work at 6:00 A.M. on December 22. Working at Weber's computer that morning, Koch said, he noticed Berwick's memo on the Helsinki threat. He said that it was the first time he had ever seen it and that it had never been distributed among the Alert staff in Frankfurt. According to the court papers, this exchange took place later between Koch and Weber:

Koch: 'What is this, after Lockerbie?'

Weber: 'Oh my God, don't worry, don't worry. It's nothing, forget it.'

Koch: 'How can I forget it? This is a warning of a potential bomb. It is my job.'

Weber: 'Just forget it. Be quiet, or you will get into trouble.'

According to the court papers, Weber backdated the Berwick memo, indicating he had received it on December 9 and distributed it to the staff shortly after; Koch says he has the original, unstamped memo, however, and he maintains that Weber distributed it to Alert personnel only after the crash in Lockerbie.

The scenario related by Oliver Koch would seem to indicate a security screwup of astounding dimensions except for one thing: The original warning on the Helsinki threat was judged by every competent authority who examined it to be a hoax. Even now, if one excludes any possible new information, the Helsinki phone call, like the presence of the U.S. intelligence officers on Flight 103, can be said to be no more than a coincidence. Bizarre it was, but a coincidence for all that. Understandably, many of the families of those who died in the crash of Pan Am 103 find this difficult to accept. Some have asserted that there is some type of cover-up about the Helsinki affair. Others, more appropriately, have called for more cogent guidelines on the dissemination of such threats to the general public. If diplomats in the U.S. embassy in Moscow could read a posted notice of a perceived threat, why shouldn't Karen Hunt, James Fuller and Michael Bernstein be accorded the same privilege?

Even after the Lockerbie disaster, U.S. officials maintain that making such warnings public is a bad idea. According to the FAA, U.S. air carriers receive an average of about 500 threats a year, and more than two dozen are usually deemed serious enough for the agency to issue a warning bulletin. Since 1986, the FAA has issued at least ninety-three bulletins, and authorities say that about a third addressed threats to specific flights.

To the families of the Lockerbie victims, such statistics mean little; perhaps if they had had an inkling of the Helsinki threat, even though it had been determined to be without merit, their loved ones might have changed their travel plans. Such superstitions, if that's all they are, have saved plenty of lives. And the families demand, quite properly, to know why that information was not made available. In their judgment, the government's answer to the question just doesn't cut it.

As the detectives dispatched by John Boyd and the FBI continued examining the circumstances in which passengers and baggage had been loaded aboard Flight 103 in Frankfurt, they found still more lapses in the security operations there. Some of the information came from the files of a separate investigation that had been conducted by the FAA. The day after the disaster in Lockerbie, FAA security inspectors were in Frankfurt, inconspicuously watching Alert personnel there and taking copious notes. The inspectors remained there, undercover, until New Year's Eve. Then they returned to Washington and put their findings in a report, which was later made available to the investigators in Locker-bie, Washington and Frankfurt. From FAA Case No. 88EU700038, Docket No. 89-254, the detectives learned these details about the security precautions taken during the loading and boarding of the first leg of the flight:

- 'During the pre-departure procedure for Pan Am Flight 103 departing Frankfurt, Pan Am failed to conduct the required search of the cargo area of the aircraft prior to loading cargo on the aircraft.'

- Because they failed to apply a uniform tracking system of passengers at Frankfurt, Pan Am security personnel allowed five passengers who should have been subjected to additional screening, according to the FAA, to board Flight 103 unchecked. Besides that, the security personnel 'did not conduct the required search of the carry-on items in the possession of [the] five passengers' and 'did not conduct the required search of [the] five passengers'.

- 'Pan Am passenger service agents, who were assigned to check in passengers at the gate for Pan Am Flight 103, checked in four interline passengers and did not refer the four interline passengers to security personnel.'

Four unchecked interline passengers, five passengers requiring further security checks that were never made, and a complete failure to examine the plane's cargo bay before loading: that left any number of ways a terrorist could have gotten a bomb on board. It was later determined, from Pan Am records, that the four interline passengers had checked either eleven or twelve pieces of luggage aboard Flight 103. And because security agents had examined so few of the total number of bags checked by the 125 Frankfurt–London passengers, the Lockerbie investigators reviewing the information months later were faced with not one mystery to solve but dozens.

Pan Am would later pay for the lapses. In the ten days the FAA inspectors were at Frankfurt Main observing the Alert system, they also documented an instance in which the bags of four passengers travelling from Budapest to Los Angeles made the trip unaccompanied, in violation of FAA regulations, because the four had missed their flight. For two other flights besides the 103, the FAA inspectors found, the ground-security coordinators of the Pan Am terminal at Frankfurt Main had 'failed to ensure that all . . . requirements relating to the security of these flights were monitored prior to departure.' Another team of FAA inspectors at London's Heathrow found even more glaring shortcomings in Pan Am's security arrangements there: Thirty-one passengers who under FAA guidelines should have been subjected to further screening had been allowed to board the 103 freely. FAA attorneys, citing the appropriate chapter and verse from the Federal Aviation Act of 1958, as amended, concluded that the violations at Heathrow and Frankfurt Main would cost the air carrier plenty. In an express-mail letter sent September 19, 1989, to Edward F. Cunningham, Pan Am's managing director for corporate security, attorneys said that the violations added up to $630,000 in fines. Pan Am could challenge the inspectors' findings, Cunningham was informed, or his employer could send a certified cheque or money order for the full amount, payable to the FAA.

Pan Am executives defended their security system vigorously. And the FAA was careful to say that none of the lapses disclosed by its inspectors was deemed to have contributed to the tragedy in Lockerbie.

The dispute between Pan Am and the FAA gave no solace to the families of those who died in Lockerbie. And it was certainly no help to the investigators under

John Boyd and Buck Revell, who had to sort through the conflicting and indeterminate information and somehow build a criminal prosecution on it. They could be certain of nothing. With their counterparts from the BKA, Scottish detectives and FBI agents interviewed the families and friends of every one of the 125 Frankfurt–London passengers. At first, because of the location of the explosion in the luggage carrier, they believed the bomb was not in an interline bag. But they couldn't be certain of that either. Baggage handlers in the Pan Am terminal were questioned and said that the interline bags loaded at Heathrow had gone on the bottom of 14L. But perhaps one hadn't. And what of the 'eleven or twelve' bags that had been interlined at Frankfurt? In London, all baggage from the first leg was offloaded. Waiting to stow the seventy bags going on to New York or Detroit aboard the *Maid of the Seas*, baggage handlers would have considered the entire lot 'Frankfurt baggage'.

Playing the odds, calculated once again on the basis of the hard physical evidence – the location of the hole in 14L – by late February the investigators had focused more closely than ever on the Frankfurt passengers; for the time being, the interline-bag theory was a runner-up. Investigators very quickly came up with a short list of suspects among the Frankfurt passengers, and they focused on it intensively.

At the top of the list very early on in the Frankfurt end of the investigation was Khalid Jaafar, the handsome young Lebanese man whose father had left the strife of Beirut behind for a new life in America. Nazir Jaafar's oldest son had been sitting in seat 53K when the *Maid of the Seas* shattered over Lockerbie. The twenty-year-old Jaafar was both a likely and an unlikely suspect. Raising the investigators' suspicions were the young man's frequent trips back to Lebanon. Why so many trips? His mother still lived there, but how many young men at that age are such devoted sons? That Jaafar was

219

a Shiite Moslem raised another question. Did he share the more radical, fundamentalist views with which the Shiites have become popularly associated? A third factor: The Jaafar family was from Baalbek, the same ancient place, famous once for its Roman ruins and now for its brisk drug trade, that is home to both the headquarters of the Iranian Revolutionary Guards in Lebanon and a training camp of terrorist Ahmed Jibril. On the other side of the ledger, most of those who knew Khalid Jaafar said he was pretty much apolitical; his were party politics, his friends said, inasmuch as he liked to have a good time. He was a car enthusiast. At home with his father in Dearborn, Michigan, he drove a Grand Prix; on visits to Lebanon, where he had been brought up by his grandparents and had graduated from an elite private school, he had the use of a Mercedes and a BMW. In the U.S., Jaafar worked in his father's truck stop near the Canadian border and took some automotive courses at a vocational school in Detroit. When he wasn't working, he liked to lift weights.

His friends described Khalid Jaafar as a good guy. They also say he couldn't have carried a bomb on board the plane in Frankfurt, and for a time at least, the Lockerbie investigators had to agree. The reason? The suitcase that contained the bomb.

In the fields around Lockerbie, in the days and weeks since the crash, the searchers directed by John Boyd and Superintendent Stuart Henderson had recovered fragments of one piece of luggage that looked nothing like any of the others. One by one, the fragments made their way to the state-of-the-art laboratory benches at Fort Halstead, where they were subjected to the most intensive scrutiny. The fragments were a whitish blue. But that hadn't been the original colour of the bag. Further examination showed that the bag had been a Samsonite, a hard-sided suitcase. Purchased new, it had been copper-coloured. In the heat and the violence of the explosion, the copper had been bleached out to a pale blue. Specialists at Fort Halstead determined conclusively that the copper-coloured Samsonite had contained the bomb in a radio–cassette player. They had found the bag that contained the bomb.

Now they had to find out to whom the bag belonged.

The investigators checking into Khalid Jaafar's background couldn't figure it. The young man's friends told the investigators that he had carried only two bags onto the plane in Frankfurt. They even had a photograph to prove it, they said. Just before he boarded a train that would take him to the Frankfurt airport, his friends had snapped a picture of him, carrying a soft-sided carry-on bag and an oversize traveller's wallet. From the fields around Lockerbie, both bags had been recovered on or immediately before January 3, knowledgeable officials say. Neither bag was very badly damaged. Neither had been involved in the explosion.

There was still another mystery. Although they had found and identified Jaafar's two bags, the investigators in Lockerbie either had not recovered or had failed to identify his body. When they finally did locate and identify it, they found nothing that would link Jaafar to the explosion, a radio–cassette player or a hard-sided copper-coloured Samsonite suitcase.

Yet he remained at the top of the list of suspects. 'Obviously, he is of interest,' Buck Revell said during the investigation. 'The young Mr. Jaafar is from Lebanon, travelled back and forth. His family [was] living in Michigan, he was in Germany. He certainly was in contact with Middle Eastern types, and [if] we hypothesize that this was caused by a Middle Eastern group, then he has to be a suspect or at least an unwitting surrogate. That doesn't mean that he is the only one, or that he should be exclusively considered. But until we can eliminate any luggage that he hadn't checked, he would have to be considered as a suspect.'

The investigators simply would not dismiss the travel

patterns to Lebanon and what they describe as a 'pattern of evidence' suggesting that Jaafar may have been involved as a courier in the narcotics traffic between the Middle East and Europe. If he was involved in that business, even in an insignificant way, it was just a small step to assume that someone, somewhere, could have given him a suitcase to carry with him on his trip.

But who?

While the investigators pondered, Nazir Jaafar tried to deal with his grief. People who knew him in the thriving Lebanese community of Dearborn called the elder Jaafar a hardworking and deeply honourable man. In Lebanon he had been a lawyer; in the United States he sold gas and repaired trucks. By his standards, it was a big improvement, a chance to rear his three children in relative safety, away from the chaos and violence of Beirut. Jaafar was deeply offended by the unfounded charges against his eldest son. In them he saw a distinct anti-Arab bias, and he resented it. The charges also deepened the pain of his loss. 'I never thought there could be anything worse than death,' he said, months after the crash in Lockerbie. 'But this is worse. The life I am living is worse than death.'

The FBI agents who came to interview him in his service station were unfailingly polite and tried to reassure him, Jaafar said. But that didn't make the pain any less.

For what it was worth, the FBI investigators genuinely did seem to have sympathized with the Jaafar family. 'I know how it would be if it was my son who was considered,' Buck Revell said. 'He was in Frankfurt, he got on board, he had a suitcase that was in that particular container. I would say, "My God, not only is my son dead, but now [he's] under suspicion of being one of the causative factors." I know how I would feel. Our position on this is that we can't eliminate anybody whose luggage was in 14L and narrow it down as to whose piece of luggage [it was]. And until we can do

222

that, everyone who fits into that category is a potential [suspect].'

In Frankfurt, the investigators continued to press other angles.

Mindful of the story of Ann Murphy, the trusting Irish woman who had very nearly boarded the El Al plane in London more than two years before, unaware her fiancé had stuck a bomb in her luggage, investigators in Frankfurt looked for similarly unwitting passengers. They found two possibilities right away.

Two college women had boarded the Boeing 727 in Frankfurt for the quick hop to London; then home to the United States. Originally they had been scheduled on a direct flight from Vienna to New York on December 21, but that flight had been taken out of service. A Pan Am representative had offered the two women another flight, from Frankfurt via London to New York.

Just as Diane Maslowski's family had been asked for numerous details about her life in London, the families of all the single women travelling on the 103 were asked a number of painful and intrusive questions. Sadly, the history of previous aircraft bombings suggested that a single woman was more apt to fit the profile of an unwitting bomb carrier. For the families who had to endure inquiries about their daughters' or sisters' social life, this may have been the most excruciating and infuriating part of the ordeal. For the FBI agents, many of whom had single daughters of their own, the questions were hard to ask. But there was no way around it.

On the other side of the Atlantic, investigators learned something that made them sit up and take notice. Two women had been friendly with a young man named Jamal, a student from the Middle East, it is believed. The investigators would go further afield chasing this lead than many other leads. Wherever they tried to find Jamal, they were told he had left.

Where had he gone? they asked.

Nobody seemed to know for sure.

Nearly everyone questioned by the investigators described the relationship between Jamal and the two women as purely friendly, not romantic. But that didn't mean he couldn't have given them a 'gift' to take home on the 103.

Like the leads on Khalid Jaafar, this one would have to be followed. After considerable time and travel by Lockerbie investigators, Jamal was located. He was described as having been a good student. He had not given the women anything to carry on the plane with them. The suspicions about the two women had been unfounded after all. Like the others killed in Lockerbie, they were innocent victims whose families had been forced to endure a terrible agony.

For Khalid Jaafar's family, the agony would not end. Frankfurt investigators brought around a photograph of the young man and an exact duplicate of the copper-coloured Samsonite, and must have asked the question hundreds of times: Had anyone seen the two together? Security people, baggage handlers, ticket agents – everyone who might conceivably have seen Jaafar in the airport was questioned.

It was the kind of grunt police work that could probably be counted on for results, but it wasn't the only thing investigators were relying on. The relatively brief history of successful terrorism investigations instructs one on the excessive importance of police procedures, but no one knowledgeable about the complicated business of counterterrorism pretends the intelligence community has no role to play. The counterterrorism experts at the CIA, FBI, State Department and Pentagon all knew that good intelligence could provide the key that would enable criminal investigators to break the case. They intended to help any way they could, but it was awfully slow going.

In January, less than a month after the crash in Lockerbie, the Pentagon had 'tasked' the Defense Intelligence Agency to begin collecting whatever new information it could about the most likely suspects in the Pan Am bombing. The DIA, naturally, focused most heavily on Ahmed Jibril and the Popular Front for the Liberation of Palestine – General Command. A common misperception about intelligence gathering is that it is done mostly by the trench-coat set, the classic covert operators of espionage fiction. In fact, most intelligence comes from regularly accredited foreign-service personnel, defence attachés and publicly available sources of information. Many of the people stationed in U.S. embassies around the world, and not just those specifically employed by the CIA, are trained intelligence officers who know which information is new, whether it might be significant, and if it is, what its implications are. Some intelligence-gathering tasks are more tricky than others, however.

On the morning of March 3, 1989, in the grim scrubland about thirty miles from Damascus, U.S. Army Colonel Clifford Ward and his assistant, Major Robert Siegel, were about to find out just how tricky such jobs can get. The military officers, who were assigned as defence attachés to the U.S. embassy in Damascus, were taking photographs with telephoto lenses when some of Ahmed Jibril's commandos came upon them suddenly, chased them through a field at the edge of the PFLP-GC training camp and, after a dizzying few minutes, took them into custody. Syrian authorities said that Ward and Siegel were carrying maps and binoculars, in addition to the long-lens cameras. Syria's foreign minister, Farouk Charaa, accused the Americans of taking photographs to pass on to Israel for use in a possible military strike at the GC training camp.

'The seriousness of this incident lies in the fact that

225

these photographs are not for the American authorities; they don't need them,' Charaa said. But he added that they 'might be channelled to the Israelis, [who] can use them in a possible air raid'.

Jibril had good reason to fear the Israelis. On December 9, 1988, the Israeli government had mounted a battalion-size attack on one of Jibril's bases just south of Beirut. Still, it was strange that the Syrian authorities took up Jibril's cause so publicly after he had been identified as the primary suspect in the Lockerbie bombing.

The United States, which through Ambassador Edward Djerejian protested vigorously the detention of Ward and Siegel, had been trying even before December to get Syrian president Assad to curtail the activities of the PFLP-GC. After Lockerbie, U.S. officials say, the protests became even more vigorous. 'Every time [Djerejian] sees him,' a State Department official recalled, 'he raises the subject of Jibril and the GC.'

Perhaps because of their embarrassment over the overt efforts by Ward and Siegel to collect information on Jibril, whom President Assad continued to defend, Syrian authorities issued a denial afterwards that the PFLP-GC had anything to do with Lockerbie. 'Jibril made a clear statement,' Foreign Minister Charaa said after the brief detention of Ward and Siegel, 'that he had nothing to do with the Pan Am tragedy.'

Not surprisingly, the intelligence officials back in Washington didn't believe Jibril, or Charaa's endorsement of Jibril's denial.

CHAPTER 14

As every good detective knows, the devil really is in the details. It is the strand of hair, the scrap of fabric, the faint stain of blood on which successful prosecutions are built; their lack is usually fatal. In Lockerbie by late March, the hundreds of searchers under John Boyd and John Orr were looking for just those kinds of clues. They had some, it was true, but not nearly enough. This was the essential conclusion of a joint meeting of the investigators and the senior members of the agencies involved. They had convened in such a forum only once before. On January 20, senior representatives of the BKA, the FBI and the British and Scottish police had gathered for a daylong session at New Scotland Yard, just a few minutes' walk from the Houses of Parliament in London. It had been early on in the investigation, and the mood had been described by participants as optimistic. In March, when the same people convened for a second meeting, this time in Lockerbie, the mood was considerably more grim. The investigation had come a long way in a relatively short time. Forensic experts at Fort Halstead and reconstruction specialists at Longtown had made great strides with the evidence already recovered from the fields around Lockerbie, but some senior members of the investigation team worried that continued conflict with German authorities was hindering their efforts. If the murderers of the 270 Pan Am passengers were to be brought to justice, it would take a lot more work.

As much as John Boyd, Buck Revell and others

monitoring the progress of the Lockerbie investigation were believers in nitty-gritty detective work, they knew they would not succeed if they relied on police work alone. Investigations of terrorist acts were different from all other criminal inquiries in that if they were to be truly successful, they had to yield not only the name of the person who'd shot the gun or planted the bomb, but also the identity of the organization that had supported, sponsored and paid for the act. One of the most disheartening things about terrorism was that there would always be another fanatic who, to further his cause, would shoot the gun or plant the bomb. Finding and convicting terrorists – or better, identifying and stopping them before they could act – was essential. But ignoring their sponsor was a mistake.

In the Lockerbie investigation, whether the problems with the Germans could be resolved or not, that meant getting the intelligence agencies fully involved. Obviously, the Dumfries and Galloway Constabulary had no intelligence-gathering capabilities in the most technical sense of the term. It had no clandestine operators or Cray supercomputers decoding intercepted communications from around the globe. Police investigators needed the itelligence agencies to help them with questions about who had sponsored the bombing – and on the other side of the coin, the intelligence agencies, ideally at least, could furnish evidentiary leads to the actual bombers and the people who had helped them carry out the attack. Although the investigators do not say so today, that was one important reason for the de facto sharing of so much decision making by Scottish and American authorities during the inquiry: the cops needed the spies, and the spies needed the cops. If one worked without the other, the Lockerbie investigation was as doomed as Flight 103.

In the best of cases, the business of intelligence officials is not so much a series of assigned tasks as it is an evolving process of understanding. For its oft cited lapses, the American intelligence community continues to provide what is arguably the most highly nuanced and trenchant reporting on events in the far corners of the world. 'It is,' says one senior U.S. official privileged to the intelligence community's most classified reporting, 'like the best one would hope for from serious postgraduate training at the best universities. It is well informed, and it is imaginative in the best sense, in the sense that where speculation must substitute for hard fact, one most often has the clear impression of very powerful minds at work.'

Because the intelligence community operates with the knowledge that its best work is often the result of long and patient accumulation of information, it came as no surprise to Buck Revell and other senior FBI officials that the CIA and the National Security Agency had had an early jump on the Lockerbie investigation. It was not just that counterterrorism analysts in Langley were poring over computer files of likely suspects within hours of the crash but also that those files contained a wealth of details. Even before the call on December 22 claiming that Pan Am 103 had been brought down in retaliation for the USS *Vincennes's* strike against the Iranian airbus in the Persian Gulf in July, some intelligence officials were pointing not just at Iran but at Ahmed Jibril himself as well. What was confusing, as the Lockerbie investigators reviewed their facts in February and March 1989, was that in the months just before the downing of the Iranian airliner, the political picture inside Iran had become much fuzzier. The tide seemed to be turning against more hardline elements of the Iranian leadership, and the Ayatollah Khomeini seemed to have given the new direction of events his blessing.

Like nearly everything else in Iran under Khomeini, the change had almost nothing to do with the United States, the 'Great Satan', and everything to do with internal politics and the long-standing bitter feud with

Iran's true archenemy, Iraq. In September 1980, Iraqi president Saddam Hussein had ordered a massive attack on Iran, and ever since, Iranian troops, when assembled for Friday prayers, had chanted the official government slogan: 'War until victory.' The war, in Khomeini's eyes, was nothing less than the defence of Islam against infidels. Saddam was a socialist, and Iraq a secular state ruled by a clique of Sunni Muslims, despite the fact that most Iraqis were Shiites. On Christmas Eve, 1986, after Iran had already lost at least half a million soldiers, Khomeini had launched Operation Karbala, publicly heralded as the 'final offensive'. But there had been other final offensives before, most of them miserable failures. This time, over fourteen weeks, Khomeini threw wave after wave of *basij* at many of Saddam's most heavily fortified positions. The *basij* were the militia volunteers, either very old or very young. In Operation Karbala, some of the *basij* were mere children, unarmed, and they were slaughtered by the tens of thousands. To many observers of Iran, Operation Karbala was the beginning of a watershed. To many Iranians too it seemed that Khomeini had gone too far. That feeling, however widespread it may have been by 1986, clearly culminated two years later when, in the afternoon of February 29, Iraq fired several Soviet-made Scud-B missiles into downtown Teheran. During the murderous eight years of conflict between Iran and Iraq, there had been several so-called wars of the cities, in which entire civilian areas had been targeted by missile and artillery fire. But this was the first time the missiles had rained on Teheran, where roughly a fifth of the entire population of the nation lived. The barrage continued until the afternoon of April 20, when it stopped as suddenly as it had begun. Thousands of Iranians protested their government's inability to protect them. By that time, it was evident that the war had embittered and disheartened most Iranians, and even Khomeini seemed to get the message: The war must end, Iran's isolation must end, the shattered economy must be patched together so that Iranians could resume something approaching a normal life.

In June 1988, several weeks before the *Vincennes* loosed its two surface-to-air missiles at the airbus, Khomeini acted. He reestablished diplomatic ties with France and prepared to do the same with the United Kingdom and Canada. In addition, Khomeini approved the elevation of the powerful speaker of the Majlis, the Iranian parliament, to the position of commander in chief of the armed forces. It was thought by many in the west that Hashemi Rafsanjani was a 'moderate', a man who could be dealt with sensibly. The Iran-contra affair had exposed that for the foolishness it was. Rafsanjani was a pragmatist, and if seeming moderation was what it took to achieve his ends, then so be it; it was just show, however, one of the many arrows in his quiver.

What the pragmatist Rafsanjani wanted in June of 1988 was an end to the war, and even as he spoke publicly of 'war until victory', he also approved final negotiations that would lead to a ceasefire and the unconditional signing of United Nations Security Council Resolution 598, which would formally end the hostilities with Baghdad. All of that was in train on the morning of July 3, when, at 10:54 local time, Captain Will C. Rogers III issued the command to fire at what he believed was a hostile F-14 approaching his ship. That changed plenty.

The fault lines in the Iranian leadership were no secret to most Iranians, and certainly to academics and intelligence officials who studied the country. Arrayed against Rafsanjani and his increasingly influential followers were the more devout and fundamentalist adherents of the powerful minister of the interior, Hojatolislam Ali Akbar Mohtashemi. Where Rafsanjani's power base was in the Majlis, Mohtashemi's was in the *komitehs*, the powerful groups of informers and govern-

231

ment officials who policed social and political conduct at all levels of Iranian society. Besides the *komitehs*, Mohtashemi also maintained enormous influence over Hezbollah, the movement of Shiite fundamentalists he had created in Lebanon between 1983 and 1985.

Mohtashemi believed devoutly in the importance of the Islamic revolution. He believed in its export to other Moslem countries, and in the literalness of the slogan 'War until victory' against Iraq. For Mohtashemi, a small man who wore glasses, 1988 had been a very bad year indeed. Devoted as he was to Khomeini (he had gone into exile with him as a student), he could hardly criticize his actions in ending the war and elevating Rafsanjani. In the downing of the Iranian airbus and the death of its 290 passengers, however, he had the perfect opportunity to brace the Ayatollah, strike out at Rafsanjani and get his beloved revolution back on track. For Mohtashemi, the airbus tragedy was quite literally a godsend. All he needed now was someone to help him take advantage of it.

The intelligence officials detailed to the Lockerbie investigation knew all of this. And they also knew who Mohtashemi's 'someone' might be. Since at least 1986, Ahmed Jibril had met on numerous occasions with senior Iranian officials in Teheran, Beirut and elsewhere. In December 1987, Western intelligence officials said, Jibril had met for four hours with Iran's foreign minister, Ali Akbar Velayati in Tripoli. What Jibril was doing, the intelligence officials say, was hustling business.

Investigators believe that although members of the Syrian intelligence establishment maintained extraordinary close contact with Jibril, there is no evidence that President Assad knew about the plot to blow up Pan Am 103. Yet in light of the fact that Syria had sponsored Jibril for such a long time and that the Syrians were aware of all of his activities, some officials believe that Syria was partially responsible. Said the State

Department's Frank Moss: 'The bottom line is that I can't believe the PFLP-GC could have done it without someone high in the Syrian government knowing about it. . . . Someone high in Assad's government would have to have known. Assad himself, perhaps not.'

Although Assad continued to provide Jibril's organization with money and logistical support for use in his proxy war against Israel, Jibril had evidently become concerned that he could wind up like Abu Nidal. After concerted pressure from the United States over Abu Nidal's unbridled campaign of terror, Assad had finally expelled him from Damascus, and he had been forced to relocate to Tripoli. If that could happen to Abu Nidal, it could obviously happen to Ahmed Jibril. He was vulnerable. U.S. intelligence officials said that Qaddafi had sharply cut back payments to the PFLP-GC – believed once to be as much as $20 million a year – as Libya wound down its war against Chad. Jibril had provided a small but highly trained commando unit to Qaddafi to deploy against the Chadians, but its services were no longer needed.

Ahmed Jibril badly needed a new source of support. Who better than the Iranians?

It is unclear, according to U.S. authorities, whether anything had come of Jibril's earlier conversations with Velayati and other senior Iranian officials. What was clear to the intelligence analysts, as they reviewed intercepted communications from a variety of sources in the early months of 1989, was that Jibril had been working hard to capitalize on the *Vincennes* incident. On July 4, he was trying desperately to arrange a meeting with members of the Iranian Revolutionary Guards in the Bekaa Valley and with a representative of Mohtashemi. Sometime immediately after that – within seven to ten days, according to U.S. intelligence sources – Jibril and his trusted aide, Hafez Dalkamouni, did meet with Iranian leaders. It was one of a series of meetings and conversations, the U.S. officials said, and almost always,

233

Jibril's pitch was the same: avenging the airbus tragedy in exchange for money. In the volumes of intercepted communications, U.S. intelligence analysts found at least one telephone call made on an open, nonsecure line. The call was from somewhere in Lebanon, perhaps in the Bekaa Valley, to Teheran. During the conversation, Jibril used elliptical language, but it is believed that he was referring, in some sort of code, to American targets in Europe.

There were other meetings in Teheran, Beirut and the Bekaa Valley, U.S. authorities said. So ardent was Jibril in wooing Iran that he was covering all bets, meeting not only with representatives of Mohtashemi and the Revolutionary Guards but with other members of the splintered Iranian leadership as well. The lines of communication got so tangled, one U.S. official said, that the Iranian chargé d'affaires in Beirut, Hosein Niknam, requested clarification from Teheran. Who, he asked, should be assigned to deal with this man Jibril.

The Revolutionary Guards got the job, although it is likely, if one considers the extent of Jibril's contacts in the leadership, that most senior Iranian officials knew of his new assignment. 'Within six to eight weeks after the [airbus] shoot-down,' said a U.S. official involved in the Lockerbie investigation, 'we believe Mohtashemi gave the go-ahead to Jibril.' It was a simple arrangement, the official said: 'It was to be an eye for an eye.'

U.S. investigators believe the idea to avenge the shooting down of the Iranian airliner by striking an American aircraft came from Teheran; everything else – the timing, the place and so on – was left up to Jibril. Apparently, Iran did not have the technical capability to carry out such an act on its own. There has been considerable speculation, and several bald but unsupported assertions, about how much Jibril was paid for his services by Teheran. Knowledgeable analysts say there is no hard information about a precise amount, however. What is known is that Jibril undertook the job

234

not out of devotion to a cause but for money and an opportunity to broaden his base of support beyond the Syrian government.

About the people who paid Jibril, there is little question of their motivation. Contracting with Jibril only confirmed the more radical elements of the leadership in Iran. If the Lockerbie investigators had any doubts about that, as they examined the intercepted communications passed along by the intelligence agencies, they were surely erased by events in the months after the crash in Scotland. In February, the Ayatollah Khomeini issued a *fatwa*, a religious edict, that 'sentenced to death' Salman Rushdie, the author of a novel entitled *The Satanic Verses*. In authorizing an award equivalent to $1 million for anyone who murdered Rushdie, Khomeini said that the author had blasphemed Islam and its founder, the prophet Mohammed. Western officials said they believed Khomeini had been unaware of *The Satanic Verses* until Mohtashemi showed him a copy. The powerful interior minister supposedly learned of the book after some 2,000 people demonstrated in Islamabad to protest its publication in Pakistan. Mohtashemi, it is thought, went to Khomeini and urged revenge against the blasphemer. The Ayatollah, outraged by the insult to Islam, agreed that revenge was appropriate. And Ahmed Jibril, not one to miss a chance, vowed publicly on March 5 to carry out the death sentence against Rushdie.

Three weeks after that, Mohtashemi notched up his campaign against the perceived enemies of Islam still further: Accommodationists and so-called pragmatists in the Iranian leadership must go. Again, Mohtashemi won the backing of Khomeini, and under his stern gaze, Mohammed Javad Larijani, the deputy foreign minister who had been conducting a very low-key dialogue with the U.S., was forced to resign. So was Mohammed Mahallati, the American-educated ambassador to the

United Nations, who was jailed upon his return to Iran. A few days after that, Mohtashemi won his greatest concession from Khomeini. On March 28, the Ayatollah Hossein Ali Montazeri, Khomeini's appointed heir as Iran's spiritual and political leader, also submitted a letter of resignation, stating in part to his fellow ayatollah that he felt 'compelled to obey . . . orders' to step down. The following day, the spiritual leader of the Moslem community in Brussels, the Netherlands and Luxembourg was gunned down with an aide on a street in Brussels. The Imam Abdullah al-Ahdal, who had objected publicly to the death sentence against Rushdie, was shot once in the head and once in the neck by a hooded man who disappeared in a van. A typewritten statement issued in Beirut the next day by an organization called the Soldiers of Justice claimed responsibility for having murdered the 'traitor' and warned others inclined to make peace with 'blasphemers' and Western-influenced opponents of Islam: 'We shall carry out just punishment against this handful of rotten heads.'

For the intelligence officials in London and Washington, it may have seemed a bit too spooky. Even as they were sorting through their most highly classified files for clues in the Lockerbie investigation, the Iran connection seemed to be manifesting itself on the front pages of the world's newspapers.

And while they proceeded with their end of the investigation, the detectives in the United States, Scotland and West Germany continued with theirs. At his home in Dumfries, after yet another long day of directing searchers and coordinating with his investigators chasing leads in a half-dozen countries, John Boyd wondered about the German end of the investigation. Professionally, he had nothing but the highest regard for the BKA. He had read of its work, of its exacting standards for collecting evidence. He could not fathom how, if the information about Marwan Kreeshat's bombs was correct, the men of the BKA had failed to find them. Buck Revell was similarly perplexed. He had worked with BKA investigators on several occasions over the past few years, and he too had high regard for them. The business about the missing bombs was frustrating. Revell had contemplated discussing the matter with FBI director Sessions and Attorney General Richard Thornburgh, but elevating matters to that level could complicate things. He knew most of the senior German law enforcement and intelligence officials, and if it were possible to resolve the question of the bombs among people at his level, it would probably be better all around. Revell remembered calling his friend Heinrich Boge, the president of the BKA: '[I] told Heinrich that we were very concerned that we weren't making any progress and that information was being withheld for reasons we couldn't understand. Heinrich said that he would look into it.'

Boge invited Dave Barham to discuss the Lockerbie investigation, and there were a few subsequent meetings of Barham, German-speaking FBI agents from Buzzard Point and the BKA investigators assigned to the Lockerbie inquiry. Revell had the impression that it was all so much talk; he decided to go to Germany himself.

He had other stops to make in Europe anyway. In Brussels and Berlin, there was FBI business to attend to, unrelated to Lockerbie. But on Friday, April 14, he met in Bonn with Hans Neusel, state secretary in the Federal Ministry of the Interior, specifically to talk about Lockerbie. Neusel was an influential man; as deputy minister of the interior, he was in charge of all police and security services in Germany. Revell was accompanied by David Keyes, his special assistant for intelligence who would become the new LegAtt in Bonn when Dave Barham's assignment ended in just a few months. Revell was always greeted cordially when he met with his counterparts in Germany. This time, however, he 'received a cold greeting', he recalled months later. Revell wanted to discuss Marwan Kreeshat's bombs, but nothing was resolved. Revell decided to try his luck elsewhere. A driver ferried him and Keyes to BKA offices in Meckenheim, where again the bombs were discussed, and once again no useful answers were forthcoming.

What no one told Revell and Keyes that afternoon was that BKA investigators had gone back to look for Kreeshat's bombs just the day before. 'At the very time I was in that building,' Revell recalled much later, 'they had pulled in additional electronic devices.' With John Boyd and others, Revell had been insisting that such a search be made. He could not understand why he was not told about it during his visit in Mechenheim. 'I think . . . they were sort of pushed by my personal visit,' he said. 'And it still didn't click that they had anything.'

Revell, like so many others involved in the Lockerbie investigation, was completely puzzled. 'The Germans are normally very proficient and capable. This certainly appeared to be an aberration. They were not willing to make a connection between Pan Am 103 and the PFLP-GC, and I said. "That's fair, that's fine. But you have to at least make the investigative assumption that there can be a connection. And we need to pursue the assumption to see if we can, in fact, find evidence."'

German authorities apparently did not want to hear it. But events would soon change their thinking. On the afternoon of April 13, when special BKA investigators returned to Hashem Abassi's old flat at 16 Isarstrasse in Neuss and to his grocery store, they asked to look at some very specific things. They wanted to see the stereo tuners that Hafez Dalkamouni had kept in his room during his stay there. Abassi, who had come to rue his friendship with Dalkamouni, accompanied the BKA men to the basement of the grocery store, where he had stored several things from the abandoned apartment, including some things Dalkamouni had left behind

238

after his arrest. There, on the basement floor, were two tuners, just as Kreeshat had described them.

With Abassi's permission, the BKA agents took the items, stowed them in the back of their official car and drove them, on a local road and through numerous towns and villages, back to the BKA office in Meckenheim. There they were placed on the desk of a detective superintendent named Klink, where they sat unattended until the following Monday morning, April 17. Incredibly, although they had finally recovered the devices described by Kreeshat, the BKA officers didn't even bother to inspect them to see if they really were rigged with explosives. And perhaps that is why no one thought to mention the search of Abassi's premises to Buck Revell.

Whatever the case, the ensuing events were tragic. On the morning of the seventeenth, a BKA technician in Meckenheim was instructed to examine the tuners that had been left on Detective Superintendent Klink's desk. Soon after he began tinkering with one of them, he heard something very peculiar, and very alarming.

The thing was ticking.

Somehow the technician had triggered the timing device. Quickly he ran the tuner through an X-ray machine. The monitor screen showed that the tuner had more wires than it should have had, and some of them seemed to be hooked up to what might be a detonator. But there was no sign of any explosives. The BKA technician knew that plastic explosives would not show up on an X-ray. He also knew he had a tuner with too many wires in it that was ticking. It had to be a bomb. Senior BKA officials in Mechenheim ordered two young officers to take the ticking tuner and the other items recovered from Hashem Abassi's grocery to BKA headquarters in Wiesbaden, where the agency's bomb experts could dismantle it safely. The two young officers refused the order. The bomb should not be moved, they argued, according to internal BKA regulations;

besides, quite understandably, they feared for their lives.

The BKA managed in one way or another to transport the ticking tuner to Wiesbaden soon after midday. In an investigation room in the basement of BKA headquarters, Hans Jürgen Sonntag, thirty-five, an experienced explosives expert, and Thomas Ettinger, twenty-nine, a junior BKA officer, began dismantling the bomb. Sonntag had done such work before. The BKA's bomb experts had handled bombs planted by the Baader-Meinhof gang, by Palestinian terrorists and, most recently, by Irish Republican Army killers operating inside Germany. Sonntag himself had worked with the FBI before. He was a close friend of Paul Clayton, an FBI agent assigned to the U.S. embassy in Bonn. Clayton, like Sonntag, was a forensic bomb specialist. With such experience, Sonntag knew what to look for to determine whether a bomb was booby-trapped. A careful check showed that there was no motion sensor inside the tuner that would have triggered an explosion. With Ettinger assisting him, Sonntag began pulling out the suspicious excess wires in the tuner. Suddenly there was a spark. And within a fraction of a second, a huge fireball engulfed the room; the explosion rocked the entire building. An ambulance and rescue helicopter rushed Sonntag and Ettinger to the emergency room at Mainz University Clinic, but within two hours Sonntag had died from his injuries. Ettinger lay critically wounded, blind and maimed. In the most tragic way possible, the BKA had finally been convinced that Marwan Kreeshat's bombs were for real.

Soon after the explosion in Wiesbaden, BKA investigators were knocking on Hashem Abassi's door once again. This time, they said, they wanted to have a look at a Sanyo television monitor, the kind that could be hooked up to a home computer. Evidently, someone at the BKA had gone back to check records of prior searches, and now all electronic gear in Abassi's possession was suspect. With Abassi in tow, the investigators returned to the basement of the grocery store, and there in plain sight, was the Sanyo monitor.

This time, the BKA decided to bring in an outside bomb expert to dismantle the device. A spokesman for the BKA said that after the kind of incident that had killed Sonntag and wounded Ettinger, it was standard procedure to request another police agency to defuse an explosive device. The spokesman said this was done 'for psychological reasons'. The Hessian state criminal police dispatched their best bomb man to Wiesbaden and, at 7:45 P.M., not long after Sonntag and Ettinger would have concluded their day's work, the Hessian policeman removed nearly 400 grams of plastic Semtex explosive from the Sanyo. Also, from the guts of the monitor, he pulled out a detonator that was wired to a barometer. Further checking showed that the second tuner was similarly laden with Semtex and a barometer-wired detonator. And both of these bombs were almost identical to the bomb in the Toshiba Bombeat that BKA men had discovered on the backseat of Dalkamouni's Ford Taurus on October 26.

If they did not know it before, they surely knew it now: German authorities had the makings of a major scandal on their hands. Alexander Prechtel, the spokesman for the Federal Prosecutor's Office in Karlsruhe, conceded after the discovery that it was now a 'theoretical possibility' that one of Kreeshat's bombs had blown up Pan Am Flight 103. But he said that that was still only a matter of 'speculation'.

Within the BKA, the death of Sonntag and wounding of Ettinger seemed to have a deep effect. In an internal BKA document, several colleagues of the two men labelled the entire episode 'the biggest police scandal in the history of the Federal Republic'. Some, resentful of the continued pressure by the Americans and Scots on the Lockerbie investigation, went so far as to blame American agents for building the bombs. But officials aware of the progress of the Lockerbie investigation say the real effect of the tragedy was a profound change of heart among many BKA officers involved in the inquiry.

Immediately after the explosion in Wiesbaden and the subsequent retrieval of the Sanyo bomb, for example, BKA investigators interrogated Hashem Abassi at length about what Dalkamouni had left behind. 'I do not know when the two tuners and the television screen came into my apartment,' he told police, according to BKA records. 'I am certain that this equipment was not in my apartment before Kreeshat and Dalkamouni came to us in October 1988. I can only assume that either Kreeshat or Dalkamouni brought the two tuners and the TV screen with them and left them in the room they used.'

For the millionth time, it seemed, Abassi told the police he had had no idea Dalkamouni, his own brother-in-law, was a terrorist. About Kreeshat's bomb-making, Abassi said, he knew nothing. The BKA agents were inclined to believe Abassi. After all, if he knew the tuners and the TV monitor contained bombs, would he have left them for months in his house, where someone could accidentally trigger them or where they might conceivably go off on their own? In the judgement of the BKA agents, Hashem Abassi was an innocent who had been cruelly used by Dalkamouni.

The BKA agents decided to ask Dalkamouni more questions. Since October 26, he had said virtually nothing to anyone who tried to interrogate him. On April 26, however, he seemed to have a change of heart, evidently after having been told that he would be charged with murder in the death of Hans Jürgen Sonntag. According to court documents in Germany, Dalkamouni told the BKA agents that Marwan Kreeshat and Ramzi Diab had brought the 'devices' into Hashem Abassi's flat. The one-legged terrorist admitted that because he himself lacked expertise in making bombs, he 'brought [Kreeshat] especially for this purpose from Amman to Germany'.

But Dalkamouni, typically, threw in a twist. The bombs, he told the BKA, were intended to be smuggled back to Israel for use there. Why build bombs in Germany for use in Israel? That seemed odd, but Dalkamouni had a ready explanation. The PFLP-GC had no one in its organization with bomb-making expertise, he told his interrogators in his Frankfurt jail cell. Therefore, he said, 'it was easier to bring them from here to Palestine'.

The 'explanation' made no sense, for several reasons. First, although Kreeshat was not known to have made bombs for Ahmed Jibril for several years before the bombing of Pan Am 103, he had a long track record, and clearly Jibril and Dalkamouni knew where to find him. Second, what use would terrorists find for barometer-triggered bombs in Israel? Jibril would say later that such bombs could be used for exploding military vehicles in mountainous terrain, but that was ridiculous. The highest point in Israel, Mount Meron, is just under 3,700 feet – not even a mile – above sea level. One would hardly need a barometer to trigger a bomb at that elevation. No, the only reason for a barometer-triggered bomb was simple: to blow up an airplane at altitude.

Frustrated with Dalkamouni's foolishness, the BKA turned its attention elsewhere. In late April, BKA agents assigned to the Lockerbie investigation initiated a new round of intelligence-gathering operations inside Germany and began taking a closer look at the men arrested in the Autumn Leaves operation and then released. German and American agents placed the pizzeria operated by Adnan Younis under rigorous surveilllance, although it is unclear whether they learned anything useful. And they aggressively set out to find Ramzi Diab. As with Kreeshat, there had been almost no identifying information on Diab's arrest documents in October. The German police, pestered time and again by the Scots and Americans, now wanted to know more about this man Diab. In late April, some very agitated BKA agents paid a visit to Angelika Berner, a woman who had shared an apartment with him in Frankfurt. Berner remembered the officers showed her a photograph of Dalkamouni and Diab together with a suitcase at their feet. The investigators were very interested in the suitcase, Berner said, but she could not tell them what was in it. She and Diab talked often about literature, she recalled, 'and a lot about religious things.' but the BKA officers weren't interested in that.

'They showed me photographs,' she recalled months later. 'They [told me] that he was a very important military head of this organization, so that maybe he had transported . . . not the bombs [but] the materials . . . to make the bombs.'

The BKA officers also asked Angelika Berner if they could dust for Diab's fingerprints in her flat; she thought that was rather unusual. They had not paid much attention to such details on October 26. '[I] gave them something from [the] flat,' she recalled. 'But I think it's too long a time between October and April to find fingerprints.'

Evidently, it was too late to find fingerprints or anything else of evidentiary value relating to Ramzi Diab: months later the Lockerbie investigators were still searching desperately for anything to lead to him. His importance to the investigation was becoming more and more clear to the investigators. Not only had Dalkamouni labelled him as the man who had transported the bomb-making materials to Germany, but Angelika Berner had told BKA officers of a trip Diab had made out of Germany, to Vienna, she thought, just prior to the time Marwan Kreeshat had begun building his five bombs.

Diab had told the same story to his German instructor, a kindly man named German Hoch. 'He told me [he was] going to Vienna in order to . . . meet with his girlfriend and to see an uncle,' Hoch recalled afterward. And when BKA officers came to pay a call on Hoch in early May 1989, he said they were very clear about their interest in learning more about his student, the mysterious Ramzi Diab: 'I had the understanding that they presumed that Ramzi could be, or was indeed, one of the men, or the man himself, who transported the explosive material . . . of the type that exploded at Lockerbie.'

CHAPTER 15

The day seemed to last forever. It was the kind of clear day that puts a spring in the step of most Washingtonians and makes visitors to the capital think they could live happily there forever. Unfortunately, for one special group of visitors on this last day of May 1989, there would be no chance to savour the balmy air along the Potomac. This was the third high-level meeting of the Lockerbie investigators, and there was no time for sightseeing or other frivolity. At the first meeting, in London in January, it had been freezing. At the second, in Lockerbie in March, it had been raining. At least this time the weather was pleasant, even if the subject under discussion was not. Lawyers from the Justice Department just across Pennsylvania Avenue from FBI headquarters had joined the Lockerbie investigators, and there was considerable discussion about the kinds of evidence they would need to take the case against the Pan Am bombers to court. After their initial scepticism, American officials were convinced there would be no difficulty with the way the Scottish detectives went about their business; their rules of evidence, in fact, were considerably stiffer than the Americans'. There would be no problem on that score.

One Scottish detective among the visitors to Washington would not be around to see the Lockerbie investigation to its conclusion. May 31 was John Boyd's last day on the case. Just weeks before the *Maid of the Seas* fell out of the sky, Boyd had been promoted. His assumption of the new job, as Her Majesty's Inspector of the Constabulary, had been delayed as long as possible while Boyd directed the efforts of the investigators in Lockerbie. On June 1, he would have to pass those responsibilities on to a successor, a well-respected career policeman named George Esson. Finally Her Majesty's constabulary could wait no longer: Boyd would have to take up his new duties as a bureaucrat in Edinburgh.

Even more than the others before it, then, the meeting in Washington on May 31 was an exercise in taking stock.

The tragedy in Wiesbaden, with the death of Hans Jürgen Sonntag and the wounding of Thomas Ettinger, had spurred the BKA to greater efforts in the Lockerbie investigation, but there were still too many unanswered questions. No one seemed to know where Ramzi Diab was, although the investigators were chasing a number of leads. And even though Marwan Kreeshat's information was being made available through the offices of intelligence officials in Jordan, there was still something fishy about his story, and he was still too far out of reach of the criminal investigation for anyone involved in it to be happy. On the Lockerbie end of things, there was some reason for cautious optimism. The search had continued in the fields and forests around the village for months now, and still more shreds of evidence – clothing, luggage, aircraft debris – had turned up. In Lockerbie and Longtown and at Fort Halstead, detectives and forensic specialists had conclusively linked most of the 700-plus pieces of luggage to their owners. Having begun with a list of 259 potential suspects who might have had a bomb in their baggage, the investigators had narrowed it down very quickly to about twenty-five. And now, as they reviewed their findings with the lawyers from Justice, they were certain that the list was a short one indeed, no more than two of three passengers at most. There was also the very real chance, which the investigators were still looking at closely, that the bomb had been placed aboard Flight 103 in a 'rogue' bag, one that might have been interlined from somewhere else and that belonged to none of the passengers and crew aboard the *Maid of the Seas*.

Here the investigators had a problem. The bags in the bottom of baggage container 14L had been interlined in London, and included the luggage of the U.S. intelligence and security officials from the Cyprus Airways flights to London on December 21. Some of Charles McKee and Matthew Gannon's luggage had been recovered by the searchers, and most of the bags interlined in London had been ruled out as suspect. The bags that had been interlined through Frankfurt were another story, however.

And in Frankfurt the investigators had their biggest problems. Because of the way the bags had been checked and loaded there, investigators still did not know exactly how many bags on the Frankfurt–London flight had found their way into the baggage hold of the *Maid of the Seas*. Was it seventy, as Pan Am's records indicated? Or was there one more?

The questions were prompted by the multiple baggage-counting systems at Frankfurt and by the less than thorough checking by the Alert personnel on the afternoon of December 21, when Flight 103 had left Germany. More specific than these concerns, however, were the questions of some investigators about the number of bags Khalid Jaafar had actually loaded. Searchers in Scotland had found the two soft-sided bags Jaafar's friends remembered him carrying to the airport. But baggage records obtained by one investigator at some point since the crash indicated that Jaafar had checked another two bags. 'That,' said a knowledgeable U.S. official, 'is the mystery.'

And on May 31 it was a mystery still. BKA agents, accompanied by FBI investigators and Scottish detectives, continued showing photographs of Jaafar and the copper-coloured Samsonite suitcase to anyone who might have seen the two together in the hours before he boarded the 103. It was something of a schizophrenic exercise. Although the BKA seemed to be pressing forward aggressively with its end of the investigation now, the official position of the German authorities continued to be that the bomb had not been loaded onto the plane in Frankfurt.

Thus the Washington meeting was not an entirely happy one. And for some, the departure of John Boyd from the team of investigators added a special note of sadness. To many officials from the United States and Germany who had worked beside him over the past months, Boyd was something of an enigma, seemingly uncomfortable with the impressive scope of the authority that had been vested in him and absolutely intolerant of the smallest obstacle that might obstruct the progress of the investigation. In a line of work filled with too many swaggerers, braggarts and camera hogs, Boyd was a bit of an odd duck. He didn't like the limelight, and he believed in sharing responsibility. 'Security is important in carrying out an investigation,' he mused after leaving the Lockerbie case to assume his new duties. 'But it should never preclude cooperation. You should never turn away people who want to help, even if it is only to bake a cake or some scones.' It may have been an unusual notion, but to many of the Lockerbie investigators, it was refreshing to have someone so interested in results that he could ignore the lure of perks and personal aggrandizement.

Late in the day on May 31, having concluded their review of the inquiry to date, the investigators packed up their files and notebooks and prepared to depart. It was still light out in Washington, but rather than have his visitors from abroad disperse by themselves to strange hotels and restaurants, Buck Revell hosted a dinner for them that night. There remained tensions among them, to be sure. The Scots had had several bitter rows with their counterparts in London. And the

249

BKA men, despite their newfound commitment to the cause since April, were still in uncertain standing among the other investigators. But there was no reason they could not all sit down over a meal as colleagues and fellow professionals. Who knew? Such gatherings might help smooth some ruffled feathers and make the difference between success and failure in the investigation.

As thoughtful as they were, such gestures as Revell's offer of dinner and Boyd's solicitous concern for his colleagues could not conceal the deeper problems still plaguing the investigation. The BKA's recent commitment to the case was heartening, but the Germans' participation overall remained problematic. Bonn's continued denial that the bomb could have come from Frankfurt was hard to fathom, for instance, and officials in Britain and the U.S. groped for explanation.

They had theories, but that was about it. One had to do with chemical weapons and terrorists. Just weeks before the crash in Lockerbie, U.S. intelligence officials had come up with hard evidence that a German firm was assisting Libya in the construction of an enormous chemical plant. William Webster, the director of Central Intelligence, had told a meeting of the World Affairs Council in Washington about the chemical plant on October 25, the day before BKA agents had arrested Hafez Dalkamouni and the other suspects identified in the Autumn Leaves operation. The coincidence was just that. But over the next several weeks, as senior State Department officials pressed their counterparts in Bonn to take action against the company, Imhausen-Chemie GmbH, the rift between Bonn and Washington grew deeper. British officials apparently had obtained information about the activities of Imhausen in Libya at about the same time as the Americans, and they too pressed Bonn for action. Public disclosure of the chemical plant would be a disaster for the Federal Republic, but that is precisely what happened. In early January, three weeks after the Lockerbie crash, the State Department and the British Foreign Office, frustrated over the apparent lack of concern by Bonn, officially confirmed earlier leaked accounts in the press, and columnists quickly began drawing parallels between the Germans' 'irresponsible' actions in Libya and the Nazis' use of poison gas in concentration camps. Just as the Lockerbie investigators were beginning to focus more narrowly on the Frankfurt connection, relations frayed still further, when the German Finance Directorate in Freiburg announced that it had conducted a three-day inquiry into the allegations concerning Imhausen's activities in Libya and found them to be without merit. Members of the German Bundestag reacted as if stuck, protesting the 'shrill tone' and the 'unfair attacks' of Washington and Whitehall. The U.S. stood by its guns, disseminating sanitized versions of the intelligence on the Libyan plant to allies and other 'interested countries', in the words of State Department spokesman Phyllis Crockett. 'We believe this information is conclusive,' Crockett said, rejecting the protests from Bonn out of hand.

Only after police found the deputy manager of Imhausen in his locked car in a forest (he had swallowed what was described as a 'massive dose' of sleeping pills) did a German prosecutor request the BKA to conduct a thorough investigation of the company's activities in Libya. And only in mid-February did Wolfgang Schaeuble, chief of staff to Chancellor Helmut Kohl, concede publicly that the Libyans had, in fact, been assisted with construction of the poison-gas plant by not one but two German companies. The new administration of George Bush professed publicly to be 'encouraged' by the German response, but privately many officials said that relations between Washington and Bonn had been deeply harmed by the episode. And

251

some officials participating in the Lockerbie investigation termed the affair 'a disaster'.

In England and Scotland, some of the investigators believed they had another explanation for what they described as the Germans' unhelpful approach to the Lockerbie inquiry. Not only had the BKA been called on to assist with the investigation, but representatives of the BfV, the interior intelligence agency, and the BND, the intelligence service operating outside Germany, also had been asked to help. Some officials in Lockerbie and London agreed with Buck Revell in believing that the BKA was 'cooperating fully with the investigation, and they placed the blame for the problems on the German intelligence community. The officials conceded they had little evidence to support their theory, but they pointed to the increasing number of attacks by the Irish Republican Army on British soldiers stationed in Germany. According to several British intelligence officials, the IRA had begun targeting the troops in Europe because their barracks were less protected and more accessible than those in Northern Ireland. The attacks had begun in 1978, but in March 1987, a massive 300-pound bomb had exploded at the joint headquarters of the British Army of the Rhine and RAF Germany in Rheinalden. German and British authorities say that marked the beginning of an increasingly violent IRA campaign against British troops in Germany that has resulted in the murder of at least eight soldiers or their dependents, and the wounding of at least fifty other people, including several small children.

BfV agents investigating the attacks discovered an IRA arsenal near the Dutch border in early 1989. But they discovered something else as well: a small team of British agents who had been shadowing the so-called 'action service unit' of the IRA that had been responsible for many of the attacks. A British intelligence official said he knew of no such team of agents dispatched to Germany, but he conceded that a team of

Special Air Service commandos could have been sent without the knowledge of the intelligence agencies in London. In March 1988, SAS commandos, evidently acting on a tip from an informant, had killed three IRA terrorists in Gibraltar, and they were fully capable of mounting a similar operation in Germany. The SAS were among the elite of the counter-terrorist forces, smart, smooth, and able to blend into virtually any background while they gathered information for their lightning-quick strikes. The typical SAS man looked like the boy next door, but he could kill you as quickly as look at you, and in a half-dozen ways.

'It wasn't us skulking around in the Federal Republic,' a British intelligence official said. 'But it could have been the baby-faced killers of the SAS. And if it was, they wouldn't tell us, and they certainly wouldn't have told Bonn.'

Miffed by the apparent discovery of a foreign paramilitary force in its own backyard, Bonn protested vigorously to Whitehall, several officials said. How much of a fuss was made is unclear, but it cannot have helped matters when the Lockerbie investigators came calling for help.

Buck Revell had his own theory of the case that, for simplicity at least, beat all else and maybe made the most sense. The hasty release of the Autumn Leaves suspects, the failure to find Marwan Kreseshat's bombs, and the death of one bomb technician and the grave wounding of another all created great humiliation for the normally efficient German authorities. 'I think there is a great deal of chagrin over the way this thing has unfolded,' Revell said, 'and it has been an embarrassment to them.'

Embarrassment among policemen has soured more than one investigation, and Revell got a taste of just how prickly the Germans had become when he attended a meeting of senior police officials in Madrid in June. There he encountered Hans Neusel, the German deputy interior minister who had given him such a chilly reception in Bonn back in April. Revell had recently spoken with a reporter from the German magazine *Stern* about the progress of the Lockerbie investigation and had stated the detectives believed the bomb had been placed on board Flight 103 in Frankfurt. Neusel was not at all pleased by the assertion. 'He was rather annoyed at me at the time,' Revell recalled. 'But what I said had already been released by the Scottish authorities, and I was simply restating our concurrence with that.'

The Germans, however, would still not admit the Frankfurt connection, and their refusal to do so only made things more difficult for the investigators.

While the policemen hashed their problems out among themselves and the intelligence officials pursued their own separate inquiries, the man who may have been ultimately responsible for the bombing of Pan Am Flight 103 went and died. On June 4, eleven months after the downing of the Iranian airbus in the Persian Gulf, the Ayatollah Ruhollah Khomeini, the Islamic holy man whose fervour had inspired his countrymen to drive Shah Mohammed Reza Pahlavi from the Peacock Throne on January 15, 1979, lay dead after surgery to stop bleeding in his digestive system.

Khomeini had been born in 1900, 1901 or 1902 (the most widely accepted date is May 27, 1900), and although few people would have given him any chance of influencing much of anything as he approached the last years of his life, he literally shaped the course of world events as he and the century entered their eighth decade together. Khomeini's followers had helped drive one American president, Jimmy Carter, from the White House. And his guile and cleverness had hobbled another, Ronald Reagan, and lured him into the arms-for-hostages negotiations in the Iran-contra affair.

As George Bush pondered the implications of

Khomeini's death in early June 1989, he certainly knew of his intelligence agencies' conclusions about Iran's involvement in the Lockerbie bombing. Indeed, he had little need of reminders. On April 3, the president had met with some of the families of the Lockerbie victims, while others held a vigil in Lafayette Park across the street from the White House. The families had asked about Iran, among many other things. Bush's schedulers had allotted just twenty minutes for the meeting, but he had wound up spending nearly an hour and a half with them, and by all accounts of those present, he had been deeply moved by their stories. A month after this meeting, Bush had a more unpleasant reminder of the tough questions posed by Iran's involvement in the Pan Am tragedy. Hashemi Rafsanjani, still Iran's preeminent politician despite the inroads made in recent months by the powerful interior minister, Mohtashemi, had shown just how radicalized Iran still was. Rafsanjani was the favourite 'moderate' of most Iran-watchers, but in early May, this 'moderate' proposed that for every Palestinian killed by Israeli soldiers attempting to put down the *intifada*, five Americans, British and French should be murdered. Rafsanjani backed off the statement a few days later, but he had achieved his objective: that no one, not even the obsessive Mohtashemi, would have more hard-line credentials than he.

While specialists at the State Department and Pentagon and on the National Security Council staff pondered how to deal with Iran, and the investigators in Britain and Germany proceeded with the incremental task of gathering and analyzing evidence, the families of the people who perished in the night sky over Scotland were not content to wait for results. They had suffered grievously, but unlike many of the relatives of others killed in terrorist attacks, these people, most of them, were organizing to ensure that some good would come

255

from their loss. Their loved ones had died so horribly, but perhaps, if they worked hard enough, the victims' families and friends believed, they could help see that others might be spared the kind of pain they were enduring.

Not every family was so strong. At least one person attempted suicide, one died of a heart attack, another developed a bleeding ulcer and kept throwing up blood. Still others suffered in silence, unable to sleep, eat and focus on the details of everyday life. To their everlasting credit, most of the families and friends of those who died in Lockerbie fought through the sense of loss and depression, and within weeks after the disaster they were meeting with one another to determine how they might translate their loss into something more positive. The result of these many separate discussions was a group called Victims of Pan Am Flight 103, and its more than 300 members meant to see that every last question raised by the Lockerbie disaster was answered. It was not enough that they were able to spend time with the president and convey their story to him. They wanted action, and they mobilized on a number of fronts to see that they got it. Government officials who met with members of the organization said it was a more cohesive and determined group than any they had ever seen, more so even than the families of the American hostages held in Iran and, later on, Lebanon.

Within Victims of Pan Am Flight 103, the members established a political action committee, a legal committee, an investigation committee and a press committee. They were not experts on terrorism, police issues or airport security, but they knew what they wanted. Their demands were simple: notification of passengers and airport and airline personnel of all serious security threats; better detection equipment, better-trained security personnel and more rigorous security procedures at airports; better coordination and communication among all government agencies responsible for gathering intelligence on and combating airline terrorism; and the establishment of mandatory crisis-management policies and procedures throughout the airline industry. They were not, the great majority of them, politically oriented people, and they were not, as one grieving father put it, 'people looking for a cause'. They were people like Stan and Norma Maslowski who, while aching with the loss of their daughter Diane, vowed that her death would not be meaningless, that whatever mistakes had been made that allowed terrorists to place a bomb on a plane and erase 270 lives must be addressed and fixed. On her blouse, like many of the other relatives of those who died, Norma Maslowski often wore a button that said: 'Pan Am 103: The Truth Must Be Known.'

Other members of Victims of Pan Am Flight 103 were Victoria Cummock, Paul Hudson and Bert Ammerman. Cummock's husband, John, a thirty-eight-year-old marketing vice-president for Bacardi Foods, was believed to have been the last person to have boarded the 103 before it backed away from Heathrow's Terminal 3. He did not have a reservation and had been scheduled to fly the following day, December 22. But he had concluded his business in London early and wanted to get back home, southern Florida, to see his wife and their three young children. The daughter of a diplomat, Victoria Cummock knew what it took to make a message heard in Washington, and she wrote hundreds of letters, testified before Congress and met with senior members of the Bush administration. Her message? 'It can never happen again.' Paul Hudson had lost his sixteen-year-old daughter, Melina, on the 103. Since then he had virtually given up his law practice to use his time and talent as an advocate for change. Bert Ammerman, a New Jersey school superintendent, had lost his thirty-six-year-old brother, Tom, in Lockerbie. He was tireless in explaining again and again the concerns and the issues of Victims of Pan Am Flight 103, and he had become the leader of the organization. 'As long as I keep doing this,' Ammerman said, months after the crash in Lockerbie, 'my brother is still alive.'

Among the other families of victims were Charles and Phyllis Rosenthal; they lost their twenty-two-year-old daughter, Andrea, who had fulfilled her lifelong dream of travelling in Asia after graduating from Brown. Daniel and Susan Cohen lost their daughter Theodora, an effervescent young woman who had been studying drama in London.

For everyone who had lost a loved one, life became virtually unbearable, a combination of unrelenting pain, guilt and loneliness. The grief was particularly acute for parents who, like the Hudsons, Rosenthals and Cohens, lost their children. On December 21, 1988, they became mourners for those they had nurtured from birth. Yet for many, the emotional paralysis gave way to a sense of mission, to ensure that those responsible for the bombing of Pan Am 103 would be brought to justice.

By early summer 1989, Victims of Pan Am Flight 103 was publishing a regular newsletter and picketing the offices of Pan Am in New York, and was well on its way to meeting with all hundred United States senators or their aides. In Britain, the families and friends of victims from there formed a similar group, called United Kingdom Families Flight 103. Its goals were almost identical to those of its counterpart in the United States, and the two groups communicated back and forth regularly. There was some friction among some members of the U.S. organization over means and methods of expressing their views (it eventually split into two), and some of those who lost loved ones in the disaster either could not participate because of the heavy emotional strain or would not, for other reasons. Bruce Smith, the Pan Am captain whose wife, Ingrid, had perished at Lockerbie, was less concerned about the more procedural issues the Victims organization was focusing on than about the simple desire that those responsible be made to pay. He had already earmarked a $100,000 settlement for Ingrid Smith's death as the down payment on what he hoped to build into a $5 million reward fund. Anyone who came forward with information that led to the capture and conviction of the Pan Am bombers would get the entire sum. That was Bruce Smith's dream, anyway. But other relatives of those who died were uncomfortable with the notion of revenge, he said. Smith carried on alone. Single-handedly, he lobbied members of Congress and officials at the State Department and the FBI to support his campaign for a government contribution to his reward fund. It was slow going. Many of those Smith approached were sympathetic over his loss but chary of what they saw as his obsession. Some officials, including Buck Revell, believed a big reward just might work, however, and they gave the Pan Am captain their support.

On June 24, six months after the crash in Lockerbie, 150 members of Victims of Pan Am Flight 103 gathered in the auditorium of Haddonfield High School in Haddonfield, New Jersey, not far from Philadelphia. They had come, several from far away, to discuss the status of the Lockerbie investigation, to commiserate with each other and to ensure that their grief was channelled into effective action. They did not consider their questions unreasonable, and they intended to put them to the government officials in attendance that morning.

Frank Moss, the State Department official who had monitored the Lockerbie investigation from the very first moments after the crash, had volunteered to come to Haddonfield that Saturday morning. It meant giving up a day off, and a three-hour drive up the highway from Washington, but Moss believed the relatives of those who had been murdered deserved answers. He had been deeply involved in the work of intelligence officials that had helped narrow the list of suspects. But he had also been in contact almost daily with various family members, and he felt their pain and anger deeply. Part of the problem that morning in Haddonfield, however, was that the anger of many of the relatives was directed at the State Department, which Moss, however much he shared their pain, was representing. He knew it would not be easy. In response to one question about the validity of the Helsinki threat, Moss explained that the call from Samra Mahayoun had been examined thoroughly at the time and reexamined several times since. There was nothing to it, Moss said; it was no more than a 'ghoulish coincidence'.

In the rear of the high school auditorium, a woman began shrieking. Her face was etched in pain, and tears were streaming down her cheeks. There was no way of consoling her, and no one even tried. They listened quietly as the woman screamed at Moss: 'How dare you! I am grieving for the loss of my twenty-year-old son. Do you understand what that means? I don't have a son anymore, and you stand up there and speak to these people in this way? How dare you!'

Clearly, there was nothing that could be said.

Among those in Haddonfield on June 24 was Ceil Buonocore. She was one of the few people who had not lost a family member or a friend in the fireball of Lockerbie. On December 28, 1985, Mrs. Buonocore had received a telex from the State Department at her home in Wilmington, Delaware. 'It is with profound regret,' the cable read, 'that we must inform you of the death on December 27, 1985, of your son, John J. Buonocore III. The Ministry of the Interior in Rome, Italy, informed the American Embassy in Rome . . . of his death from injuries sustained during a terrorist attack at the Rome Airport.' The attack had been carried out by Samir Kadar, the Professor, of the Abu Nidal terrorist organization. John Buonocore had been among the twelve people killed. Sixty more had been wounded.

In Haddonfield, Ceil Buonocore told of her horror on

receiving the State Department cable and of learning the terrible details of her son's death. There were indignities as well, she told the people in the auditorium. To obtain her son's body, she had had to send a Western Union money order for $900 to the State Department immediately. On receipt of the cheque in Washington, the 'remains' of her son would be returned to the United States, where she could claim them. The auditorium was perfectly silent as Mrs. Buonocore told her story. The friends and family of many who died in Lockerbie had similar tales of sorrow and outrage. But that was not what Ceil Buonocore had come to talk to them about. Her message, she said, had to do with her life in the years since her son's death. She had pressured Washington to learn more about what precautions were being taken against future terrorist attacks. Her efforts were about as effective, she said, as 'dropping a rose petal down the side of the Grand Canyon and waiting to hear an echo'. But she had persisted, she told the people in Haddonfield, because life, despite the pain of loss, has to continue. Life must continue, Ceil Buonocore said in conclusion; there is no alternative.

The families and friends of those killed in Lockerbie gave Mrs. Buonocore a standing ovation that morning. And later in the afternoon, at a reception at Stan and Norma Maslowski's house, a small clutch of friends and relatives of the Lockerbie victims were still talking about her. 'She, unlike most of us, has come to grips with being happy again,' one woman said. Suddenly, out of nowhere, Mrs. Buonocore appeared. In a spontaneous gesture, everyone in the group hugged her.

Like his predecessor, George Esson began each day in the Lockerbie investigation the same way. Behind his big, well-ordered desk in the Incident Control Centre, he sat down promptly at 9:00 A.M. with John Orr, the senior investigating officer, to lay out the day's tasks. When John Boyd's promotion to Edinburgh had been made known, senior police officials announced that applications for the Dumfries and Galloway job would be accepted from appropriately credentialled officers. The deadline for filing the applications was December 21, 1988. George Esson had gotten in just under the wire.

Six months later, having been awarded the job and having assumed control of the most exhaustive counter-terrorism investigation ever, he might reasonably be pardoned for wondering what he had gotten himself in for. Esson, a squarish, compact man with a pleasant smile and carefully barbered hair, professed to be undaunted by the task. Not only did he have John Orr to rely on to maintain the continuity of the inquiry, but he himself was one of the most highly regarded policemen in the ranks of the Scottish force. He was also no stranger to disaster investigations. Two years before Lockerbie, he had directed the inquiry into the crash of an RAF Chinook helicopter that had crashed near Aberdeen, killing forty-four people. Before that, he had assisted in the investigation of an Occidental Piper-Alfa that had crashed with 162 people on board. Still, Esson readily conceded that Lockerbie was beyond the scope of anything he had ever experienced. 'What you've got is a murder inquiry times 270,' he said shortly after assuming direction of the Lockerbie investigation. 'It is complicated by international aspects, by interline baggage. . . . You have thirty-one nationalities, [the] majority Americans, causing great concern there. You put all that potpourri together, and you have a criminal inquiry that is unique.'

By the end of June, the search teams directed by George Esson and John Orr numbered just about a hundred. The HOLMES-generated computer files bulged with detailed descriptions of clothing, luggage and other personal belongings. And still new clues were coming in, prompting flurries of phone calls between Lockerbie, London and Buzzard Point. 'You have a lot of things,' Esson said, 'that take you down the road of routine police work.' It would make or break the Lockerbie investigation.

In the middle of June, the police thought they might have their break. In a dense wood, one of the searchers had recovered a lock that appeared to have come from a Samsonite bag. The lock was locked, the key and anything else that might have connected it to the copper-coloured Samsonite that held the bomb were missing. If the key could be found, however, it could be the critical link to the passenger who had checked the bag. Perhaps the key had already even been found. There were plenty of keys among the possessions of the 259 people on Flight 103. They were checked to see if they fit the lock, and the HOLMES computers whirred as detectives examined property logs to see if there were keys not yet attributed to any of the passengers.

Nothing. Evidently, try as they might, the detectives found no match for the mystery lock, or they concluded that the lock itself was irrelevant to the investigation. Whatever the case, the discovery had generated a spark of enthusiasm among the investigators and gave them renewed energy to keep going through July.

In the middle of July, one of the stalwarts of the Lockerbie investigation, Angus Kennedy, received devastating news. Since late December he had worked the same long hours as other Lockerbie investigators. With the shattered families of the victims, he had been patient and gentle. With unruly reporters, he had been firm and helpful, but unyielding on points of principle, of which the essential one was: Do nothing to upset the bereaved unduly. Through it all, he had been a professional, a policeman's policeman. When some families complained about tardy return of the belongings of their loved ones and others griped about the complicated Scottish legal system, it was Angus Kennedy who had been dispatched to the United States to meet with them. Patiently, he had explained how the investiga-

263

tion was being conducted and why, if the families hoped to see convictions of those who murdered their loved ones, certain procedural rules of evidence must be followed. It was not an easy line to sell. But many family members said they accepted the word of Detective Superintendent Kennedy because of his fundamental decency and honesty, and because of his obvious participation in their grief, almost as if it were his own.

Angus Kennedy could have been excused if he no longer found room in his big heart for the grief of others. His wife, Katie, had been feeling poorly, and she was diagnosed as having a weak gallbladder. When she went into the hospital to have it removed, surgeons discovered the real reason for her poor health: she had a cancerous growth so extensive she was given just two days to live. Katie Kennedy fought bravely for much longer than that, but Angus knew it was only a matter of time before she was gone. All that he could do now was make her as comfortable as possible in the short time left.

After Lockerbie, further loss seemed just too hard to bear.

But the investigators carried on, and their efforts were finally rewarded by a real break in the case. Strangely enough, though, it led not to Frankfurt, but to Malta. In Lockerbie, at one of their 9:00 A.M. sessions toward the very end of July, George Esson, John Orr and Stuart Henderson got out their maps.

CHAPTER 16

It is a small place, Malta, as different from Lockerbie as any place could possibly be. A tiny archipelago in the central Mediterranean, some sixty miles south of Sicily and 200 miles north of Libya , Malta, like Lockerbie, does not normally find itself in the main run of the world's events. In the late fall of 1989, George Bush and Mikhail Gorbachev would hold a shipboard summit in the storm-roiled waters just off Malta, but in early August, when Harry Bell, a Scottish detective, stepped off a plane at Malta's tiny international airport, the place was quiet, the weather brutally hot, and the one parallel with Lockerbie that really meant anything – the size of the place – manifested itself almost immediately. Just as most people in Lockerbie know a bit about their friends' and neighbours' business, they are quick to learn of a stranger's presence in the village. So it is in Malta. Within a week of Bell's arrival, an FBI special agent from squad C-3 was also in Malta, and soon stories of detectives with funny accents and FBI men in freshly pressed tropical-weight suits began making the rounds. Within a week, the local *Times*, desperate for any news in the dog days of August, even ran a brief item on the policeman's visit. The islands were abuzz. And the Lockerbie investigators were aghast.

After months of steady but slow progress, the Malta connection was a big break, and they didn't want to blow it because of untimely publicity. Unfortunately, there was not much they could do but go about their business as quietly as possible and hope for the best.

265

Not surprisingly, the trail to Malta had begun with the searchers still crawling through the fields and the forests around Lockerbie. With spring's turn to summer, and temperatures approaching 100 degrees on some days, the bright green fields had begun fading to brown; and for the first time in recent memory, trout and salmon had virtually disappeared from the abundant streams and rivers of southern Scotland, avoiding the torpid weather in cool deep pools, too hot even to eat.

The weather had not prevented George Esson and John Orr from pressing on with the search for evidence, however; indeed, the clue that would lead the investigators to Malta was recovered on one of the worst of the very hot days. In appearance, it seemed no more remarkable than the 10,000 other items recovered from Lockerbie and catalogued in the HOLMES computer system. Like the other scraps and shards, the remnants of the 270 lives shattered in the crash, this one spoke painfully of the force and violence of the explosion. The piece of evidence in question was a jumpsuit, designed to be worn by a small baby.

The small bit of blue cotton fabric that had survived after the crash is said to have been scorched and burned. Nothing special there; so much of the clothing and other debris that fell in and around Lockerbie was charred by fires on the ground. What was special about the jumpsuit is that the manufacturer's label had somehow remained intact despite the explosion and the long fall to earth. The label read 'Babygro', and Lockerbie investigators seized it eagerly. Preliminary checking showed that Babygro was a label used by Yorkie Clothing Ltd., a Maltese clothing manufacturer. Further investigation determined that the jumpsuit recovered in Lockerbie was one of a batch of only 500. Some of those 500 had been kept for sale in Malta, the rest shipped off to stores and shops in Ireland. That set bells ringing. Perhaps the investigators had been wrong from the very beginning. Maybe the destruction of Flight 103 was not the doing of Palestinian terrorists in Germany, but more of the bloody piecework of the Irish Republican Army. One of the first, false leads brought investigators to Dublin.

Meanwhile, forensic specialists at the Royal Armaments Research and Development Establishment at Fort Halstead continued with their analysis. Authorities knowledgeable about the investigation would not give precise information on this point, but they said that laboratory tests showed conclusively that the Babygro jumpsuit was inside the copper-coloured Samsonite suitcase that contained the bomb. The evidence that might establish such a link might include residue of the Semtex explosive or traces of the hot gases given off in the explosion.

In any case, the discovery added yet another question to the investigators' already long list. It would be unlikely, at the very least, that a male passenger would have a baby's jumpsuit in his belongings. It had to be one of the women on board the 103, perhaps one of the young college women, who might have been given a suitcase to carry for a friend or acquaintance. The investigators, who had been focusing on the possibility that Khalid Jaafar or another male passenger had carried the bomb aboard, shifted their focus once again.

The only way they could resolve the questions for sure was by going to Malta. For the Scots and the Americans, Malta was very far from the worst of places to conduct such inquiries. Although the island nation still maintains rather close ties with Libya, which added a certain element of danger for the investigators, it also has a strong and healthy relationship with the United Kingdom. A former Crown Colony, Malta suffered heavy aerial bombardment in World War II and was awarded the George Cross in 1942 by King George VI. The bonds had frayed considerably since then, but by the late 1980s, things were improving once again. In

May 1987, Prime Minister Fenech Adami publicly announced his intention to establish closer ties with the United States and Western Europe. And in September 1988, Adami met with Prime Minister Margaret Thatcher to discuss further improvement in bilateral relations. Thus British and American police officials had a solid political footing on which to begin. Now, if only they could keep their visit quiet for a while, they might have a bit of luck. Fortunately, the Malta *Times* item seems to have gone virtually unnoticed, even in the capital of Valletta, where the investigators were staying. Even so, they would take precautions. With the cooperation of Maltese police authorities, at least two of the witnesses questioned by the investigators would be put under twenty-four-hour armed guard. There were reports that the investigators themselves were armed during their stay in Malta, but that could not be confirmed. 'The fear,' said one investigator, 'was [not for us], but for the people there.'

As they began work in Malta, the investigators paid one of several visits to Yorkie Clothing. There they spoke with Victor Calleja, who easily identified the jumpsuit as one of his own. We have a ticket we put on all our clothes, Calleja said, according to informed sources. That enabled him to determine roughly when an article of clothing was manufactured and where it was distributed.

Evidently, Calleja or someone else was able to determine that the Babygro recovered in Lockerbie had been sold not in Ireland but in Malta. Like so many other leads, the IRA link was thus deemed to be without merit, the blue cotton jumpsuit pointing to Belfast yet another red herring. From Yorkie's records, the investigators obtained a list of all the shops and boutiques on Malta that sold its clothing. Malta was a small place, and it was not long after the investigators had fanned out to talk with shopowners that they came up with a winner.

At a pleasant family-run boutique on Tower Road in the resort village of Sliema, not far from the capital, one of the investigators obtained a positive match on the jumpsuit. The store was called Mary's House, and the shopkeeper there said he was certain he remembered the man who had purchased the Babygro jumpsuit. The man was muscular and spoke with a Libyan accent. He was clean-shaven, with dark eyes and neatly trimmed hair; he appeared to be in his middle to late thirties, maybe a bit older. After some thought, the shopkeeper placed the man's visit on November 23.

But the shopkeeper remembered the man who bought the jumpsuit for another reason, he told investigators: the good fortune of the man's visit. He had come in off the street and started buying 'an unusual selection', in the words of one of the investigators. He had purchased not only the jumpsuit but a pair of pyjamas, a pair of men's pants and a heavy tweed jacket as well. No two items the man bought were the same size, the shopkeeper recalled. The merchant then showed the investigators two pairs of pants he still had in stock. Mary's House had purchased only three pairs, the shopkeeper said; the customer had bought the one pair, and the remaining two were from the same batch. The investigator noted the batch number. What the shopkeeper remembered most about the man's purchases was not the pyjamas, the pants or the jumpsuit, but the tweed jacket. In Malta's usually warm weather, the heavy sports coat was a dog; for nearly seven years Mary's House had been unable to sell it, no matter how often it cut the price. The man with the strange shopping habits had bought it all.

As his acquisitions were being wrapped, the shopkeeper recalled, a heavy squall blew up; he had asked his customer if he needed an umbrella. The man said he would indeed like one, and after he'd paid, he tucked his parcel of clothing under his arm, snapped open his new umbrella and ducked out into the blowing wind and rain.

It was an astonishing piece of luck, such a detailed recollection. Now the investigators had plenty more to go on. In Lockerbie, detectives waited anxiously by a fax machine for a police sketch of the visitor to Mary's House. When the fax finally came through, a detective groaned. 'It looks like Qaddafi,' he said. Within a day or two after the visit to Mary's House a HOLMES technician had sent the powerful computer whirring, searching for references to the kinds of clothing described by the helpful shopkeeper in Malta.

At Fort Halstead, forensic specialists went back to the lab bench. The testing process would be as exacting as ever, but this time they knew precisely what to look for. And after a relatively brief but painstaking examination they had it: The tweed jacket, apparently, had been blown into bits by the bomb, but fragments of it had been recovered from shards of the copper-coloured Samsonite. The HOLMES had pinpointed fragments of an umbrella recovered by the searchers, and lab technicians at Fort Halstead subjected it to a thorough microscopic analysis and came up winners again: fibres from the Babygro jumpsuit had been blasted into the fabric of the umbrella.

There was only one conclusion: the umbrella, the tweed jacket and the blue cotton jumpsuit had been purchased for one purpose and one purpose only, to wrap around the radio–cassette player bomb concealed in the suitcase. Whoever had bought those clothes, the investigators surmised, knew plenty about the bomb and, probably, who planted it.

This meant also that the assumption that the bomb was carried aboard by a woman passenger was not necessarily valid. It could have been carried aboard by anyone. And it could have been interlined from Malta through Frankfurt and on to London. This was maddening. Every new lead, it seemed, yielded dozens more questions.

The Lockerbie investigators already knew that a flight from Malta had landed in Frankfurt just under four hours before the first leg of Flight 103 had departed Germany. One of the first things they had done in examining the ways a bomb might have been put on board the 103 in Frankfurt was to look at all connecting flights that day. Air Malta Flight KM 180 had left Valetta at 10:15 A.M. on December 21 and arrived at Frankfurt Main shortly before 1:00 P.M. Pan Am 103 from Frankfurt hadn't left until 4:50 P.M. Air Malta records showed that, of the thirty-nine passengers on KM 180, most were stopping in Frankfurt, but one was going on to Düsseldorf, two to Münster, one to Bremen, four to Prague and four to Miami. The Miami-bound quartet had booked tickets initially on Pan Am 103 to New York, where they were to have taken a connecting flight to Miami International. That was interesting.

Further checking by the investigators in Malta, however, showed that the four passengers, all relatives of an Air Malta employee, had changed their travel plans at the last minute, and booked a quicker and more convenient Lufthansa flight through to Miami.

The investigators continued interviewing airline and airport staff in Valletta, but they were hampered by what one of the investigators described as a 'terribly sloppy' record of the passengers and baggage on KM 180. An Air Malta statement asserted that its 'computer check-in tallies match *precisely* the physical count made by the staff loading bags onto KM 180 on 21 December 1988' and that, of the fifty-five pieces loaded onto the plane, all were properly accounted for and none had been interlined to London or the United States.

The investigators were not so sure. There were some anomalies, they said, that had to be looked into. A four-man television film crew, for instance, was shown to have checked seventeen pieces of baggage, although

271

the records indicated each had checked only one suitcase of personal belongings. The rest, it turned out,
had been film and camera gear, and they had spread it
among themselves.

Because so many of the KM 180 passengers had dead-
ended in Germany, the Lockerbie investigators were
obliged to conduct interviews there with their counterparts from the BKA. Once again, according to knowledgeable officials, there were problems in coordination
and in gaining access to people in a timely manner.
Lockerbie investigators were unable to locate or interview about a half-dozen of the thirty-nine KM 180 passengers, and there were further complaints that the
German authorities had reason to believe the Malta connection was important well before Scottish and American investigators had gone to Malta in August. A
senior official in the United Kingdom says there is no
merit to the latter complaint, but he concedes that there
was deep frustration over the failure to interview all the
passengers on the Air Malta flight, so much so that the
matter of the Germans' cooperation in the Lockerbie
inquiry was raised with Prime Minister Thatcher.

Among the most puzzling questions raised by the
Malta connection to Lockerbie was that of interline baggage. Although Air Malta's records might well have
been correct, in that no bags were interlined on KM 180
through Frankfurt to London, investigators in Malta
would later discover evidence of what appeared to be
a smuggling operation using 'mules', or unwitting air
passengers, to carry suitcases containing Lord knows
what to Europe.

A British couple who had been on vacation in Malta
in the autumn of 1989 read a news account of the investigators' suspicions about a Maltese link to the Lockerbie tragedy and telephoned the agents to relate their
own suspicions. Three weeks before the departure of
Air Malta KM 180 on December 21, Geoffrey and Christine Middleton had gone to Valletta to recover from

the death of their son. Later, they recalled sitting in a waterfront bistro in Sliema – the picturesque village where the Mary's House boutique is located – and watching as a buxom blonde and an Arab man made their way around the bar, approaching several patrons with questions about a suitcase.

'It was most peculiar,' Geoffrey Middleton, a BritRail depot manager in south London, recalled later. 'She was very brassy and dripping in jewelry. We thought she was on the make she had so much front.'

According to the Middletons, who were interviewed by a team of Lockerbie investigators, the woman approached at least three people at the bar, saying she had asked a friend to take a suitcase to the airport in Malta. The suitcase, she said, was full of fluffy toys, but her friend had failed to show up and collect it. The woman then asked one of the three patrons, a drunken Englishman according to the Middletons, if he would bring her suitcase to London. The Middletons left the bistro before the Arab man and the blonde could approach them, but they had a good idea what the couple was up to. Drugs, they figured, it had to be that. After they learned of the connection to Malta, they figured again.

And so, for a time, did the Lockerbie investigators.

CHAPTER 17

Malta was far from the strangest place investigators ventured, chasing this or that oddball lead. By late August 1989, members of the Lockerbie team had travelled to nearly forty countries, including several in the Far East. Some of the Scottish detectives, who before rarely had had occasion to venture as far as London, were fetching up now, suitcase in hand, pockets jammed with maps, in cities from Athens to Singapore. If they failed to get the evidence they needed to catch and convict the murderers of Lockerbie, it would not be for failure to run down clues. They chased everything. So anxious were some American officials at the Scots' tenacity that several Justice Department memoranda in the autumn of 1989 reflected concerns that the FBI was not keeping up with the Scots. Scottish investigators were first in Malta, and they moved on several other leads before even telling the Bureau. 'We were worried,' said one Justice Department lawyer, 'that we weren't protecting our prosecutive equities.'

There was one lead, however, to which neither the Scots nor the Americans had paid much attention early on. Pursuing it did not mean arduous travel to hostile places; it involved a brief flight to one of the world's most civilized, if expensive, countries. The place was Sweden.

On the morning of May 18, 1989, more than a hundred special agents of the Säkerhetspolis, the Swedish government security agency known as SAPO, had raided several apartments in Stockholm, Göteborg and

Uppsala and arrested fifteen people described as members of a radical Palestinian terrorist organization known as the Palestine Popular Struggle Front. A small offshoot of the Palestine Liberation Organization, the PPSF had been created after the June 1967 Arab–Israeli war and had moved its headquarters to Damascus in 1982. The Lockerbie investigators initially paid little attention to the Swedish arrests because the PPSF was believed to be a bitter rival of Ahmed Jibril's Popular Front for the Liberation of Palestine – General Command. It seemed highly improbable that two rival terrorist organizations would collaborate on an operation, even if it were directed against a common enemy, in this case the United States.

By midsummer at the latest, the Lockerbie investigators seem to have begun reevaluating that assumption. And then they quickly became very interested in the Swedish connection. Scottish and American investigators visited several times to consult with the police in Stockholm. By August, the peripatetic Buck Revell had also made a visit.

What the Lockerbie investigators learned surprised them. The trail from Lockerbie was like one of those Chinese firecracker snakes, squiggling this way and that with no apparent rhyme or reason. First Frankfurt, then Malta, now Sweden.

The arrests by the SAPO agents in May had marked the culmination of a surveillance operation that had begun just the month before, following an alert from the BKA. There was, it turned out, a definite link between Sweden and Germany.

The bomb from Hashem Abassi's grocery store that had exploded, killing Hans Jürgen Sonntag and critically wounding Thomas Ettinger, had set some BKA agents hurrying back to examine the surveillance records of the Autumn Leaves operation, while others began reinterviewing Hafez Dalkamouni, his jailmate Abdel Ghadanfar and the beleaguered Hashem Abassi,

275

who police continued to believe was the most hapless of innocents in the whole affair.

From these interviews, supplemented by the review of the Autumn Leaves records, BKA investigators now had a better fix on some of the visitors they had watched coming and going from 16 Isarstrasse. On October 14, twelve days before they wrapped up the Autumn Leaves investigation, BKA agents had seen a white Volvo sedan with Swedish licence plates outside the address. The Volvo, they learned, belonged to a man named Martin Imandi. At the time, the agents had duly noted the car and the three people carrying packages and suitcases in and out of the building. But they did not know what to make of it. They knew that Dalkamouni was staying in the flat with Abassi. And they knew that Abassi's brother, Ahmed, had come from Uppsala to serve as Dalkamouni's translator. But who were the other people in Imandi's Volvo?

Only after the death of Sonntag and the wounding of Ettinger did the BKA agents find out. From Ghadanfar's and Dalkamouni's statements and from a search of German and Swedish police and immigration records, they established this chronology: On September 5, 1988 – even before Operation Autumn Leaves had begun – a Syrian Arab Airlines plane from Damascus had touched down just after 7:00 P.M. in Munich; Martin Imandi waited anxiously in the airport's international-arrivals lounge. Aboard the flight had been his two brothers, Ziad and Jehad, and a cousin, Samar Ourfali. Although none of the three had proper immigration papers, evidently they'd had no difficulty clearing customs and immigration, and Martin Imandi had soon had them all heading north by train to Sweden. According to the reconstruction of events by BKA agents, the party of four had gotten off the train in Denmark, intending, apparently, to sneak into Sweden, where Imandi lived, without going through customs.

In Denmark they decided to take a ferry. Police there

interrupted their plans, however. As the four men waited nervously at the ferry depot in Rodwhavm harbour, a police officer asked to see their passports. There were indications that several had been altered. And sure enough, further checking by Danish police confirmed the suspicion: The passports were forged. Martin Imandi's three relatives were sent back to Munich, where the oldest brother, Ziad, soon boarded a plane back to Damascus. Imandi himself, who had a valid Swedish passport, returned to Uppsala. And according to Swedish intelligence officials, his younger brother and his cousin soon telephoned Imandi in Uppsala. This was in late September or early October. Intelligence officials say it was not possible to determine conclusively whether it was Martin Imandi's voice they heard as they listened in on the conversation, but whoever it was gave the two men precise travel instructions. Go to Hashem Abassi's grocery store at 14 Neumarkt in Neuss, the man on the phone said. At the grocery store, apparently, Abassi directed the two men to his flat at 16 Isarstrasse. Now things were beginning to make sense.

Two of the men in Imandi's Volvo outside Abassi's flat now had names. They were Jehad, Imandi's younger brother, and Samar Ourfali. But who had been behind the wheel when the Volvo left? From their interviews with Dalkamouni, Ghadanfar and Hashem Abassi in April, the BKA agents had learned that it had not been Martin Imandi. Apparently, he had been nervous about returning to Germany after his run-in with the police in Denmark. Instead, he had sent a friend, a man named Mohammed Mougrabi. From Neuss, Mougrabi and his two passengers had headed back to Sweden, taking the ferry from Kiel to Göteborg. And this time they had made it through.

Despite their obvious concerns about Dalkamouni and their suspicions about the activities inside the Isarstrasse flat, for two weeks the German authorities made no mention of the passengers in Imandi's Volvo to their

Swedish counterparts. Finally, on October 30, four days after they had terminated the Autumn Leaves operation, the Germans said something to the Swedes about the three visitors to Hashem Abassi's flat. Coincidentally, this was just a day after a BKA officer had finally taken the time to examine the Toshiba Bombeat recovered from the backseat of Dalkamouni's Ford Taurus and discovered that it was a bomb.

The BKA might have delayed telling the Swedish authorities for several good reasons. Even when they had concluded Autumn Leaves on October 26, senior BKA investigators still had not been entirely sure what Dalkamouni and the others were up to. And if they alerted the Swedes too early it could have compromised their own surveillance operation.

Whatever the reason for the delay, when they finally did alert the Swedes, it was too late. Swedish police immediately moved in on Martin Imandi's apartment in Uppsala and arrested him, Mougrabi and five others, including Ahmed Abassi, Dalkamouni's translator, who had been arrested in Germany by the BKA just the week before and then immediately released. In fact, it was almost as if Autumn Leaves had been a model for the Swedish case: within forty-eight hours after their arrest, all of the people apprehended – including Imandi, Mougrabi and Abassi – were set free. The reason, once again, was 'insufficient evidence'. In searching Imandi's flat in Uppsala and several other apartments, the police had found no explosives or weapons, nothing that would indicate involvement in the kinds of terrorist activities to which Dalkamouni and company were clearly connected. Swedish detectives complained privately that the four-day delay by the BKA could have enabled Imandi and the others to clear any incriminating evidence out of their apartments. They were suspicious enough about the activities of Imandi and those associated with him that they decided to keep them under loose surveillance. It was simply a matter of precaution on their part.

Swedish authorities had several reasons to be nervous. For one thing, if they had a Palestinian terrorist cell operating in Sweden, they wanted to know about it. Pope John Paul II was scheduled to visit Stockholm in June, and he could conceivably be a target of such a group.

Scandinavia had long been immune from the threat of terrorism, and even most kinds of violent crime. But that had begun to change in recent years. On June 22, 1985, two explosions had rocked downtown Copenhagen, damaging a Northwest Airlines office and a synagogue. One person had been killed and twenty-two wounded. A third bomb, discovered that same day at the offices of El Al, had failed to explode. Less than a year after that, Stockholm had been the target. On the evening of April 7, 1986, a bomb had exploded outside the offices of Northwest Airlines. This time no injuries were reported. But police determined that the bomb had been the same type as that used in Copenhagen, and although there were no public claims of responsibility, intelligence received by the police led them to conclude that a small international terrorist group operating within Sweden had been responsible for both attacks. The discovery of several sizeable arms caches in Sweden since then seemed to reinforce the suspicion.

More important than that, however, was the background of some of those arrested by the Swedish police in October. German authorities say they warned their counterparts in Stockholm that while they had no reason to be suspicious of Hashem Abassi, they were very concerned indeed about his brother, Ahmed. The Swedes had reasons of their own to be worried about some of the others picked up, and this seemed to be the real reason for their decision to keep closer tabs on them and their activities.

Martin Imandi, especially, was a real source of interest. Police detectives in Copenhagen and Stockholm had reason to believe that it was he who had been behind the bombings in 1985 and 1986. An odd series of events had led the detectives to this conclusion, but it seemed to make sense nevertheless. In downtown Copenhagen, just a few days before the bombings of the synagogue and the Northwest offices in June 1985, a man walking in front of the El Al ticket office had slipped a plastic Northwest tote bag into the doorway and began to stroll away. An elderly Danish woman, thinking the man had forgotten the bag, had rushed after him with it, grabbed his arm and attempted to give it back to him.

Wordlessly, the man had grabbed the bag from the woman and, dodging pedestrians, had run down the street to Nyhavn Canal, where he had flung it in the water. People on a nearby sailboat had witnessed the incident and reported it to the police, and divers had been sent to recover the mystery bag. In it were three bombs wrapped in a Swedish newspaper and nails of a type purchasable only in Sweden. Forensic specialists had been able to lift only one fingerprint from the soaked newspaper. But detectives did obtain detailed descriptions from the eyewitnesses who had seen the man take the bag from the elderly woman and toss it into the water.

Copenhagen police later found other witnesses who described a man fitting the description given to the Danish detectives. The witnesses said the man had boarded a ferry back to Stockholm the same afternoon as the incident in Nyhavn Canal. The police evidently lacked enough evidence to link Martin Imandi conclusively to the Copenhagen and Stockholm bombings, but they began looking into his background. And what they discovered was that his name wasn't Martin Imandi at all.

Imandi's real name was Imad Shaaban, and he had

been born in Syria in 1956, of Palestinian parents. He had graduated from high school in Syria, gone to work for an oil company in Lebanon and then moved to England and later Sweden, where he worked as a part-time dishwasher and custodian in the university town of Uppsala. Just forty miles north of Stockholm, Uppsala boasts Sweden's oldest and most prestigious university. A handsome city of 120,000, it is home to a polyglot population that includes thousands of Palestinian, Lebanese and Iranian exiles. In Uppsala, Shaaban eventually acquired part-ownership of a grocery store. An internal Swedish Corrections Department file said that Shaaban suffered from 'psychological problems', including depression, and that he had attempted suicide once. A weightlifter, he was described as a loner. What he was not described as was a terrorist. That would come later.

In late August 1989, as the Lockerbie investigators reviewed the files on those arrested in May by SAPO agents, they were especially interested in Imandi and two other men. Of the fifteen people arrested, only five had been detained by the authorities, and four would be held for trial on charges related to the 1985 and 1986 bombings. The four were Martin Imandi, Mohammed Abu Talb, Mohammed Mougrabi, and his brother, Mustafa. It was Mohammed Mougrabi who had gone to Neuss in October in the white Volvo to collect Imandi's younger brother and cousin. Here was a definite link to the Dalkamouni network in Germany.

The Lockerbie investigators were very interested in the others the SAPO agents had picked up. What was the evidence against them? What did Swedish police know about them? Just weeks before, it had seemed highly unlikely these suspects could have had anything to do with the 270 murders in Lockerbie. Now it was looking more and more as if that were the case.

From Imandi's apartment after his arrest in May, detectives had lifted fingerprints that matched conclusively with the single print lifted from the newspaper wrapped around the bombs recovered in Copenhagen. Understandably, Scottish and American police officials were less interested in the Copenhagen and Stockholm bombings than in the connections to Lockerbie, and Imandi's ties to the Mougrabi brothers made those connections very intriguing indeed. The Mougrabis came from a family of terrorists, if such a thing can be said to exist. One sister had attempted to murder the Iraqi ambassador to Great Britain, and had been caught, convicted and imprisoned there. Another had been killed in the Gaza Strip while attempting to blow up an Israeli bus.

A third sister, Jamilla, had been married for several years to one of the four men detained for trial in Stockholm, Mohammed Abu Talb. From his apartment in Uppsala, forensic specialists had recovered traces of what was described as 'metal dust' that they linked conclusively to the explosives used in the 1985 and 1986 bombings. When he was arrested, SAPO agents found four passports in his name and the smouldering remains of two more. For some reason, Abu Talb had tried to destroy them when the police began banging on his door. Unfortunately, police lab experts had had little success in reconstructing the two burnt passports, but from the four undamaged ones they learned some very interesting things. Immigration stamps showed that Abu Talb had travelled to Cyprus on October 3, 1988, and stayed until the eighteenth. The next day, the stamps in his passport showed, he had gone to Malta, where he had remained until October 26.

The Malta connection jumped out immediately to FBI and Scottish investigators. But so did the date he had left there. On October 26, BKA agents were concluding Operation Autumn Leaves and taking Hafez Dalkamouni, Marwan Kreeshat and others into police custody. The Lockerbie investigators wanted to know more about Mohammed Abu Talb immediately.

Swedish police records showed that he had come to the country initially in February 1986 on a forged Moroccan passport. He had asked for, and been given, political asylum. Abu Talb gave authorities various accounts of his early life, but this much seems to be true: He had been born in Port Said, Egypt; he had lived with his parents and eight brothers until 1968 and at age eighteen had joined the Egyptian army as a volunteer to fight against Israel. In 1969 he had been sent to the Soviet Union, where he'd received training to use SAM-3 antiaircraft missiles. After eighteen months, he had returned to Egypt; he had left again in 1973 to join the Palestine Liberation Organization in Lebanon. In 1977 he'd become a bodyguard in the Palestine Popular Struggle Front. And in August 1980 he'd returned to the Soviet Union for one year to study political organization and recruitment. According to Swedish records, Mohammed Abu Talb had been seriously wounded at least three times in his life, most recently in 1988, when he had been stabbed in the back by what was described as an 'unknown assailant'. The Swedish documents say Abu Talb told investigators that if he returned to Lebanon, he would be murdered. His nom de guerre, Intiqam, translates roughly as 'the man who takes revenge'.

Scottish and American investigators, naturally enough, wanted to know what part, if any, Abu Talb had played in what they believed was revenge for the July downing of the Iranian airliner in the Persian Gulf. Unfortunately, their Swedish counterparts seem to have been considerably less interested in that question. The Swedish foreign minister, Sten Andersson, had invested considerable time and effort in nurturing the tentative dialogue between the United States and the PLO, and American law enforcement officials and Swedish sources said they believed pressure may have been brought to bear on police and prosecutors in Stockholm to contain the investigation against Imandi,

283

Abu Talb and the Mougrabi brothers to the 1985 and 1986 bombings. As the trial against the four men was scheduled to proceed on October 9 in a Stockholm court, Lockerbie investigators were convinced that they could link Abu Talb to the strange batch of clothes purchased at Mary's House in Malta. The description given by the shopkeeper, notwithstanding the faxed police sketch resembling Qaddafi, fitted Abu Talb to a tee: He was muscular and clean-shaven. He was in his mid-thirties and spoke with an accent that could easily have been mistaken for Libyan. The date of Abu Talb's visit, in October, didn't quite jibe with the shopkeeper's recollection, but that could have been a trick of memory. In any case, without a search of Abu Talb's residence, what Lockerbie investigators were left with was intriguing theories, but hardly the type of evidence one could hope to present in court. They needed proof.

Swedish authorities seem to have been profoundly uninterested in the investigators' needs. On the opening day of the trial in Stockholm, prosecutor Stefan Karlmark was asked by a reporter about any connection between his criminal case and the Lockerbie inquiry. 'I have charged the four men with the [1985 and 1986] bombings,' Karlmark replied blandly. 'That is enough for me.'

But it wasn't good enough for the investigators from Lockerbie, London and Washington. In fact, within days of the start of the trial, a story broke in Washington, perhaps indicating just how serious the government had become about proceeding against enemies of American interests overseas. On October 13, the *Los Angeles Times* reported that the Justice Department had reversed a ruling dating back to the Carter administration, which had denied the FBI authority to apprehend criminals in foreign countries without first obtaining the consent of the foreign government involved. The Carter ruling had even gone so far as to warn that FBI agents could face kidnapping charges abroad if they used such tactics. The new ruling, requested by Attorney General Richard Thornburgh and drafted by his chief legal advisor, William P. Barr, carried the rather grand and cumbersome title 'The Authority of the FBI to Override Customary or Other International Law in the Course of Extraterritorial Law-Enforcement Activities'. Some administration officials called it simply the president's 'snatch authority'.

The 'snatch authority' could yet play a role in the Lockerbie investigation, but by late autumn, American and British officials were still hoping to prevail through less controversial means. They had begun making progress with the Germans, after all, only because they had been patient and determined to avoid publicly embarrassing them. In Stockholm, the same approach was worth trying. If it didn't work, they could try more forceful means later.

While the investigators attempted to determine how best to manoeuvre the levers in the legal and diplomatic community in Stockholm, they were blindsided in perhaps the most bizarre way imaginable. For the families of those who died in Lockerbie, this was also one of the cruellest developments since the tragedy. Most of the victims' families had sued Pan Am over the disaster, and if a judgement is ultimately returned against the airline, it could easily be in the millions if not hundreds of millions of dollars. In seeking to defend itself against the lawsuits, Pan Am has retained a team of attorneys, who in turn contracted with an investigative agency, Interfor, Inc., in New York City, to begin assembling information that could be used in a trial.

In November 1989, as police investigators continued to pursue a variety of leads while attempting to clear up the dispute with Swedish authorities, a report of an Interfor investigator named Juval Aviv leaked into the press. An Ohio congressman, of all people, was responsible for revealing five pages of Aviv's twenty-seven-page report, and it could only be termed an unfortunate occurrence. How Representative James Traficant, Jr., obtained the report, prepared for Pan Am's lawyers, was unclear. What the report itself was based on was similarly murky. Its conclusions, investigators say, were patently ridiculous.

What was clear is that in attempting to show that it was not responsible for the events that allowed a bomb to be placed on one of its jets and blown up, Pan Am went pretty far afield in its search for evidence, issuing subpoenas to the CIA and five other U.S. government intelligence-gathering agencies. The subpoenas sought to elicit information government officials may have had about warnings of a bomb attack on U.S. aircraft before the crash of Flight 103. It was certainly a reasonable line of inquiry.

The premise on which the subpoenas were based, however, was false, according to officials in the U.S. and Britain and elsewhere. Essentially, the premise, as outlined in Juval Aviv's report, was this: That rogue CIA officials in Frankfurt had struck a deal with a Syrian arms merchant named Monzer al-Kassar, allowing him to smuggle a quantity of heroin into the U.S. in exchange for his assistance in securing the release of some or all of the American hostages in Lebanon. Knowing of this 'protected' route, Interfor's report said, the terrorists who carried out the bombing planted the explosives in the piece of luggage that was to have contained the drugs, switching one bag for another at the last moment in the baggage-loading area at Frankfurt Main Airport. 'We do not know exactly when this decision was made,' Aviv wrote in the report, 'but the dates point to two [to] three days before the flight.' Aviv's conclusion? U.S. intelligence officials, believing the luggage contained drugs and not explosives, deliberately underplayed warnings of a bomb threat, allowing the fatal Samsonite to be loaded aboard Flight 103. It was, according to intelligence officials and police investigators, a classic 'spitball', a messy amalgam of known facts, clever suppositions and wholesale fabrications. Interfor even offered to apprehend the Pan Am bombers.

Once again, rumours of spies and drugs had grown like barnacles on the hide of the Lockerbie tragedy. And once again the barnacles had to be scraped off. The CIA described the allegations as 'rubbish'. And the families of the victims, having endured so much already, were subjected once again to a case of the what-ifs. If a loved one hadn't travelled, if the State Department had warned, and now, if the CIA hadn't been swapping drugs for hostages, life would be as it always had been. There wouldn't have been the death and sadness. There wouldn't have been a Lockerbie. Such feelings were perfectly understandable. But in this instance, based as they were on such flawed assumptions, the questions the families put to themselves were particularly unnecessary, and the cause for their having been asked especially regrettable.

Among the police officials assigned to the Lockerbie case, the business about a CIA-orchestrated drugs-for-hostages swap caused some consternation, but they kept on with their inquiries. By early December 1989, they had taken 14,181 statements from witnesses, relatives, potential suspects and anyone who might have any knowledge about the tragedy. In the HOLMES computer, more than 16,000 pieces of property had been identified and logged. And at Longtown, nearly eighty-five percent of the fuselage of the *Maid of the Seas* had been assembled over an enormous skeleton of metal scaffolding. At Fort Halstead, the forensic people were still examining bits of wreckage and personal belongings under microscopes. In short, despite the frustration in Sweden and the flap over the private investigator's report in the States, the Lockerbie investigators were sticking with what worked. What they needed was not wild theory but hard fact. And that would come mainly from solid police work.

If Swedish authorities would grant them access to Abu Talb's Uppsala apartment and permission to take clothing samples with them back to England, where the forensic team at Fort Halstead could run tests on them, they might be close to making a case that could be presented in a courtroom.

Out of the tangled trail from Lockerbie, the Malta and Stockholm threads were finally coming together, the investigators believed. Now they needed only the Swedes to help them prove it. Sometime in November, officials from Scotland Yard met secretly in a two-hour session with Swedish security officials in Stockholm to press their case. The session was never officially disclosed, but it is known that the British representatives asserted forcefully and in detail why they believed Abu Talb had been involved in the Lockerbie disaster. And apparently, the Scotland Yard presentation was effective.

While the owner of Mary's House remained under round-the-clock guard in Malta, the Lockerbie investigators applied formally through the Swedish Foreign Office for a warrant to search Mohammed Abu Talb's apartment. On November 27, three Scottish detectives, accompanied by seven SAPO agents, entered the apartment and spent several hours inside. When they emerged, they had fifteen large black plastic garbage bags – bags that looked very much like the body bags in the fields and lanes of Lockerbie – full of Abu Talb's clothing. Over the next two days, Swedish police searched two other places for clothes belonging to Abu Talb: they visited his ex-wife, Jamilla Mougrabi, in Uppsala and his prison cell. More clothes were taken. But still that was not enough.

Under Swedish law, foreign police cannot take evidence from a resident of the country out of Sweden without court approval. A magistrate would now have to bless the seizure, and Abu Talb's lawyer was objecting strenuously. Representing the police in a fifteen-minute court hearing on December 1, prosecutor Ulf Forsberg argued that the confiscation of the clothing was legal. If absolutely necessary, Forsberg said, the materials could be examined in Sweden, but in any case it was essential to determine whether there was a link to Lockerbie or not.

On December 4, Swedish judge Gunnar Graberg ruled that the Scottish police could take Abu Talb's clothes to Malta and then to Scotland. On December 7, three officers from Scotland Yard took possession of the clothes; they brought them to Malta and took them to Mary's House. But none of the clothes from the apartment were found to have been purchased there.

Meanwhile British agents from Scotland Yard questioned Martin Imandi, the Mougrabi brothers and Abu Talb about the Pan Am bombing. All denied having anything to do with it.

With respect to Abu Talb at least, the evidence suggested a definite link to Malta and thus to Lockerbie. Investigators learned that in the raid on his apartment on May 18, SAPO agents had recovered a plane ticket from Malta to Stockholm via Rome. Swedish police documents show that Abu Talb had used the ticket to return to Stockholm on November 26, 1988. That meant Abu Talb had made not one trip to Malta, but two. And November 26 was just three days after the owner of the boutique in Malta had sold the jumble of clothes that wound up in the copper-coloured Samsonite.

There was more. In police evidence against Abu Talb, Jamilla Mougrabi is quoted as telling a SAPO agent that her ex-husband had travelled to Malta in November to recover from a knife wound and that while he was there he 'visited a friend who owns a bakery and a brother of his named Salam'. Salam, according to the notes of the SAPO agent's interview with Jamilla Mougrabi, 'owns a clothing business where Abu Talb bought some clothes'.

The lid would close still tighter. Police investigators in Sweden say they have a recording of a telephone call between Jamilla Mougrabi and some unidentified friends. The call was placed soon after Abu Talb's arrest on May 18, and during the conversation, Mougrabi told her friends to 'get rid of the clothes'.

Finally, there was Abu Talb's own calendar, which contained a bit of circumstantial evidence that is more eerie than anything else. Abu Talb had circled the date of December 21.

That's all. Nothing more.

Exactly one year to the day after that, December 21, 1989, Mohammed Abu Talb stood in the front of a Stockholm courtroom with his friend, Martin Imandi. On the last day of his trial, Abu Talb had risen before the judges to make a final statement. 'If being a lifelong combatant for Palestine is terrorism,' he said, 'then I am one of the world's biggest terrorists.' Now, as he stood awaiting judgement, Abu Talb seemed considerably less sure of himself.

The verdict against Abu Talb had already been announced: guilty of murder of the one person who had died in one of the 1985 bombings in Copenhagen. Now it was time for the sentence: life in prison, the Swedish judges ordered. Martin Imandi received an identical sentence. And the judges, in concluding the proceedings, said that the actions of Mohammed Abu Talb and Martin Imandi had been 'directed against the lives and property of innocent people. Society must react very strongly against such crimes.'

A year to the day after the Lockerbie tragedy, it was difficult to imagine a more fitting or appropriate message.

CHAPTER 18

Mohammed Abu Talb is in jail in Sweden. Hafez Dalkamouni is cooling his heels in West Germany. More than a year after the tragedy, here is what else we know.

There is virtually no disagreement among the investigators or intelligence officials involved in the Lockerbie inquiry that Ahmed Jibril's organization was responsible for the bomb that blew up Flight 103. Jibril, in interviews, denies he had anything to do with it. 'You shot down the Iranian airbus in cold blood,' he said, in response to questions about the Lockerbie bombing. 'Your media accused us of blowing up Flight 103 . . . even before they knew whether it was sabotage. That means the accusation was prepared in advance.' Jibril said that the weapons seized in the Autumn Leaves operation in Germany were 'intended for defence against [Israeli] agents; others were to be sent to Palestine. We look for every possible way to smuggle arms to our land,' he continued. 'The barometric detonators are not only used for planes. For instance, you can place these devices aboard a ship, and when the materials these devices are hidden in are transported to a mountainous region, we can use them to blow the [explosives] up. We know the accusation [that the PFLP-GC blew up Flight 103] is not true and the CIA knows it, but they want to sully our reputation. They want Yasir Arafat to go forward with his concessions to the Israelis without having a credible substitute.' By which Ahmed Jibril meant himself.

Jibril's 'explanations' about blowing up barometer

bombs on mountaintops are nonsense, according to explosives experts. His angry reference to the Iranian airbus and his abhorrence of Arafat are more telling. According to intelligence officials who assisted with the Lockerbie investigation and who have studied Jibril and his organization for years, the airbus and the faint prospect of peace in the Middle East are the small reason and the large reason, respectively, for the bombing of Flight 103. Authorities familiar with the National Security Agency's exhaustive analysis of intercepts in connection with the Lockerbie inquiry concede that despite the tens of thousands of man-hours spent, the evidence linking Jibril and Dalkamouni to the hard-line elements in Teheran is voluminous but inconclusive. From other sources, however, U.S. intelligence officials can document chapter and verse about Jibril's ties to Iran, and they say that information clearly bolsters the evidence discovered by police in West Germany, Sweden, Yugoslavia and Malta linking the PFLP-GC conclusively to the Pan Am bombing.

While he professed his innocence, Ahmed Jibril also professed to be worried about American retaliation, and Israeli intelligence sources have said he has become increasingly religious, praying as often as five times a day – an indication that he has become close to his new sponsors in Iran. Jibril would seem to have reason to pray for deliverance, but not so much from American vengeance as from the terrorists within his own ranks and increasing pressure from Damascus, of all places. More than a year afer the Lockerbie incident, intelligence sources say, the Popular Front for the Liberation of Palestine – General Command is riven with dissent. According to an intelligence official, a 'serious schism' erupted within the organization, pitting those who favour increasing their alliance with Iran against those who preferred to stay closer to Syria. The division parallels the fighting that broke out between Syrian and Iranian loyalists in Lebanon in January 1990. In southern

Lebanon, the Syrian-backed Amal Moslem militia fought the Iranian-sponsored Hezbollah. Hundreds were killed or wounded. Intelligence officials believed the fighting was actually a proxy war between Iran and Syria. The Hezbollah, prodded by Iran's former interior minister Ali Akbar Mohtashemi – who had recently been reelected to the Iranian Parliament – was determined to prove that it was in the forefront of the battle against Israel, while Amal, encouraged by Syria, wanted to demonstrate that it controlled its adjacent territory.

Mohtashemi himself visited Lebanon and met with Hezbollah leaders in late November 1989. At the same time, the Iranian cleric met with Jibril in a secret rendezvous in the Bekaa Valley. The purpose of the meeting was to strengthen their year-old relationship. It was shortly after this meeting that intelligence officials picked up evidence that Jibril, a longtime atheist, had suddenly become a born-again Moslem.

Try as he might, Jibril was unable to force all of his fighters to follow in his footsteps. To many of them – trained and nurtured by the Syrian government – Syria remained their ultimate patron and they refused to change loyalties. In Lebanon, Jibril's organization was ripped apart by the conflict. And back in his home territory, Syria, the split degenerated into a battle with his longtime sponsor Hafez al-Assad. The Syrian president publicly warned that if the PFLP-GC had been involved in some way with the Lockerbie bombing, Jibril would be expelled from Syria and punished. And in fact, a year after the bombing, a dozen PFLP-GC members had been jailed in Syria – on charges unrelated to Lockerbie.

To some intelligence officials, Assad's warning and the arrests were indications of the severe pressure brought to bear on him by the United States, Great Britain and West Germany. Yet other intelligence officials believed that Assad's actions were contrived, designed to demonstrate disingenuously to the West his exasperation with Jibril and mask the fact that Assad's regime had provided components and logistical support to Jibril to carry out the bombing of Pan Am 103.

Nevertheless, for Jibril, the turn of events within Syria must have seemed as if his worst nightmare had come true. Jibril himself was trying desperately to get back in Assad's good graces. On January 10, 1990, at a hastily arranged news conference in West Beirut, Jibril blasted the Lockerbie investigators and the finger-pointing at the PFLP-GC.

'We believe that this campaign is aimed at blackmailing Syria and President . . . Assad,' he told reporters, 'because the United States and [President] Bush believe the time is ripe to settle scores with countries and movements hostile to imperialism. But they do not want to face Syria outright, so they did it indirectly by trying to implicate us in the [Lockerbie] bombing. We say it loud and clear,' Jibril continued, 'Assad is not a Noriega and Syria is not a banana republic.'

It was an impressive show, but it was also anyone's guess whether Assad put much stock in it. Jibril must have been praying harder than ever.

Had Lockerbie never happened, it is not unreasonable to believe that Jibril's extensive network of operatives across Europe would still be in existence today. Largely through the efforts of two key figures, Hafez Dalkamouni and Abdel Ghadanfar, the PFLP-GC was able, by early 1988, to establish an impressive web of bank accounts, safe houses and operatives in Frankfurt, Bonn, Rome, Stockholm, Barcelona, Athens, Malta, Cyprus and Yugoslavia.

In Cyprus, according to intelligence officials, one of Jibril's aides, Nabil Maksumi, had constructed an elaborate operations base. Maksumi, a big, burly, bearded Palestinian, had served several years in an Israeli prison after being caught trying to blow up an Israeli industrial plant. Maksumi had been released with Jibril in the 1985

Israeli prisoner exchange and had immediately gone to work for Jibril's organization; he soon became a top aide to Dalkamouni. According to Scottish and U.S. officials, it was Maksumi who had set up the telephone-relay system that enabled Jibril to talk directly to Dalkamouni in Europe, evidently in an effort to avoid electronic eavesdropping. But German agents succeeded in recording many of Dalkamouni's conversations during October, including key conversations held with operatives in Damascus and elsewhere through the relay stations set up on Cyprus.

Intelligence officials have evidence that Cyprus was an important way station for Jibril, convenient for shipping arms and perhaps explosives to and from Europe. Weapons, for example, were shipped to Cyprus, under the guise of being 'toys', and then to Damascus. Barcelona was another important cog in Jibril's European operation. German and Israeli officials said that Nabil Maksumi made extensive use of an apartment ostensibly occupied by a Spanish woman whose son was half Palestinian. Intelligence officials said the apartment was actually used to store weapons and put up PFLP-GC members, who were believed to be gathering information on American, Israeli and Spanish targets, presumably for a much bigger terrorist operation.

The heart and soul of Jibril's network were not full-time terrorists who plotted or participated in operations every minute. In a real sense, they were much more like the 'sleeper' agents of classic espionage theory. These were people who held jobs, waved to the neighbours and, in some cases, even headed families, living outwardly normal lives until they were suddenly summoned to action. The most effective sleepers in the spy business are typically those who have lived the cover for long periods of time, for years and sometimes decades. Jibril's people in Europe, by contrast, seem to have been relative newcomers in highly transient jobs. They were used-car salesmen, as was Martin Kadourah in Frankfurt, or pizza chefs, as was Abu Tarek in Berlin, or building custodians, as was Martin Imandi in Uppsala. Dealing in used cars seems to have been an especially effective cover for terrorists in Europe. It provides a legitimate means and reason for frequent travel, is convenient for moving people, weapons and explosives from place to place, and offers a ready excuse for having large sums of ready cash around. Others among Jibril's operatives, according to investigators and intelligence officials, worked as electricians, bakers, mechanics and videocassette salesmen, although some had more permanent jobs. Investigators identified one man, Mukhadeen Joban, as a Palestinian chemical engineer in Yugoslavia; he had held a job there for twenty-seven years before he became active in assisting with the logistical planning for Dalkamouni's anticipated autumn bombing campaign in Europe.

Although it is not immediately relevant to the Lockerbie investigators and their chances of bringing to count an indictable case against the bombers, one of the most intriguing questions raised by the inquiry has to do with Marwan Kreeshat's bombs. Most investigators accept as fact that Kreeshat constructed five bombs, although a minority view holds that six were built. (If there was a sixth bomb, investigators believe, it might still be in the possession of terrorists.) There was the bomb found in the backseat of Dalkamouni's Ford Taurus; the bomb in the stereo tuner that exploded, killing Hans Jürgen Sonntag, and the two other bombs, one in the tuner and one in the Sanyo television monitor, that had been defused safely. The fifth bomb, investigators believe, blew up in baggage carrier 14L at 7:03 P.M. local time on December 21, 1988, in the belly of the *Maid of the Seas* over Lockerbie.

This is not just a matter of surmise on the investigators' part. By late December 1989, forensic technicians at Fort Halstead had conclusively linked a bit of melted plastic residue from the crash of Flight 103 to the casing of one of three alarm clocks Hafez Dalkamouni had purchased on his mysterious shopping trips around Neuss. Another bit of printed circuit board was also positively identified as having come from a Toshiba radio-cassette player, although forensic specialists and police investigators have concluded that it was a different Toshiba model from the Bombeat found in Dalkamouni's car. The Toshiba that held the bomb that blew up Flight 103 is believed to have had two speakers; the Bombeat had only one.

That accounts for five bombs. If there was a sixth, its whereabouts remain unknown to Lockerbie investigators. Either way, however, the number of bombs raises the question of what they were to have been used for.

The answer, according to American law enforcement and Israeli intelligence officials, is mass murder, on a scale even more terrible than Lockerbie. They have little hard evidence, but these officials believe that Jibril's mission to avenge the downing of the Iranian airbus was just one part of a larger and more diabolical operation that may have involved placing barometer-triggered bombs on as many as four airplanes on the same day. One theory of the intelligence officials, who would not reveal on what the theory is based, is that the bombs were intended to go off on the day of the American elections, November 8, 1988; the planning for such an operation probably would have been completed by September 1, and it would have involved several terrorist cells in Europe, each carrying out a small part of the operation and having no knowledge of the other parts.

Several intelligence officials have said they believe they have identified one of Jibril's other targets besides Pan Am 103. According to these officials, Dalkamouni, who had visited a PFLP-GC safe house in Barcelona, decided that Iberia Flight 888, from Madrid to Tel Aviv with a stop in Barcelona, would be a relatively easy target. The elaborate operation called for someone to board the flight in Madrid with the bomb in carry-on luggage and leave the plane in Barcelona, with the bomb still on board. After the Autumn Leaves arrests, the intelligence officials said, the operation was evidently abandoned.

Like the use of barometer bombs and the network of sleeper operatives established by Dalkamouni, the highly compartmentalized operation showed the sophistication of Jibril's organization. What the Lockerbie investigators know for certain is that in late 1988, before his arrest in the Autumn Leaves sweep, Hafez Dalkamouni was a very busy man. BKA surveillance documented many of his movements, and Scottish detectives and FBI agents have since pieced together many more. In August, September and early October, investigators found, Dalkamouni travelled to Barcelona, Malta, Yugoslavia, East Berlin and Cyprus, alerting the network of PFLP-GC operatives and giving them their instructions. In Cyprus, some investigators believe, Mohammed Abu Talb got his instructions directly from Dalkamouni and was told to travel to Malta to purchase clothing for the suitcases that would carry Marwan Kreeshat's bombs.

The operation was designed to be so highly compartmentalized, with Dalkamouni's giving each person his instructions in person, that if one operative was caught, he would not know enough to jeopardize the entire plan. This too could explain why Flight 103 was blown up even after Dalkamouni, Ghadanfar and the others had been arrested in West Germany. That also leads to the conclusion that Autumn Leaves, for all its evident failings, may have inadvertently saved several hundreds, if not thousands, of lives. Israeli intelligence officials believe that if Jibril had carried out his plan for simultaneous aircraft bombings in the autumn of 1988, as many as 1,000 people could have died. If they are correct, it would have been the single worst terrorist attack ever, dwarfing by far the June 1985 Air-India plane bombing that killed 329 people.

But that still doesn't explain how the bomb that blew up over Lockerbie was built and smuggled aboard the *Maid of the Seas*. This is what the Lockerbie investigators believe. When Marwan Kreeshat arrived in Frankfurt from Jordan on October 13, 1988, most of the material to build his bombs was already in Germany. On October 19, BKA agents listened in on a telephone conversation in which Kreeshat said that he had 'made some changes in the medicine' and that it was 'better and stronger than before'. Clearly, the Semtex and most of the bomb components, and the Toshiba Bombeat, had been purchased or built already.

U.S. intelligence officials now believe that the barometer-timers were built by Jibril's technicians in the laboratory of the camp outside Damascus where U.S. Army Colonel Clifford Ward and Major Robert Siegel were detained as they attempted to shoot photographs and gather other evidence about the PFLP-GC's operations in March 1989.

One theory of the Lockerbie investigators is that the barometer-timers were smuggled from Damascus to Germany by Ziad Shaaban and Samar Ourfali, Martin Imandi's brother and cousin. They arrived in Munich on September 5, 1988, on the Syrian Arab Airlines flight from Damascus. The carrier had been used to smuggle weapons before, according to U.S. and other law enforcement officials. They say they have documented several instances, the most recent in Denmark in 1988, in which the Damascus-based carrier has carried weapons to Europe inside diplomatic mail bags. An even stronger possibility, intelligence officials say, is that the fuses, which are extraordinarily sensitive to movement, were smuggled into Germany via Iranian diplomatic pouch.

Lockerbie investigators have traced the trail of explosives right to the source, and they believe they know

299

how the Semtex found its way into Marwan Kreeshat's nimble hands. Semtex, it is true, is made in Czechoslovakia, but U.S. and other Western intelligence officials say that Jilril's people obtained the batch Kreeshat used from Iran, and that it, like the fuses, was smuggled from the Middle East via Iranian diplomatic pouch. But with the Semtex the route was not directly to West Germany, but to Yugoslavia and the city of Belgrade.

From there, according to several knowledgeable officials, it went by car to a dingy flat in the village of Kruševac, not far from the Bulgarian border. On October 26, when BKA agents burst into the apartment at 28 Sandweg in Frankfurt, they found an enormous cache of guns and explosives. Among them were six automatic rifles, five made in Hungary, and the sixth assembled from pieces of two or three other rifles. One part of the sixth rifle, next to the breech lock, was made in Yugoslavia. So was one of seven rifle-fired grenades taken from the apartment.

European intelligence officials say there was something about these Yugoslav weapons that caused the Bonn government to press Belgrade for assistance in the investigation of Dalkamouni and the other suspected PFLP-GC members. Four weeks after the Autumn Leaves raid, Yugoslav police shipped Martin Kadourah, a suspected PFLP-GC member wanted for questioning by the BKA, back to Frankfurt. A few days after that, on or about December 1, Yugoslav police, presumably acting on information provided by Kadourah, raided the flat in Kruševac and discovered seven and a half kilos of Semtex, two kilos of Soviet-made dynamite, 484 detonators and several yards of fuse. There was also a 'recipe', according to one intelligence official, for making Semtex. The flat had been occupied by Mukhadeen Joban, the Palestinian chemical engineer who, evidently, had been activated just recently by Jibril or Dalkamouni.

Lockerbie investigators did not fully understand the

significance of the raid on Kruševac until April 1989, after one of Marwan Kreeshat's bombs exploded, killing the German explosives technician Sonntag. After the other two bombs were safely disarmed, lab technicians analyzed the Semtex in them, compared it with the Semtex in Dalkamouni's Bombeat bomb and with the Semtex found in Kruševac. All had come from the same batch. Not only that, the formula corresponded exactly to the recipe found in Joban's flat.

Clearly, another batch had already been smuggled from Joban's apartment in Kruševac to Hashem Abassi's flat in Neuss. The Lockerbie investigators believe that the Semtex was smuggled either through East Germany or directly from Kruševac. Intelligence officials have documented at least one meeting in East Berlin between Dalkamouni and Iranian government officials. Dalkamouni could have been given the Semtex by those officials, the investigators believe, and could have smuggled it back to Neuss in his plastic leg. Ever since his leg had been amputated in Israel in 1969, Dalkamouni had had difficulty with the prosthesis he had been given. Since his release from an Israeli prison in 1979, he had made numerous visits to a clinic in East Gemany to resolve the problem, and several Lockerbie investigators now believe that Dalkamouni could have used one of the visits as a pretext to meet with Iranian officials and get the Semtex.

Others among the Lockerbie investigators believe that the Semtex could have been smuggled directly from Kruševac by Martin Kadourah, the used-car salesman who was arrested in Yugoslavia and detained for questioning by the BKA in the Autumn Leaves investigation. Kadourah was also a frequent visitor to Yugoslavia and is believed to have lived there for a time. His car trips might have provided ready opportunities for smuggling explosives. Still another theory is that Dalkamouni smuggled it directly from Kruševac. He is known to have stayed in Joban's flat on October 5, 1988, and to have travelled back to Neuss by car.

With the Semtex, the barometer-timers and the Toshiba waiting for him in Neuss, Marwan Kreeshat had only to wire the bomb together.

BKA agents documented several of the shopping trips Dalkamouni and Kreeshat made around Neuss to purchase last-minute odds and ends. Some intelligence officials believe Ahmed Abassi, the greengrocer's brother, purchased the radios and tuners Kreeshat converted into bombs. CIA officials believe it was Abdel Ghadanfar who bought the electronic devices. Whoever bought them, the Lockerbie investigators believe that some of the purchases for the bombs had been completed and the devices delivered to Dalkamouni in the flat at 16 Isarstrasse by October 11.

Kreeshat arrived in Neuss on October 13. And the very next day, BKA agents photographed Mohammed Mougrabi coming out of 16 Isarstrasse carrying packages. Mougrabi had come to Neuss ostensibly to pick up Martin Imandi's brother and cousin and take them back to Sweden in Imandi's white Volvo. Kreeshat would have had a day to wire the Toshiba radio to the Semtex and the barometer-timer; explosives experts say that is plenty of time. In was known, from a phone conversation intercepted by the BKA on October 24, that Kreeshat had not completed wiring all the bombs, but he could have wired the first one. When Mougrabi left 16 Isarstrasse, he was not followed by BKA agents, and he soon arrived back in Sweden. Scottish detectives and FBI agents say it is possible that Mougrabi never even knew he was transporting a bomb. In any event, they believe that the bomb that blew up Flight 103 was removed from the apartment before the October 26 arrests.

What happened to the bomb from this point on has the investigators stumped. On October 30, 1988, four days after the Autumn Leaves arrests, the BKA finally alerted their counterparts in Sweden about Mougrabi and the suspicious Volvo. By this time the trail was dead cold.

Thanks to Dalkamouni's cleverly conceived operation, the machinery was already set in motion that would carry the bomb aboard Flight 103. But why didn't the Autumn Leaves arrests derail the whole thing? With Dalkamouni in jail and most of his operatives scattered, how did the bomb get on the plane?

U.S. and Scottish officials believe that when the BKA agents concluded Operation Autumn Leaves, they did so for a good reason. They had a bomb-maker, a known terrorist and evidence of bombs being made. The Lockerbie investigators believe also that the BKA had a tip from an informant that the terrorists were poised to strike. Who was the informant?

The CIA learned shortly after the crash in Lockerbie that Marwan Kreeshat had returned to Jordan and was talking to intelligence officials in Amman. West German authorities say they also were told that Kreeshat was an informant for Jordanian intelligence. U.S. officials say now that they are not sure what to believe, but some in the intelligence community are skeptical of the story that Kreeshat passed his information primarily or exclusively to Jordan. Despite Bonn's protestations to the contrary, some senior American officials believe that Kreeshat may have been working also for one of Germany's intelligence services, probably the BfV, and that the release of so many of the Autumn Leaves suspects and the unusual treatment accorded Kreeshat during his detention (there was virtually no information on his arrest documents that could give him away) was intended to disguise that fact. Thus the story about Kreeshat's phone call to Jordan from the police interrogation room in early November could have been yet another layer in the cover the Germans were providing for him.

The only problem is, Kreeshat didn't seem to be

giving much back. Several U.S. and Israeli intelligence officials believe that while working for the Germans, he was not telling them the truth. Kreeshat, said one intelligence official who has worked closely with the German intelligence services, 'was running circles around his German handlers and reporting back to Jibril about what he was reporting to the Germans'. Other intelligence officials said they believe Kreeshat was primarily a Jordanian informant and that his information was passed on to the Germans from officials in Amman.

Thus, investigators have concluded, the likelihood is that Kreeshat was a double, maybe even a triple, agent. 'We may never know who he was really working for,' conceded an American investigator after more than a year on the Pan Am case. Whatever the truth is, investigators believe, Kreeshat probably never reported about every one of the bombs he built in Neuss. Whether he did or not, U.S. and Scottish officials do not think Kreeshat tipped the BKA to finish up Autumn Leaves on October 26; they believe there was a second informant among the Autumn Leaves suspects.

As with Kreeshat's arrest documents, German authorities listed virtually no information on the arrest sheet for Ramzi Diab. Dalkamouni later identified Diab as a critical player in the bombing operation, a courier of some of the bomb-making materials. Lockerbie investigators would like to find Diab, but they have been unable to do so. Some senior officials in the Lockerbie investigation believe that Diab prompted the Autumn Leaves arrests on October 26. Once the arrests were made, evidently, the Germans were told by Diab's handlers that everything was under control, that the terrorist operation had been interrupted. The senior officials think that even if Ramzi Diab was telling his handlers the truth, it would not have made any difference in the end, because he seems to have known of only one small part of the operation. Thus, other parts of the Dalkamouni machine kept functioning, and almost eight weeks after the arrests, Marwan Kreeshat's fifth bomb blew up the *Maid of the Seas*.

If Ramzi Diab was the second informant, as some investigators believe, he may not have known about Kreeshat's other four bombs, and if that is so, German authorities would have been using Diab's partial truth to confirm Kreeshat's wholesale lie.

For whom was Diab really working? Again, as with Marwan Kreeshat, American investigators are not sure. Some believe that he had convinced the Germans that he was genuinely working for them. Others believe he may have been an informant for Israel. Some intelligence officials believe that, in an even stranger twist, there were Syrian informants in or connected to Dalkamouni's network. One or more may have been reporting back to Syrian intelligence agents who – because of their close working relationship with Jibril – had been able to infiltrate his organization and keep abreast of all of his activities, just in case he was not as forthcoming as he had promised.

For the Germans, Operation Autumn Leaves – as well motivated as it may have been – seems to have been afflicted with several major flaws. There were gaps in the electronic surveillance and the misinterpretations of the coded language used by Dalkamouni and others in the conversations intercepted by German agents. The Germans had attempted to keep track of Dalkamouni twenty-four hours a day. Hundreds of hours of video-tapes and tape recordings had been made. But because of Dalkamouni's evasive measures – it is almost certain that he suspected he was under surveillance – and because of the technological limitations of electronic listening devices, German agents were not able to hear everything Dalkamouni said, especially in his subterranean personal visits with other members of the PFLP-GC in Germany. In several key meetings, Dalkamouni could be seen – but not heard – for hours at a time.

Yet German investigators were confident that any gaps in their personal surveillance of Dalkamouni would be compensated for by their intercepts of his telephone calls with other members of the PFLP-GC. In those conversations, intelligence officials say, Dalkamouni and others used coded language. He, for example, spoke of 'apples' and 'presents'. At the time of the intercepts, German agents felt confident they could decipher the tapes and figure out what Dalkamouni was referring to. Intelligence experts believe that 'apples' meant grenades and that 'presents' were bombs. Dalkamouni is also said to have mentioned 'aunts', 'uncles', 'sons' and 'cars', but agents were unable to determine what those signified.

However, on the basis of what they had overheard in these conversations – in conjunction with the assurance they had received from their informant that everything was under control – the Germans felt that the October 26 raid had preempted future terrorist operations. In retrospect, though, other Western intelligence services believe that the Germans had a difficult time in uncoding Dalkamouni's references and that, despite suspicions to the contrary, the Germans ultimately failed to conclude correctly that Dalkamouni and Kreeshat had made more than one bomb. Abetted by disinformation provided by their informants, the German agents decided the bomb they had seized in Dalkamouni's car was the only one he had helped prepare.

Transcripts of Dalkamouni's conversations were provided to American analysts after the bombing of Pan Am 103. And those transcripts, studied in great detail, show that Dalkamouni had referred indirectly to at least five bombs in his possession. Yet German agents steadfastly refused to believe that he had made five bombs – notwithstanding repeated American assertions. It was only after the death of one of their bomb specialists and the maiming of another in April 1989 that West German intelligence officials finally discovered Marwan

Kreeshat for the liar he was. By that time there wasn't much they could do about it.

In fact, the Germans may have had their own suspicions, as evidenced by a revealing yet little-noticed statement made by Alexander Prechtel, the spokesman for the West German Federal Prosecutor's Office, on December 23, 1988 – right after the Lockerbie bombing. Asked about the possibility that any of the PFLP-GC members arrested in October could have been responsible, Prechtel said, 'Naturally, you can see a connection. . . . They may have built several of these bombs.'

American and Israeli intelligence officials believe that within a week or so after the bombing of Pan Am 103, German agents realized that they had come to a terribly wrong conclusion in October, based on both a misinterpretation of the phone taps and misinformation provided by Kreeshat and Diab. The bomb and the bomber had been in their clutches, and the Germans had unknowingly let them go.

Having now recognized the magnitude of their error, German intelligence services embarked on a cover-up to hide their mistakes. And that is why, American and Israeli officials believe, in the weeks and months immediately following the Lockerbie bombing, German intelligence agencies refused to cooperate with American and British investigators and even provided misinformation to the FBI.

For the Scottish detectives and FBI agents, accustomed to dealing more in fact than theory, trying to read the entrails of an intelligence operation such as this, with its multiple agencies and jumbled lines of responsibility, is a thankless task. For all the hard evidence the investigators have developed against considerable odds, more than a year after the downing of Pan Am 103, they are left with theories.

On January 10, 1990, investigators gathered in Lockerbie to review the evidence and to test their theories against it. Now, for the first time, prosecutors from

Germany, Scotland and the United States sat down with the investigators. Some of the American participants in the meeting had been pushing to get the lawyers involved for months. At a meeting of investigators on September 14, held at BKA offices in Meckenheim, Chief Constable George Esson had caused a bit of flap. According to several of those present, Esson stood up and announced that he believed, after reviewing the investigators' findings in Malta and Sweden, that there was enough evidence to seek an indictment. 'I nearly fell out of my chair,' said one of the American officials in attendance. 'That was way out of line.' As much as they applauded the fast and thorough work of the investigators, the lawyers believed that some police officials would push for an indictment before the evidence actually warranted such a move. For this reason they wanted to be present at the meeting in Lockerbie. Lawyers from the U.S. Justice Department and the Scottish Lord Advocate's staff had been involved in the investigation from day one, advising the police and FBI on the finer points of legal procedure and filing court papers where necessary to free up information from reluctant foreign governments. They didn't want to see the inquiry blown by the inadvertent slip of a police officer somewhere along the line.

In Lockerbie, however, George Esson once again managed to irritate some investigators. The night before the conference, many of them had gathered in a Lockerbie bar to reacquaint themselves and to greet some of the people who had joined the investigative team since the last meeting. Malta, for instance, had two police representatives at the meeting. There were several people from Sweden too. Word soon circulated that Esson planned to allow television cameras to film the beginnings of the proceedings. Some investigators, concerned about being publicly identified as police agents, were aghast. Esson heard of their concerns, and the next morning he said that anyone who didn't like the idea of being on TV could simply leave the room before the camera crews began filming. According to those present, fifteen officials got up and walked out.

That was a minor irritant, however. The day after the investigators concluded their meeting, Scottish, German and American prosecutors sat down without the investigators to review the case. By and large, several of those present said, they had reason to be optimistic; things were on the right track, the investigators had come a long way. Still, they did not have the answer to the critical question: How did the bomb get on the plane?

In trying to answer that question, investigators looked very carefully at the barometer trigger on the bomb. Very simply, a barometer measures atmospheric pressure. The further away from the earth's surface, the lower the air pressure. Investigators believe the barometer that blew up Flight 103 was probably the same type as that in the Toshiba Bombeat found in the back-seat of Dalkamouni's Ford Taurus.

An analysis of the Bombeat showed that the barometer was set to activate the timer at 9,000 feet. According to German police documents, the barometer was marked '750 mb'. A Millibar, or mb, is a unit of atmospheric pressure, and thus may indicate altitude; 750 mb is air pressure at an altitude of 9,000 feet.

The barometer Marwan Kreeshat used in the Bombeat is believed to have been an aneroid type: it acts like an accordion, expanding as air pressure decreases. When the barometer expands to a preset position – in this case, 750 mb – it closes an electric circuit, activating the timer.

If the aircraft on which the bomb was placed descended to an altitude below the preset level on the barometer, the electric circuit would be broken and the timer would stop. The timer, obviously, could be set for as long as desired, twelve hours on a normal watch, twenty-four on a military watch. If the goal were to blow up an airplane over water, however, the timer would most likely be set to activate after a relatively short period, considerably less than six hours, the time it takes for a jumbo jet to fly from London to New York.

That sounds tricky enough. What Lockerbie investigators soon discovered, however, was that Marwan Kreeshat was no ordinary bombmaker. To fool airport security machines, which subject checked luggage to 'preflight low-pressure chamber checks', Kreeshat had rigged the Bombeat bomb so that the barometer would not activate the timer until after it had been subjected to continuous pressurization for thirty-five minutes. Pressurized for just a few minutes by airport security machines, the barometer would not activate.

This was puzzling to investigators. If the bomb that had blown up Flight 103 had been rigged exactly as the Bombeat bomb found in Dalkamouni's car, it would never have gone off. Because outside the plane neither passengers nor crew could function at the altitudes normally flown by commercial aircraft, the cabin is pressurized to simulate a maximum altitude of just 7,000 feet, or 768.36 mb. This meant that cabin pressure on the *Maid of the Seas* would never have reached 9,000 feet, and the aneroid barometer never would have swelled to the fatal 750-mb mark. Lockerbie investigators, some of whom knew next to nothing about barometers and physics when they began the investigation, concluded that the 750-mb mark referred not to internal cabin pressure, but to the actual altitude of the plane, which would have been reflected as a differential between external air pressure and air pressure inside the aircraft cabin. In other words, anytime the barometer bomb was above 9,000 feet for more than thirty-five minutes, it could activate the timer, which would then, ultimately, detonate the bomb. A senior Scottish official said investigators now believe that the 750-mb mark was intended to remind Dalkamouni's carriers not to transport the bombs at elevations above 9,000 feet. This is strange, since none of the Alpine passes that can be travelled by car is above 8,500 feet.

The information about the barometers was of little value to the investigators, however, because they had no way of knowing for how long Kreeshat had set the timer. There was no reason to assume he would have set all five bombs exactly the same way: the only concern was to ensure, as much as possible, that they exploded over water. That narrowed the time constraints some, but not much.

When investigators discovered the Lockerbie link to Malta, in late July 1989, there was considerable speculation that the bomb had been loaded on the Air Malta flight to Frankfurt and then interlined to London with no accompanying passenger. The confusion over Air Malta's baggage records made the Malta link appear even more likely. But the triple play, Malta to Frankfurt to London, seemed a bit ambitious even for the likes of Marwan Kreeshat. On December 21, Air Malta Flight KM 180 had been scheduled to depart Valletta at 9:45 A.M., but it had been delayed about a half-hour. During the two-and-a-half-hour flight to Frankfurt, the jet would have been above 9,000 feet for at least ninety minutes. With the thirty-five-minute delay Kreeshat had built into the bomb, the timer still could have been activated for nearly an hour before the barometer deflated and the circuit was broken, stopping the timer.

If the bag had been interlined to London from Frankfurt, the timer would have been reactivated for exactly one hour and one minute, the precise time the first leg of Flight 103 was above an altitude of 9,000 feet. The fact that the bomb finally did explode over Lockerbie exactly thirty-eight minutes after departure from Heathrow, at thirty-eight seconds after 7:03 P.M., makes it appear that Kreeshat would have been cutting things awfully close by setting the barometer-activated timer for anything under three hours.

To the investigators in Lockerbie, this seemed to

argue against the theory that the bomb had been loaded in Malta. The fact that the Malta link meant smuggling Marwan Kreeshat's fifth bomb off the continent and taking it, on a plane, to Malta also seemed to argue against it. Malta was important to the Lockerbie investigators' case. But it was not, it seemed, where the bomb was smuggled aboard a plane eventually to end up on the 103.

That place, investigators still believe, is Frankfurt.

That jibes with the conclusions of forensic specialists. American authorities had been especially helpful in reconstructing baggage carrier 14L, and on the basis of their work and interrogations of baggage loaders at Heathrow, they were pretty confident that the bomb was in a bag loaded in Frankfurt. But because so many baggage handlers in London gave confused statements about the loading of 14L, the Heathrow connection has not been ruled out, and it remains a plausible theory. What American investigators knew about the barometer now made that seem all the more certain. And their suspicions were further confirmed in December 1989, in a court proceeding against Hafez Dalkamouni. Hashem Abassi's wife was asked to give evidence against Dalkamouni. He was Mrs. Abassi's brother, but he had also dragged her family through a hell of repeated questions from police investigators and chilly stares from neighbours. It is impossible to know how much that might have played a part in Somaia Abassi's answers in court, but when the prosecutor asked her what she knew about Dalkamouni and Marwan Kreeshat, she replied that Kreeshat had had a brown Samsonite suitcase when he had arrived from Amman on October 13, 1988.

Now, apparently, investigators could connect the suitcase that held the bomb with the man who had built the bomb.

Next question: Did Marwan Kreeshat give the Samsonite with the bomb in it to Mohammed Mougrabi on

October 14? According to several officials involved in the Lockerbie investigation, it is a strong possibility.

What happened then?

Investigators believe that an unwitting Khalid Jaafar wound up with the deadly Samsonite. It is still unclear who might have given him the bag, or why he might have taken it without examining its contents. This, in a nutshell, is the biggest mystery of the Lockerbie investigation. But Scottish detectives, FBI agents, U.S. intelligence officials and the forensic specialists who assisted with the inquiry now believe that the copper-coloured Samsonite was one of the two mystery bags Jaafar checked aboard the first leg of Flight 103 when he arrived at Frankfurt Main Airport. Those two bags remain unaccounted for. Another very real possibility is that a corrupt baggage handler in Frankfurt threw a 'rogue' bag onto the plane. According to statements of baggage handlers in London, the Samsonite with the bomb in it was among the last loaded in Frankfurt and among the first of the Frankfurt bags stowed in baggage container 14L. It was that Samsonite bag, investigators say, that disintegrated into fragments at 7:03:38 local time at 31,000 feet above the village of Lockerbie.

Israeli intelligence officials believe that Mougrabi and Abu Talb were not involved in the bombing of Pan Am 103. Rather, the Israelis say they were planning other terrorist acts to be carried out in the autumn. Still, how did the bomb get on board the *Maid of the Seas*? These officials believe it was through one (or more) of those arrested by West German authorities in late October 1988. After being set free by the Germans, who felt that the suspected terrorist no longer posed a danger, this person managed to retrieve the bomb that eventually blew up Pan Am 103. According to this view, whoever was the mastermind had devised a series of contingency plans in case he got caught.

The ending, according to these investigators, was the same. Somehow, the bomb was given to young Jaafar.

For the investigators, the questions still remaining are the biggest ones. They are, quite simply, the difference between success and failure.

For Buck Revell, who is retiring in 1990 after a quarter-century with the Bureau, the Lockerbie investigation is a fitting capstone to an extraordinary career. When he joined the FBI, an ambitious young man from Muskogee, Oklahoma, there was really no such thing as terrorism as it is known today. Terror was inspired by awful wars abroad. At home in the United States, there were shootings and stabbings and other violent crimes, but nothing like blowing up airplanes with hundreds of innocent people aboard. That was one measure of how the world had changed in twenty-five years. The holes remaining in the Lockerbie investigation are a source of frustration for Revell. But in his years of police work, in which he has assisted in most of the Bureau's biggest terrorism investigations, he had learned to take the long view. Getting to the bottom will take time, Revell says, but it will happen.

Speaking, in his large, spare office on an upper floor of St. Andrew's house, the Scottish Home Office in Edinburgh, John Boyd is of the same view. 'With all the help and assistance from so many different parties, good, solid police work will get us there. It has not been easy, and it won't be easy. But it will happen.' As Her Majesty's Inspector of the Constabulary, Boyd is on the go more than he likes these days, travelling to the far corners of Scotland to check up on things. He has been back to Lockerbie on numerous occasions, and the shock of the events of the night of December 21, 1988, has not left him. 'I feel, we all feel, so badly for those who lost their loved ones that night. . . . We owe them the duty of finding and bringing to justice those who are responsible.' For his work on the Lockerbie investigation, Boyd has been named Commander of the Most

Excellent Order of the British Empire, a title just below knighthood.

Darrell Mills, the FBI's legal attaché in London, is scheduled to return to the States in 1990, leaving behind more friends and wellwishers than he can possibly number. For Mills, Lockerbie was an eye-opener. He will never forget the horror and the pain of the families' loss. But then there were also the efforts of so many people, the searchers in the fields, the morticians and the people of Lockerbie themselves. 'Never,' Mills says, 'have I seen people turn out to help like that.'

Like Mills, Special Agent Tim Dorch, the first FBI representative on the ground in Lockerbie, is returning to the States. One of his sons has already begun college in Washington, D.C., and FBI regulations require that Dorch rotate through headquarters, if only briefly, before returning to New York.

Special Agent Tom Thurman, the Bureau's explosives expert who spent so much time on the Lockerbie inquiry, remains in Washington, as does the FAA's Walter Korsgaard. Since Lockerbie, Korsgaard has travelled to Africa, the Middle East and Latin America investigating other aircraft disasters, some natural, some the result of terrorists' bombs. He will never forget Lockerbie, however. 'It was the most phenomenal investigation,' he says, 'that I have ever seen.'

In Scotland, Angus Kennedy has been awarded a medal by the Queen for his service in the Lockerbie investigation. A neighbour had to ride a bicycle two miles through driving rain to notify Kennedy of the honour. It does not mean as much, he says, as the gratitude and friendship of the families of those who died in Lockerbie

Inspector George Stubbs too was awarded the Queen's Police Medal. Stubbs had one of the most painful jobs in the hours and days after the bombing of Pan Am 103: escorting families of the victims in the area where bodies were discovered. The families cannot say enough about the depth of his compassion, and his diligence and conscentiousness.

In Lockerbie itself, George Esson and his senior investigating officer, John Orr, continue to meet each day at 9:00 A.M., to plan the day's activities. Their detectives, working with FBI agents and German police, continue to turn up in strange parts of the world from time to time, although not as often as they once did. The focus of the Lockerbie investigation has narrowed, and now, they have told colleagues, it is simply a matter of dogged police work and persistence in amassing evidence.

In Edinburgh, Lord Peter Fraser, the Scottish lord advocate, is waiting for the final pieces of evidence that will give him a court case, if all parties agree to try it in Scotland. It is a frustrating business, though. 'While encouraging progress continues to be made toward our goal of criminal prosecution,' he said in a new conference in mid-December 1989, 'we have not yet reached the stage where proceedings are immediately in prospect.'

That's lawyer talk. George Esson, a politically savvy official who knows the cost of failure, put it more graphically. 'What we are doing, in effect, is trying to piece together an international terrorist jigsaw. We have some of the pieces,' Esson said. 'Some we are trying to place. And some we are trying to find.'

Ironically, it is not just the terrorists who hold all the answers. West German authorities, who sincerely thought they had permanently disrupted the terrorist plans of the PFLP-GC in Operation Autumn Leaves, undoubtedly know more than they have told the Americans and British. Either their informant betrayed them or that informant was simply not in the loop. Nevertheless, the Germans are still reluctant to provide details of their relationship with their 'sources' and informants within the PFLP-GC cell they arrested. They may have an obligation to protect the identity of these sources, but according to Western intelligence officials, the German reluctance has been reinforced by a fear that any disclosures would confirm to the world that they blundered in Operation Autumn Leaves.

A break in the investigation could come if Hafez Dalkamouni decided to tell what he knows. But he spent ten years in an Israeli prison, and he is accustomed to privation. More to the point, perhaps, the man who knows all the details of the bombing of Flight 103, may have no reason to talk to Lockerbie investigators now. Dalkamouni and Abdel Ghadanfar have been charged with the bombings of the two American troop trains in Hedemünden, West Germany, in 1987 and 1988. And Dalkamouni, at least, is certain to be charged in connection with the deaths of Hans Jürgen Sonntag and the wounding of Thomas Ettinger. The evidence against Dalkamouni and Ghadanfar from the Lockerbie investigation seems overwhelming, but much of it is the kind of circumstantial flimsiness a good lawyer can brush away with a few well-crafted briefs.

In Sweden, Mohammed Abu Talb and Martin Imandi also may have no reason to tell what they know about the Lockerbie bombing. Abu Talb has appealed his conviction, but he and Imandi are serving life prison terms for the 1985 and 1986 bombings in Copenhagen and Stockholm. They are likely to be charged eventually in connection with the Lockerbie murders, but that doesn't mean they will have any incentive to cooperate with the police. The Mougrabi brothers are also doing time; Mustafa, the younger, testified against Mohammed, who is serving an eight-year prison sentence. Investigators say it is possible the Mougrabis may cooperate, but so far that has not been the case.

Which means the Lockerbie investigators will probably keep doing exactly what they have been doing until they get the answers they need. As Buck Revell noted, the few successful terrorism investigations to date have taken years to come to fruition. Revell recalled the case against Mohammed Rashid, the terror-ist from the 15 May Organization who planted a bomb on the plane that exploded in Hawaii. 'I go back to the Pan Am bombing in 1982,' he said. 'It took us four years to solve that, get a warrant, and it took us two more years to get him into custody.' Even now, although Rashid is in jail in Greece, U.S. officials have been frus-trated in seeking his extradition, and he remains out of their grasp.

The Rashid case is a sore point for those who fight against terrorists. While it is a tribute to a splendid effort by police and intelligence officials, it cannot yet be called a success. In the Lockerbie investigation, the same kinds of questions arise, only with more force and urgency.

To many American officials who have assisted in the investigation into the bombing of Flight 103, the lesson of Lockerbie is simple. In the war against terrorism, these officials say, the United States can no longer play by the old rules. First of all, there should be absolutely no dealings, diplomatic, economic or otherwise, with states such as Iran, Syria and Libya, that sponsor terror-ist activity. But beyond that, confining the American response to terrorism to the legal system is, in their view, unreasonable. Where possible, the U.S. and all other nations should rely on courts and evidence; but where courts and evidence prove useless, other mea-sures should be used.

Among the officials within the Pentagon, State Department, CIA, FBI and other government agencies involved in coordinating policy against terrorists, there is a great range of views on how to deal with terrorists. But there seems to be growing concern among these officials that the U.S. has boxed itself in by precluding the use of violence against them. The view in support of the use of force has been born as much out of frus-tration as out of fear, however, and some officials point out that that is hardly the best foundation for delicate foreign policy decisions.

There is more agreement in the area of police procedure. A senior U.S. official with long experience in investigations of terrorism says there is a growing sense, based on a review of the Autumn Leaves operation, that terrorism cases should not be treated as any other police matter. In drug investigations, for instance, detectives occasionally allow a shipment of narcotics to pass into smugglers' hands to learn more about the distribution network and sources of financing. Terrorism cases, this official said, cannot be handled that way. When there are too many questions and evidence of unaccounted-for bombs or weapons, arrests should be made quickly. Monday-morning quarter-backing of police investigations is a dreary business; there is always another lead that should have been followed more aggressively, or a clue that was missed. In this instance, however, officials say the lesson seems apt: when in doubt during an investigation of terrorism, police should move sooner rather than later. Several U.S. officials point also to the difficulty the FBI has encountered in assisting with terrorism investigations overseas. The Lockerbie inquiry was facilitated not only by the close relationship between London and Washington, but also by the strong ties that the FBI legal attachés had established with West German and British law enforcement agencies. Although Darrell Mills and Chief Constable John Boyd didn't know each other before the Lockerbie case, Boyd knew of the contributions the Bureau could make to the inquiry and wasted no time in asking for help. To better U.S. chances in terrorism investigations in the future, U.S. officials suggest, the FBI ought to strengthen the LegAtt program: expand it to countries where it as yet has no representation and beef it up in those where it already exists.

Another area of consensus is airport and airline

security. Airlines fly planes, serve food and generally do a pretty good job of getting people from one place to another. They are not equipped to fight wars, however. And that is precisely what terrorism is. If the U.S. is serious about fighting terrorism, a growing number of officials in Washington say, it should get directly involved in the security arrangements for air carriers operating inside and outside its borders. It is unfair and unwise, in the view of these officials, to ask air carriers to serve as the front line in the terrorists' war against the West.

For the families of those who died in Lockerbie, this does not seem too much to ask. It will not bring back Diane Maslowski, Suruchi Rattan or Michael Bernstein. But for all who died on Flight 103, and for the families who have since dedicated themselves to seeing that some good comes of the tragedy in Lockerbie, it seems only fitting that the government address those questions that still have not been answered.

For people like Bruce Smith who have lobbied long and hard for a reward fund for information leading to the bombers of Flight 103, there can be only one end to the Lockerbie investigation. 'It is not revenge,' Smith says. 'It is simply a statement, that we as a civilized people will not allow the people responsible for these kinds of crimes to get away with them. It is not revenge but justice.'

Some of the families of the victims remain too overcome by their loss to care much about such broad concerns. Some, says Ceil Buonocore, the woman who lost her own son to a terrorist attack some years before and came to Haddonfield, New Jersey, in the summer of 1989 to help the families of the Lockerbie victims with their loss, will just 'not make it'. Just as the Lockerbie investigators have holes in their case, the families of the victims have holes in their lives, and many will never be filled. To an outsider, to one who has never suffered the kind of loss they have suffered, the intensity of their grief is frightening, the depth of their passion deeply humbling.

In Lockerbie itself in 1990, the scars have begun to heal slowly. In Sherwood Crescent, where eleven houses vanished in a fireball, contractors have put the finishing touches on eleven new ones. In Rosebank Crescent, Ella Ramsden's house is nearly as good as new. And with another spring and the lambs in the fields, it seems, on some days, as if the whole terrible tragedy never happened.

But it did. And if the lessons of Lockerbie are not learned, it could well happen again.

NOTE ON SOURCES
AND METHODOLOGY

In attempting to reconstruct the investigation into the bombing of Pan Am Flight 103, we interviewed more than 250 people in Europe, the United States and the Middle East. In every instance, we attempted to conduct the interviews on the record and for attribution, that is, in such a way that the information would be linked to its source by name and/or title so that the reader can evaluate its validity for himself. In a great many cases, despite the fact that we were reporting on what was an ongoing criminal investigation, we were successful; in many others, because of the strict constraints on the investigators as far as disclosing information and the sensitive nature of the inquiry, we were not. Those who spoke with us on the record, for example Oliver Revell of the FBI and John Boyd of the Scottish police, did so because they believed that there is merit in explaining to the public just how important and difficult it is to investigate acts of terrorism and make a legal case in a court of law against those responsible. In each instance, those who assisted us with our research confined their comments to procedural matters related to the inquiry, explaining how detectives were assigned to various tasks, for instance, and helping us understand the tricky business of forensics. As to quotations, our rule was straightforward: Statements made directly to us, or contained in government documents, court papers or the like appear in the book within quotation marks. Statements that were reconstructed for us by a third party, and which we were unable to confirm directly, are attributed to the appropriate individual but do not appear in quotation marks.

In several cases, where we came into possession of information the investigators deemed potentially harmful to a legal prosecution of the terrorists responsible for the Lockerbie bombing, we agreed to withhold that information, and it is not included here. We alone decided what to print and what not to print, however. In each case, our yardstick was the same: If disclosure could jeopardize the efforts of the investigators to apprehend and convict the Lockerbie killers, we chose not to publish.

As is frequent in reporting on national security and intelligence matters, it was often difficult to distinguish what was true from what was false or misleading. We were fortunate during the course of our reporting to have had access to internal government documents in the United States, West Germany, Sweden, Israel and elsewhere. This enabled us to check the necessarily tentative conclusions of intelligence officials against harder evidence contained in surveillance records, arrest documents and internal logs of law enforcement agencies. Where this was not possible we had to content ourselves with cross-checking the conclusions of one intelligence agency with those of others. We were fortunate as well to have had access to senior and mid-level intelligence and law enforcement officials in the United States, Great Britain, West Germany, Israel, Finland, Sweden and France. For obvious reasons, many of those people are unnamed in the book, but they are not unthanked. In each case where these intelligence officials provided information cited in the book, we have identified them by the country with which they were affiliated; where officials from more than one European country provided corroborating information, they were identified as 'European' intelligence officials; where U.S. and European officials agreed on a point of information, it was attributed to 'Western' intelligence officials. Nowhere in the book was any use made of pseudonyms.

Because there were often conflicting versions of events from various parties and it was not possible to determine which was correct, we have related all of the versions related to us and highlighted the contradictions among them. Where law enforcement or intelligence officials were uncertain of events but were willing to advance theories of how something might have transpired, we have included those as well, referring to them clearly as theories. Our reason for doing this was simple. In attempting to explain the extraordinary complexity of counterterrorism work, we believed it was important to show how investigators must work from the flimsiest of evidence and how they are often led by it to tentative and sometimes incorrect conclusions. Underlying the tragedy of Pan Am Flight 103 is a story of disagreement and, in some cases, deception among the various intelligence and police agencies assisting in the investigation. To the extent that deliberately misleading information may have been passed from one of those agencies to another and then to us, we too have been victims of disinformation. Despite that possibility, and notwithstanding the generous help extended to us by so many people, we alone are responsible for the information contained in this book.

In our attempt to reconstruct the Lockerbie investigation and tell its story through the eyes of those involved in it, we have used the standard journalistic technique of beginning with the public record and amplifying or amending its contents with our own reporting. In chapters 1 through 6, the accounts of events in Lockerbie in the aftermath of the crash are based on interviews with Lord Peter Fraser, Chief Constable John Boyd, Chief Constable George Esson, Superintendent Douglas Roxburgh, Superintendent Angus Kennedy, Dumfries and Galloway Firemaster Barry Stiff, Assistant Divisional Fire Officer Alan Riddet, social worker Mike Combe,

324

Lockerbie residents Ella Ramsden, Jimmie and June Wilson, Robin and Sally Devlin, Ian Stewart, Paul Thomas, Chris Graham, Foster Dodd and Dorothy Adamson, deputy head of the Lockerbie Primary School. In addition, five Scottish police officials and one fire department official in Lockerbie provided accounts of the crash and details of the ensuing investigation. All agreed to interviews on the condition that their names would not be used. The account of the disappearance of Flight 103 from the radar screens in the Air Traffic Control Centre in Prestwick comes from air traffic controller Alan Topp. Officials from Pan Am and the Air Accident Investigations Board in London confirmed the details related to us by Topp.

The account of the early U.S. response after the crash of Flight 103 is based on interviews with Oliver Revell, executive assistant director of the Federal Bureau of Investigation; Bob Ricks, the FBI's deputy assistant director for counterterrorism; James Fox, the assistant director in charge of the FBI's New York field office; Douglas Gow, the special agent in charge of the Washington Field Office; Darrell Mills, the FBI's legal attaché in London; David Barham, the FBI's legal attaché in Bonn; Tim Dorch, an assistant legal attaché in London; Frank Moss and Clayton McManaway of the U.S. Department of State's Office for Combatting Terrorism; Walter Korsgaard, the Federal Aviation Administration special agent assigned to investigate the explosion of Pan Am Flight 103; and Monte Belger, an associate administrator of the FAA in charge of security. In addition, more than a dozen officials of the FBI, five officials of the Pentagon and two officials of the Central Intelligence Agency provided information.

The accounts of the response of victims' families to the crash in Lockerbie and their subsequent interactions with the investigators in Lockerbie, London and Washington is drawn from interviews with Bruce Smith, Stan and Norma Maslowski, Suzi Maslowski, Bert Ammer-

325

man, Robert and Peggy Hunt, Dr. Shachi Rattan, Beulah McKee, Stephanie Bernstein, Nazir Jaafar, Charles and Phyllis Rosenthal, and Daniel and Susan Cohen. More than three dozen other families or friends of those who died in Lockerbie were interviewed.

The account of the downing of Iran Air Flight 655 by the USS *Vincennes* in July 1988 is drawn from a Pentagon investigative report on the incident, as well as from a report from the Institute of Naval Proceedings. The account of the August 1988 downing of the C-130 Hercules with President Zia of Pakistan on board is drawn from the Pakistani government's executive summary of its investigative report, as well as from a separate review conducted by the U.S. Department of Defense.

The accounts of the activities of terrorist groups listed as suspects in the Lockerbie bombing, in addition to the Popular Front for the Liberation of Palestine – General Command, are drawn from unclassified files of the U.S. Department of State, the Pentagon and the Central Intelligence Agency, supplemented by interviews with American, French and Israeli intelligence officials. In addition, information contained in *The Age of Terrorism* by Walter Laqueur, *Best Laid Plans* by David Martin and John Walcott, *The Agency* by John Ranelagh, and *In the Name of God* by Robin Wright provided valuable insights into the history of terrorist organizations and their operations in the Middle East, Asia and Europe. The account of the arrest of Japanese Red Army terrorist Yu Kikumura is based on interviews with police and federal prosecutors in New Jersey, as well as transcripts of the federal court proceedings in which Kikumura was convicted and sentenced.

The biographical information on Ahmed Jibril, and the history of his involvement with terrorist organizations, is drawn from Israeli intelligence files, considered the most authoritative and comprehensive on Middle East terrorism, and from Defense Intelligence Agency documents. The account of Chesai Shai's imprisonment by

Jibril is based on interviews with Shai and Israeli intelligence officials. That information was supplemented by interviews with terrorism specialists from the CIA, the FBI, the Department of State and the Pentagon. French intelligence officials provided additional information on the recent history of the PFLP-GC and its increasingly tense relations with Iran. The account of Hafez Dalkamouni's activities in Europe on behalf of Ahmed Jibril and the PFLP-GC is drawn from internal West German police agency files we were fortunate to review, as well as from information provided confidentially by intelligence officials in the United States and law enforcement authorities in Israel, Finland and Sweden. The account of the Autumn Leaves surveillance operation in West Germany is drawn similarly from records and internal logs of the Bundeskriminalamt that were made available to us on a confidential basis. That information was supplemented by interviews with Achim Thiele, a West German prosecutor specializing in terrorism cases in Frankfurt; and Alexander Prechtel, the spokesman for the Federal Prosecutor's Office in Karlsruhe, which handles most terrorism cases in West Germany. Under West German regulations, we were denied permission to speak with Hafez Dalkamouni and Abdel Ghadanfar in prison, but we were able to obtain transcripts of some of the interrogations of Dalkamouni, Ghadanfar, Hashem Abassi, Martin Kadourah and Marwan Kreeshat. Other information was drawn from public police records in Stockholm, as well as from confidential law enforcement records there. In Germany we also interviewed Gerhard Siegele, head of the Interior Ministry's section for combatting terrorism, and Joachim Rott, a senior official in the Interior Ministry.

The account of the recovery of the Central Intelligence Agency papers that were said to refer to American hostages in Lebanon was provided by two Scottish officials who participated in the searches around Lockerbie and were present when the papers were found. The account of the intelligence-gathering activities of Matthew Gannon and Charles McKee in Lebanon is based on information provided by three officials in the Pentagon who spoke to us in general terms and only on the condition that they not be identified by name. Their information was confirmed, in part, by Beulah McKee and verified by an official of the CIA and two officers in the U.S. Army's Intelligence and Security Command.

The account of Pan Am's security problems at London's Heathrow Airport and at Frankfurt Main Airport is drawn from interviews with security and intelligence officials in London and Frankfurt, supplemented by Federal Aviation Administration records and by court documents filed in connection with the lawsuits by families of the victims who died on Flight 103 in Lockerbie. In addition, Fred Ford, the first president of Alert Management Systems, Inc., provided documentation of the security problems at both airports.

The account of the Malta connection to the Lockerbie investigation is drawn exclusively from interviews with Scottish and American officials. An interview with Christine Middleton, a British holidaymaker in Malta who later volunteered information to the Lockerbie investigators, confirmed a report of her and her husband's visit first published in the newspaper *The Independent*. Further documentation was drawn from court documents filed in connection with the litigation between the families of those who died in Lockerbie and Pan Am.

The account of the events in Sweden involving Mohammed Abu Talb and Martin Imandi and the suspected connection of Hafez Dalkamouni's operations in West Germany are drawn from public court records in Stockholm and interviews with senior law enforcement officials there, and from the records of the Autumn Leaves surveillance operation made available after the death of Hans Jürgen Sonntag. Scottish and American authorities confirmed much of the information from these sources and provided additional details of their own.

THE VICTIMS OF PAN AM 103

AIRLINE STAFF

Cockpit Crew

Captain: MacQuarrie, James Bruce, 55, Kensington, New Hampshire. American

First Officer: Wagner, Raymond Ronald, 52, Pennington, New Jersey. American

Flight Engineer: Avritt, Jerry Don, 46, Westminster, California. American

Pursers

Murphy, Mary Geraldine, 51, Twickenham, England. British

Velimirovich, Milutin, 35, Hounslow, England. Czechoslovakian

Flight Attendants

Avoyne, Elisabeth Nichole, 44, Croissy-sur-Seine, France. French

Berti, Noelle Lydie, 41, Paris, France. French

Engstrom, Siv Ulla, 51, Windsor, England. Swedish

Franklin, Stacie Denise, 20, San Diego, California. American

Garrett, Paul Isaac, 41, Napa, California. American

Kuhne, Elke Etha, 43, Hannover, West Germany. West German

Larracoechea, Maria Nieves, 39, Madrid, Spain. Spanish

Sources: 'The Darkest Day', *The Post-Standard* (Syracuse, New York), May 7, 1989; Victims of Pan Am 103; United States Department of State.

Macalolooy, Lilibeth Tobila, 27, Kelsterbach, West
  Germany. Filipino
Reina, Jocelyn, 26, Isleworth, England. American
Royal, Myra Josephine, 30, Hanwell, London, England.
  Dominican Republic
Skabo, Irja Syhnove, 38, Oslo, Norway. Finnish

PASSENGERS

Ahern, John Michael Gerard, 26, Rockville Center, New
  York. American
Aicher, Sarah Margaret, 29, London, England.
  American
Akerstrom, John David, 34, Medina, Ohio. American
Alexander, Ronald Ely, 46, New York City. Swiss
Ammerman, Thomas Joseph, 36, Old Tappan, New
  Jersey. American
Apfelbaum, Martin Lewis, 59, Philadelphia,
  Pennsylvania. American
Asrelsky, Rachel Marie, 21, New York City. American
Atkinson, Judith Ellen, 37, London, England. American
Atkinson, William Garreston, 33, London, England.
  American
Bacciochi, Clare Louise, 19, Tamworth, England. British
Bainbridge, Harry Michael, 34, Montrose, New York.
  American
Barclay, Stuart Murray, 29, Farm Barnard, Vermont.
  American
Bell, Jean Mary, 44, Windsor, England. British
Benello, Julian MacBain, 25, Brookline, Massachusetts.
  American
Bennett, Lawrence Ray, 41, Chelsea, Michigan.
  American
Bergstrom, Philip, 22, Forest Lake, Minnesota.
  American
Berkley, Alistair Davis, 29, London, England. British
Bernstein, Michael Stuart, 36, Bethesda, Maryland.
  American

Berrell, Steven Russell, 20, Fargo, North Dakota. American

Bhatia, Surinder Mohan, 51, Los Angeles, California. Indian

Bissett, Kenneth John, 21, Hartsdale, New York. American

Boatman-Fuller, Diane Anne, 35, London, England. American

Boland, Stephen John, 20, Nashua, New Hampshire. American

Bouckley, Glenn, 27, Liverpool, New York. British

Bouckley, Paula, 29, Liverpool, New York. American

Boulanger, Nicole Elise, 21, Shrewsbury, Massachusetts. American

Boyer, Francis, 43, Toulosane, France. French

Bright, Nicholas, 32, Brookline, Massachusetts. American

Browner (Bier), Daniel Solomon, 23, Parod, Israel. Israeli

Brunner, Colleen Renee, 20, Hamburg, New York. American

Burman, Timothy Guy, 24, London, England. British

Buser, Michael Warren, 34, Ridgefield Park, New Jersey. American

Buser, Warren Max, 62, Glen Rock, New Jersey. American

Butler, Steven Lee, 35, Denver, Colorado. American

Cadman, William Martin, 32, London, England. British

Caffarone, Fabiana, 28, London, England. Argentinian

Caffarone, Hernán, 28, London, England. Argentinian

Canady, Valerie, 25, Morgantown, West Virginia. American

Capasso, Gregory, 21, Brooklyn, New York. American

Cardwell, Timothy Michael, 21, Cresco, Pennsylvania. American

Carlsson, Bernt Wilson, 50, New York City. Swedish

Cawley, Richard Anthony, 43, New York City. American

Ciulla, Frank, 45, Park Ridge, New Jersey. American

Cohen, Theodora Eugenia, 20, Port Jervis, New York. American

Coker, Eric Michael, 20, Mendham, New Jersey. American

Coker, Jason Michael, 20, Mendham, New Jersey. American

Colasanti, Gary Leonard, 20, Melrose, Massachusetts. American

Concannon, Bridget, 53, Banbury, England. Irish

Concannon, Sean, 16, Banbury, England. Irish

Concannon, Thomas, 51, Banbury, England. Irish

Corner, Tracey Jane, 17, Millhouses, England. British

Cory, Scott, 20, Old Lyme Court, Connecticut. American

Coursey, Willis Larry, 40, San Antonio, Texas. American

Coyle, Patricia Mary, 20 Wallingford, Connecticut. American

Cummock, John Binning, 38, Coral Gables, Florida. American

Curry, Joseph Patrick, 31, Fort Devens, Massachusetts. American

Daniels, William Allen, 40, Belle Mead, New Jersey. American

Dater, Gretchen Joyce, 20, Ramsey, New Jersey. American

Davis, Shannon, 19, Shelton, Connecticut. American

Della Ripa, Gabriel, 46, Floral Park, New York. Italian

Di Mauro, Joyce Christine, 32, New York City. American

Di Nardo, Gianfranca, 26, London, England. Italian

Dix, Peter Thomas Stanley, 35, London, England. Irish

Dixit, Om, 54, Fairborn, Ohio. Indian

Dixit, Shanti, 54, Fairborn, Ohio. Indian

Dornstein, David Scott, 25, Philadelphia, Pennsylvania. American

Doyle, Michael Joseph, 30, Voorhees, New Jersey. American

Eggleston, Edgar Howard III, 24, Glens Falls, New York. American

Ergin, Turhan, 22, West Hartford, Connecticut. American

Fisher, Charles Thomas IV, 34, London, England. American

Flick, Clayton Lee, 25, Coventry, England. American

Flynn, John Patrick, 21, Montville, New Jersey. American

Fondiler, Arthur, 33, West Armonk, New York. American

Fortune, Robert Gerard, 40, Jackson Heights, New York. American

Freeman, Paul Matthew Stephen, 25, London, England. Canadian

Fuller, James Ralph, 50, Bloomfield Hills, Michigan. American

Gabor, Ibolya Robertine, 79, Budapest, Hungary. Hungarian

Gallagher, Amy Beth, 22, Quebec, Canada. American

Gannon, Matthew Kevin, 34, Los Angeles, California. American

Garczynski, Kenneth Raymond, 37, North Brunswick, New Jersey. American

Gibson, Kenneth James, 20, Romulus, Michigan. American

Giebler, William David, 29, London, England. American

Gordon, Olive Leonora, 25, London, England. British

Gordon-Gorgacz, Linda Susan, 39, London, England. American

Gorgacz, Anne Madelene, 76, Newcastle, Pennsylvania. American

Gorgacz, Loretta Anne, 47, Newcastle, Pennsylvania. American

Gould, David, 45, Pittsburgh, Pennsylvania. American

Guevorgian, André Nikolai, 32, Sea Cliff, New York. French

Hall, Nicola Jane, 23, Sandton, South Africa. Australian

Halsch, Lorraine Frances, 31, Fairport, New York. American

Hartunian, Lynne Carol, 21, Schenectady, New York.
American

Hawkins, Anthony Lacey, 57, Brooklyn, New York.
British

Herbert, Pamela Elaine, 19, Battle Creek, Michigan.
American

Hilbert, Rodney Peter, 40, Newton, Pennsylvania.
American

Hill, Alfred, 29, Sonthofen, West Germany. West
German

Hollister, Katherine Augusta, 20, Rego Park, New York.
American

Hudson, Josephine Lisa, 22, London, England. British

Hudson, Melina Kristina, 16, Albany, New York.
American

Hudson, Sophie Ailette Miriam, 26, Paris, France.
French

Hunt, Karen Lee, 20, Webster, New York. American

Hurst, Roger Elwood, 38, Ringwood, New Jersey.
American

Ivell, Elizabeth Sophie, 19, Robertsbridge, England.
British

Jaafar, Khalid Nazir, 20, Dearborn, Michigan.
Lebanese/American

Jeck, Robert van Houten, 57, Mountain Lakes, New
Jersey. American

Jeffreys, Paul Avron, 36, Kingston-upon-Thames,
England. British

Jeffreys, Rachel, 23, Kingston-upon-Thames, England.
British

Jermyn, Kathleen Mary, 20, Staten Island, New York.
American

Johnson, Beth Ann, 21, Greensburg, Pennsylvania.
American

Johnson, Mary Alice Lincoln, 25, Wayland,
Massachusetts. American

Johnson, Timothy Baron, 21, Neptune, New Jersey.
American

Jones, Christopher Andrew, 20, Claverack, New York. American

Kelly, Julianne Frances, 20, Dedham, Massachusetts. American

Kingham, Jay Joseph, 44, Potomac, Maryland. American

Klein, Patricia Ann, 35, Trenton, New Jersey. American

Kosmowski, Gregory, 40, Milford, Michigan. American

Kulukundis, Minas Christopher, 38, London, England. British

LaRiviere, Ronald Albert, 33, Alexandria, Virginia. American

Leckburg, Robert Milton, 30, Piscataway, New Jersey. American

Leyrer, William Chase, 46, Bay Shore, New York. American

Lincoln, Wendy Anne, 23, North Adams, Massachusetts. American

Lowenstein, Alexander Silas, 21, Morristown, New Jersey. American

Ludlow, Lloyd David, 41, Macksville, Kansas. American

Lurbke, Maria Theresia, 25, Balve Beckum, West Germany. West German

McAllister, William John, 26, Sunbury-on-Thames, England. British

McCarthy, Daniel Emmet, 31, Brooklyn, New York. American

McCollum, Robert Eugene, 61, Wayne, Pennsylvania. American

McKee, Charles Dennis, 40, Arlington, Virginia. American

McLaughlin, Bernard Joseph, 30, Bristol, England. American

Mack, William Edward, 30, New York City. American

Malicote, Douglas Eugene, 22, Lebanon, Ohio. American

Malicote, Wendy Gay, 21, Lebanon, Ohio, American

Marek, Elizabeth Lillian, 30, New York City. American

Marengo, Louis Anthony, 33, Rochester, Michigan. American
Martin, Noel George, 27, Clapton, England. Jamaican
Maslowski, Diane Marie, 30, New York City. American
Melber, Jane Susan, 27, Middlesex, England. American
Merrill, John, 35, Hertfordshire, England. British
Miazga, Suzanne Marie, 22, Marcy, New York. American
Miller, Joseph Kenneth, 53, Woodmere, New York. American
Mitchell, Jewel Courtney, 32, Brooklyn, New York. Guyanese
Monetti, Richard Paul, 20, Cherry Hill, New Jersey. American
Morgan, Jane Ann, 37, London, England. American
Morson, Eva Ingeborg, 48, New York City. German
Mosey, Helga Rachael, 19, Warley, England. British
Mulroy, Ingrid Elizabeth, 25, Lund, Sweden. Swedish
Mulroy, John, 59, East Northport, New York. Irish
Mulroy, Sean Kevin, 25, Lund, Sweden. American
Noonan, Karen Elizabeth, 20, Potomac, Maryland. American
O'Connor, Daniel Emmett, 31, Boston, Massachusetts. American
O'Neil, Mary Denice, 21, Bronx, New York. American
Otenasek, Anne Lindsey, 21, Baltimore, Maryland. American
Owen, Bryony Elise, 1, Bristol, England. British
Owen, Gwyneth Yvonne Margaret, 29, Bristol, England. British
Owens, Laura Abigail, 8, Cherry Hill, New Jersey. American
Owens, Martha, 44, Cherry Hill, New Jersey. American
Owens, Robert Plack, 45, Cherry Hill, New Jersey. American
Owens, Sarah Rebecca, 14, Cherry Hill, New Jersey. American

Pagnucco, Robert Italo, 51, South Salem, New York. American

Papadopoulos, Christos Michael, 45, Lawrence, New York. Greek/American

Peirce, Peter Raymond, 40, Perrysburg, Ohio. American

Pescatore, Michael, 33, Solon, Ohio, American

Philipps, Sarah Suzanne Buchanan, 20, Newtonville, Massachusetts. American

Phillips, Frederick Sandford, 27, Little Rock, Arkansas. American

Pitt, James Andrew Campbell, 24, South Hadley, Massachusetts. American

Platt, David, 33, Staten Island, New York. American

Porter, Walter Leonard, 35, Brooklyn, New York. American

Posen, Pamela Lynn, 20, Harrison, New York. American

Pugh, William, 56, Margate, New Jersey. American

Quiguyan, Crisostomo Estrella, 43, London, England. Filipino

Ramses, Rajesh Tarsis Priskel, 35, Leicester, England. Indian

Rattan, Anmol, 2, Warren, Michigan. American

Rattan, Garima, 29, Warren, Michigan. American

Rattan, Suruchi, 3, Warren, Michigan. American

Reeves, Anita Lynn, 24, Laurel, Maryland. American

Rein, Mark Alan, 44, New York City. American

Rencevicz, Diane Marie, 21, Burlington, New Jersey. American

Rogers, Louise Ann, 20, Olney, Maryland. American

Roller, Edina, 5, Hungary. Hungarian

Roller, Janos Gabor, 29, Hungary. Hungarian

Roller, Zsuzsana, 27, Hungary. Hungarian

Root, Hanne Maria, 26, Toronto, Canada. Canadian

Rosen, Saul Mark, 35, Morris Plains, New Jersey. American

Rosenthal, Andrea Victoria, 20, New York City. American

Rosenthal, Daniel Peter, 20, Staten Island, New York.
American
Rubin, Arnaud David, 28, Waterloo, Belgium. Belgian
Saraceni, Elyse Jeanne, 20, East London, England.
American
Saunders, Scott Christopher, 21, Macungie,
Pennsylvania. American
Saunders, Theresa Elizabeth, 28, Sunbury-on-Thames,
England. British
Schauble, Johannes Otto, 41, Kappellenweg, West
Germany. West German
Schlageter, Robert Thomas, 20, Warwick, Rhode Island.
American
Schultz, Thomas Britton, 20, Ridgefield, Connecticut.
American
Scott, Sally Elizabeth, 22, Huntington, New York. British
Shapiro, Amy Elizabeth, 21, Stanford, Connecticut.
American
Shastri, Mridula, 24, Oxford, England. Indian
Sheanshang, Joan, 46, New York City. American
Sigal, Irving Stanley, 35, Pennington, New Jersey.
American
Simpson, Martin Bernard Christopher, 52, Brooklyn,
New York. South African
Smith, Cynthia Joan, 21, Milton, Massachusetts.
American
Smith, Ingrid Anita, 31, Berkshire, England. British
Smith, James Alvin, 55, New York City. American
Smith, Mary Edna, 34, Kalamazoo, Michigan. American
Stevenson, Geraldine Anne, 37, Esher, England. British
Stevenson, Hannah Louise, 10, Esher, England. British
Stevenson, John Charles, 38, Esher, England. British
Stevenson, Rachael, 8, Esher, England. British
Stinnett, Charlotte Ann, 36, New York City. American
Stinnett, Michael Gary, 26, Duncanville, Texas.
American
Stinnett, Stacey Leeanne, 9, Duncanville, Texas.
American

Stow, James Ralph, 49, New York City. American
Stratis, Elia G., 43, Montvale, New Jersey. Sudanese
Swan, Anthony Selwyn, 29, Brooklyn, New York. Trinidadian
Swire, Flora Margaret, 24, London, England. British
Tager, Marc Alex, 22, London, England. British
Tanaka, Hidekazu, 26, London, England. Japanese
Teran, Andrew Alexander, 20, New Haven, Connecticut. British/Bolivian
Thomas, Arva Anthony, 17, Detroit, Michigan. American
Thomas, Jonathan Ryan, 2 months, Southfield, Michigan. American
Thomas, Lawanda, 21, Southfield, Michigan. American
Tobin, Mark Lawrence, 21, North Hempstead, New York. American
Trimmer-Smith, David William, 51, New York City. British
Tsairis, Alexia Kathryn, 20, Franklin Lakes, New Jersey. American
Valentino, Barry Joseph, 28, San Francisco, California. American
van Tienhoven, Thomas Floro, 45, Buenos Aires, Argentina. American
Vejdany, Asaad Eidi, 46, Great Neck, New York. Iranian
Vrenios, Nicholas Andreas, 20, Washington, D.C. American
Vulcu, Peter, 21, Alliance, Ohio. Romanian
Waido, Janina Josefa, 61, Chicago, Illinois. Polish
Walker, Thomas Edwin, 47, Quincy, Massachusetts. American
Weedon, Kesha, 20, Bronx, New York. American
Weston, Jerome Lee, 45, Baldwin, New York. American
White, Jonathan, 33, North Hollywood, California. American
Williams, Bonnie Leigh, 21, Crown Point, New York. American

Williams, Brittany Leigh, 2 months, Crown Point, New York. American

Williams, Eric Jon, 24, Crown Point, New York. American

Williams, George Waterson, 24, Joppa, Maryland. American

Williams, Stephanie Leigh, 1, Crown Point, New York. American

Wolfe, Miriam Luby, 20, Severna Park, Maryland. American

Woods, Chelsea Marie, 10 months, Willingboro, New Jersey. American

Woods, Dedera Lynn, 27, Willingboro, New Jersey. American

Woods, Joe Nathan, 28, Willingboro, New Jersey. American

Woods, Joe Nathan, Jr., 2, Willingboro, New Jersey. American

Wright, Andrew Christopher Gillies, 24, Surrey, England. British

Zwynenburg, Mark James, 29, West Nyack, New York. American

BRITISH RESIDENTS OF LOCKERBIE

Flannigan, Joanne, 10.
Flannigan, Kathleen Mary, 41.
Flannigan, Thomas Brown, 44.
Henry, Dora Henrietta, 56.
Henry, Maurice Peter, 63.
Lancaster, Mary, 81.
Murray, Jean Aitken, 82.
Somerville, John, 40.
Somerville, Lyndsey Ann, 10.
Somerville, Paul, 13.
Somerville, Rosaleen Later, 40.

INDEX

345

348

350

All Futura Books are available at your bookshop or newsagent, or can be ordered from the following address:
Futura Books, Cash Sales Department,
P.O. Box 11, Falmouth, Cornwall TR10 9EN.

Please send cheque or postal order (no currency), and allow 60p for postage and packing for the first book plus 25p for the second book and 15p for each additional book ordered up to a maximum charge of £1.90 in U.K.

B.F.P.O. customers please allow 60p for the first book, 25p for the second book plus 15p per copy for the next 7 books, thereafter 9p per book

Overseas customers, including Eire, please allow £1.25 for postage and packing for the first book, 75p for the second book and 28p for each subsequent title ordered.